AN IDIC

The Utterly Useless Guide to Mediterranean Sailing.

by
Bob Newbury
(Shamelessly plagiarising the diaries of Liz Newbury)

Two unsuspecting liveaboards blunder their way to Turkey
by sailing boat.

Cover design by Carmelline Matriano

What's with the title?

Many years ago I was at the gym with a friend of mine. We were doing bench presses and I decided to increase the weight from 15 kilos to 20 kilos. This level of unnecessary detail is, of course, mere showing off. It was also, as I said, several years ago. Nowadays I would have trouble bench pressing a couple of budgies stapled onto a long perch.

The bar was supported by two stands, each just inside of the weights. On each side I needed to replace a five kilo weight and a two and a half kilo weight with a single ten kilo weight. So I took all the weights off one side. It wasn't that I had no understanding of the concept of moments or first order levers. It was just that I had switched off critical thinking mode. Of course, the obvious happened. The bar up-ended and hurtled to the floor, scattering the stacks of dumbbells and narrowly missing braining my friend before knocking some expensive looking chunks out of the parquet.

He looked over at the chaos and destruction wrought around him, shook his head, and in a quiet, resigned and world-weary voice just commented 'physics teacher!' This incident exemplifies a recurring theme in my life (and hence, in this book) - having a modicum of intelligence and a rough working knowledge of how the world works in no way prevents me from being an idiot.

Frequently.

Warning & Disclaimer

This is definitely not one of those 'How to' books that give vast amounts of useful advice on cruising. I can say that with confidence as we have read all of them and forgotten most of what we read. What we haven't forgotten we misinterpret.

If you do find any apparently useful information in here regarding boat handling, heavy weather tactics, collision avoidance, victualling, sail trim, ropework, navigation, anchoring, diesel engine maintenance or any other of the myriad skills required for successful cruising then it must have slipped through the proofreading process and I apologise unreservedly.

Should you come across any such inadvertent advice please disregard it completely and immediately. The fact that we managed to get (relatively) unscathed from the English Channel to Turkey by boat is no indication of expertise on our parts. It merely demonstrates that incompetence and ignorance are no match for blind luck and cowardice. Our knowledge and skills are so lamentable that following our advice on cruising would be about as productive as taking public speaking lessons from George W. Bush and John Prescott.

This is despite the fact that we have been avid readers of Practical Boat Owner for many years. I'm sure that for the majority of the magazine's readership this is an apt and accurately descriptive title. Not so for us. We read PBO articles with a similar sense of wonder and awe as a puppy watching an electrician at work - "*I love you. I don't know what you're doing, but it ain't half clever!*" In truth, a magazine designed to capture our demographic as a readership should more appropriately be titled Clueless Yottie. Now there's an opening for niche publishing.

In fact, we strongly identify with yottie as a label. We contrast ourselves with proper big hairy sailors and yottie is a suitably disparaging, but mildly affectionate term which describes our type of cruiser to a T. Henceforth, yotties we are.

This book doesn't attempt to answer the question 'How do I do it?', but rather the question 'What is life like as a live-aboard cruiser on the 'milk run' from Northern Europe to the Med?' It tries to give a flavour, from the cruiser's viewpoint, of the countries encountered on the voyage: the highs, the lows, the sublime and the absurd, the customs, cultures, idiosyncrasies, bureaucracies, (oh – the bureaucracies) and food; but most of all the people.

It is a commonly held misconception that the combination of mass communications and the EU has effectively erased the differences between cultures, especially within Europe. This is far from the case, as becomes obvious to the cruiser, who tends to call into areas situated less squarely on the tourist route. In fact, if you scratch beneath the surface it becomes apparent in tourist areas as well. Perhaps cruisers tend to find this to a greater extent as they are more likely to find themselves having to deal with the minutiae of everyday life than are those on a two week holiday. If you're staying at the Hotel Splendido you don't often find yourself spending the hottest part of the day scouring the dusty, fly-blown outskirts of town for the parts you need to fix your toilet. Although, I don't know – perhaps you do. I've never stayed at the Hotel Splendido.

The Novelty Junkies

Is that all there is?
Is that all there is?
If that's all there is my friends
Then let's keep dancing
Let's break out the booze and have a ball
If that's all there is.

Do you ever find yourself like a dog with a bone, gnawing away at a nagging question along the lines of that Peggy Lee classic? I do. Frequently. A lot of people, when they hit this existential impasse, decide to have children. We usually decide to bugger off on an ill-considered adventure. It's the journey, not the destination, that counts. The paths of glory and all that.

In line with this philosophy, we seem to have had some hare-brained scheme or other on the go ever since we met. The first one, in our twenties, was to travel overland to New Zealand by motorcycle. We got as far as Turkey before getting ourselves snowed in. We followed this up by buying *Minivet*, a tiny (seven metre) wooden sailing boat, with the intention of taking her through the French canals to the Mediterranean and then on to the Greek Islands. We lifted her out of the water and spent over a year preparing her. On putting her back in she leaked like a sieve and nearly sank before she could even get out of the harbour.

After a short interlude of proper jobs, we upped sticks and decamped to the Algarve to run a bar-restaurant. It only took us five years to work out that catering was not our *métier* so we decided to give up on all this frivolous dilettantism, return to Jersey and get stuck into some proper careers.

The novelty of this situation lasted about five years. We were sitting down after dinner, indulging in our favourite post-prandial pastime of bemoaning the petty politics and bloody minded managerial incompetence of our respective workplaces. The Peggy Lee moment had obviously been simmering away for a while as we both came out with it at the same time – *"There's got to be something more to life than this"*. There had to be something more satisfying, more meaningful, than clawing our way up the greasy pole before falling off the top into retirement and an endless round of golf, gardening and Good Morning Britain.

We wanted a challenge. We wanted a plan. We wanted a light at the end of the tunnel. We wanted another adventure.

A back of the envelope calculation indicated that if we managed to wangle retirement in about another ten years we could just about have enough time to pay for a boat and equip it in the manner to which Liz would like to become accustomed.

Two months later we drove from Margate to Falmouth and back, calling in to just about every yacht brokerage we could find. We saw *Birvidik*, fell in love with her and bought her. We then spent the next ten years and more money than we could afford paying off the loan and fitting her out for long term liveaboard cruising.

Unusually for us, events fell into place more or less as expected. There is a French proverb that roughly translates as the first third of life is for learning, the second is for achieving and the third is for living.

We were going to put that to the test.

Preamble

A short digression on alternative lifestyles and

bureaucracy:

This book has Buddhist tendencies. It has been through many incarnations in its journey to the Nirvana of publication. Each incarnation spawned another title. It started off as *'Second Wind'* which I considered a witty allusion both to sailing and the idea of having another go at life in our dotage. Unfortunately, I had to discard it when it became apparent that the sailing bit was actually pretty incidental to the main thrust of the book.

In the end, the constraints and demands of search engine algorithms in Amazon and Google forced my hand to the current title. A bit clunky it may be, but By God it's got a shedload of search terms shoe-horned into it.

Up until then it was a close run thing as to whether it would be called *'No Fixed Abode'* or *'No Direction Home'*, both of which encapsulated the nomadic and rootless nature of the cruising life. This was apt. Being full time liveaboards put us in the minority.

It is fairly unusual for cruisers to have no land base at all. Most retain a house or flat in their home country. The majority do not live aboard all year, but come out to cruise for varying periods of the year. Some live on board most or all of the year, but intend to return to their home base after a few years. At one point I considered calling the book *'Burning Bridges'*.

Despite the 'living the dream' rhetoric, in our current world it is not possible to escape the insidious, grasping tentacles of bureaucracy entirely. Governments have got most things pretty well tied up, for the average Joe at least.

In order to get away without paying taxes you've either got to have no money at all, or prodigious amounts of the stuff.

Or be dead, and that doesn't always stop them.

On top of that, I for one would not want to be completely isolated from some of the many benefits of developed societies, such as modern medical science, clean diesel, the internet, efficient rubbish disposal, light engineering, telecommunications, the BBC and decent beer. On the other hand, I can happily live without wide screen TVs in bars and restaurants, muzak, invitations to increase my penis size (how did they *know*?), the whole of the British tabloid press, cheesy compilations of Christmas songs in shops, reality television and the advertising industry in all its scrofulous entirety.

The problem is that the full time cruising lifestyle lies outside the rather narrow limits of the bureaucratic mindset. I suppose another alternative title could have been '*Not 2.4 children*'. Take, for example, the small matter of bankers. (Yes, I appreciate that I have broken with modern journalistic and conversational etiquette here, and that the plural noun 'bankers' should normally be preceded by a string of at least five derogatory adjectives, one of which should be 'greedy' although 'avaricious' is a permitted alternative for Guardian readers). There will now be a short recess while everyone has a quick rant and gets things off their chests.

...

Better?

Good.

Right, to continue: it is increasingly difficult, if not impossible, to function in a modern society without at least one bank account. Try opening a bank account if you enter 'No fixed abode' in the address field. . You'd probably have more success if you put 'child pornographer' under 'occupation'. This is despite the fact that, according to the Local Government Finance Act of 1988 'No Fixed Abode' is a valid residential address.[1]

Even having an accommodating friend or relative allowing you to use their address is no solution. Anti money laundering regulations imposed on the banks require proof of residence at a given address. Utility bills in your name are normally demanded. Full time liveaboards don't have any of these. On top of that, the banks require a written, signed and sealed confirmation from an upstanding member of society that you are an upright, law-abiding chap and all-round good egg. Certainly not an international terrorist, drug smuggler, white slaver, African warlord, recently deposed Middle Eastern despot or Mark Thatcher.

The abovementioned affidavit has to be signed by someone really, really trustworthy and important. As we found to our cost, senior hospital managers and heads of large secondary schools are far too suspect. No, it's got to be someone totally above suspicion. So, who do they suggest? I'll tell you, since you ask - they suggest a banker

(pause for ritual 2 minutes hate)

or

(wait for it) ...

A lawyer!

As if anyone with the inclination and the wherewithal to launder large amounts of cash isn't going to have an entire retinue of bent lawyers at his beck and call, all of them doing their level best to get their noses as far up his arse as possible.

Never mind though – we managed it in the end and are willing to share our secrets in exchange for a suitable

---

[1] No fixed abode does not mean 'homeless', although it is often used as a euphemism for it. The term was originally enshrined in legislation to cater for those who had homes, but whose homes did not remain in one place. Examples given were seamen, showmen and nomadic peoples. The act actually states that: "If a person has no fixed abode he shall be treated as having his sole or main residence in the place where he is at any particular time." Try telling that to a bureaucrat.

donation in brown envelopes *á la* Neil and Christine Hamilton.

Departure

At 06:30 on the seventh of May 2006, just eleven years into a ten year plan, *Birvidik* sailed out through the pier heads of St. Helier. She cleared into Turkey just over three years later. Many yachts have circumnavigated the globe in less time.

It is just over 1800 miles as the crow flies from St. Helier to Marmaris. You could fly that in around four hours. By road it is around 2500 miles and in a halfway decent car you could get there in just over a couple of days. Hell – you could walk it in twelve weeks. We took three years.

We logged almost exactly 6000 nautical miles. That's just over 7000 statute miles, or almost three times the road distance. Over those three years she carried us to seven countries and nearly 200 ports and anchorages.

This slow rate of progress was no accident. Few non-sailors appreciate just how slow a mode of transport sailing usually is. Unless you are an Ellen McArthur or a Pete Goss, with millions of pounds' worth of multihull straining at the leash beneath your feet, you will be lucky to do much more than about seven knots. Your average speed is more likely to be around three to four knots. Or two to three knots if you're as much of a wimp regarding weather forecasts as we are: *"Go out in a predicted force five? – Good God man, are you completely mad?"*

Let's put that into perspective. Seven knots is around eight miles per hour and three to four knots is just over three miles per hour. So if you are hurtling along parallel to the shore at seven knots you could be overtaken by someone having a leisurely bicycle ride along the promenade. Most of the time, at three to four knots, you would be keeping pace with someone taking a gentle stroll. You can, however, take some comfort in the fact that you're steaming past the jellyfish. Well, most of them.

Yachts do, though, cover large distances. Even at four knots they could cover those 7000 miles in a whisker over two months. They do this by keeping going, day and night, for days and even weeks on end. We don't. In fact we don't go in for long passages at all if we can help it. Over the whole three years we only did four night passages.

We spent far more time in port or at anchor than we did at sea. Our longest passage was crossing Biscay, which involved just two nights at sea. Most of our sailing consisted of day hops, rarely lasting more than about eight to ten hours. Nelson famously said that harbours rot both ships and men. That may be the case, but they are far more interesting. It is in and around them that you meet the people and experience the country.

I would like, at this point, to reinforce the warning given in the preface. When we set off we were singularly unqualified, both formally and personally, to undertake such a project. Our sailing had been limited to short hops around the Channel Islands and Northern Brittany and we had never done a night passage.

Reading the pilot books brought us out in a cold sweat: *"The approach to Port Doom is simple enough for the experienced mariner once he manages to weather the hazards of Point Horror. Care must be taken of the overfalls off Cape Catastrophe, as well as the 9 knot tidal race which invariably sweeps the yacht onto the barely visible rocks of Dead Man's Shoal. Once clear of these, keep a close lookout while crossing the inshore shipping lanes where fast ferries and supertankers carrying explosive cargoes appear out of nowhere at high speed. Thick fog often descends without warning.*

Leading marks are frequently absent or can easily be confused with the recently disused gibbets hanging in the town square. Following these in error leads the boat over a submerged training wall with iron spikes protruding at all angles. Take care to avoid the new piranha farm close to starboard as you enter the harbour. It is reported that the local fishermen have now, to all intents and purposes, abandoned piracy. A night approach is not recommended."

We countered this stomach-gnawing anxiety with

obsessive preparation and excessive caution. I drew up passage plans in ludicrous detail. Tidal streams were identified and built into the plan so as to be either favourable or, preferably, non-existent. I obtained weather forecasts from at least eight different sources and took the most potentially disastrous as the best we could possibly hope for.

As a result, most of our passages took place in flat calm conditions without even enough wind to fill a handkerchief, let alone a sail. That's another reason it took us so long - and so much diesel. We probably have a carbon footprint the size of Ecuador.

France

All human cultures seem to harbour stereotypes of other nationalities. Some are patently untrue and blatantly slanderous. Others though, despite the existence of many individual exceptions, do seem to contain a kernel of truth. This is possibly because they reflect, in an exaggerated caricature it is true, some fundamental attitudes, beliefs, norms, manners or customs of the culture in question. Being wishy-washy liberals we refuse to think in stereotypes. We prefer to rejoice in the wide diversity of human nature and to judge each individual on his or her merits.

The stereotypical Frenchman is a stylish, elegant, sophisticated, cultured, arrogant, smug, snobbish epicure who looks down condescendingly on all other nationalities, especially the British and the Germans. He's not too keen on the Dutch either. His idea of slobbing out is to sit in a dark smoky café discussing abstruse philosophical concepts over a glass of absinthe. He is fluent in at least four languages, including English, but refuses to speak anything but auctioneer speed French to any foreigner who has the temerity to attempt to engage him in conversation. He has the uncanny ability to make exquisite good manners and politeness deeply insulting and humiliating. He has a frequent, varied and imaginative sex life and at least four lovers, as has his wife – a fact with which he is perfectly comfortable. He takes his pleasures very seriously. He vigorously defends his self interest and will strike, demonstrate or riot at the drop of a hat.

Only some of which is true.

Northern Brittany - St. Quay to L' AberWra' ch

May 7th 2006 – May 31st 2006.

Brittany is about as representative of France as a whole as Merthyr Tydfil is of England. It has its own language, Breton, which is of the same Celtic family as Welsh and Cornish. Welsh speakers are able understand it and make themselves understood, as would have been the case for the last remaining native speaker of Cornish if she hadn't died in 1777.

Despite the strenuous efforts of Paris to eradicate it, the Breton language hangs in there, and nowhere is this more apparent than in the place names. Nearly everywhere starts with 'Ker' - Kernival, Kernaval, Kerperroch, Kerlivan, Kerdruc, Kerfany, Kerroch' – the list is endless. On top of that, most of the rest are other 'K's. I harbour a fantasy concerning a Breton A to Z. It would comprise four pages of A-J and four pages of L-Z sandwiching 852 pages of Ks. Paris really hates this as traditionally French has no letter 'K', except in foreign imports such as 'klaxon', which are looked down upon by the *Academie Francaise* with particularly expressive Gallic disdain.

The area has long claimed to be legally distinct from the rest of France. However, when the Duchy of Brittany was abolished during the French Revolution, the locals (who had up until then been agitating for independence from the French crown) took umbrage at this revolutionary slight and promptly retaliated by turning the place into a hotbed of Royalist and Catholic resistance. The independence movement continued throughout the nineteenth and twentieth centuries, linking with similar movements in Scotland, Ireland and Wales. The Breton National Party, however, made a bit of a *faux pas* (if they'll excuse the French) when it picked the wrong side in the Second World War and allied itself with the Nazis. That set things back a just a smidgeon in the immediate post war period.

St. Quay was our first port of call, and we were promptly weather-bound for four days. On the second day we took a stroll from the gale-lashed harbour into the gale-lashed town. Approaching the gale-lashed main street the sound of car horns, occasionally interspersed with short whoops of sirens, got louder and closer. All traffic had ground almost to a halt; the entire town centre was blockaded by protesting ambulance, taxi and lorry drivers. A faint blue haze of acrid exhaust fumes assailed our nostrils, causing paroxysms of coughing and sneezing and making our eyes water. Perhaps the ambulance drivers were trying to drum up a bit of extra custom: *Bon, Henri - encore trois asthmatiques.*

This protest, according to the posters and flyers that abounded, was completely spontaneous. The professional nature of said posters and flyers, together with the logistical challenge of bringing such a disparate and congenitally unco-operative bunch of road users together at the same place and time did bring the purported spontaneity into question somewhat. The flyers proclaimed that the protesters' livelihoods were being jeopardized by the astronomical and totally unreasonable price of fuel. It seemed particularly inappropriate then, that the protest took the form of driving in convoy all round the town at walking pace in first gear. It must have cost them a fortune.

Round one to the stereotype.

Once the winds and rain had subsided I confidently announced to Liz that the next leg would be a relaxing trip to Paimpol, leaving at the civilised hour of about two in the afternoon. She found this difficult to believe. Experience had led her to assume that the tides invariably conspire to ensure that we get up at four in the morning and grope around in the cold and dark (and usually wet) preparing for sea.

Uncharacteristically then, we slumped out of bed at about nine and pottered about getting ready. I strolled down to the Capitainerie to pay for the previous night. I found the harbourmaster, a lean, weather-beaten man with grey, wiry hair, hooded eyes and the obligatory Gauloise drooping from the side of his mouth. I informed him that we would be leaving in about four hours' time.

"I very much doubt that you will" he said with just a hint of Antoine de Caune on his perfect English. "If I were you I would be leaving now."

After I had spent a few seconds wondering how many native Anglophones would even recognise the subjunctive mood in English, let alone employ it as he had, I considered the possibility that I'd made a complete pig's ear of working out the tides. It seemed unlikely that even I could be that far out.

"Why's that?" I asked.

"Because, M'sieu, our local fishermen are going to blockade the port in about half an hour."

This turned out to be in protest at the extortionate price they were expected to pay for diesel (just under 20p a litre – it was 56p a litre duty free in Jersey and God knows how much in the UK and for everyone else in France). I was beginning to experience the peculiar phenomenon of *déjà vu*.

Stereotype 2; wishy-washy liberals 0.

I hurriedly stuffed the money in his hand and ran back to the boat.

"*Bon chance!*" he called out laconically.

Unfortunately, we were still in caravan mode.

Life on a boat involves two basic *modi operandi*, sea-going and harbour based (or 'caravan mode' as we refer to it). Sea-going mode, in our case anyway, is based on the premise that disaster can, and probably will, strike at any time, almost certainly at the most inopportune moment. Preparing for sea-going mode involves starting from a worst case position and working backwards. The boat is made as watertight as possible with all hatches and windows closed. Everything that could possibly be needed - charts, flares, emergency beacons, boathooks, knife, shark repellent, white flag, prayer book, etc - is placed readily to hand in its allotted place.

Fenders are tied out of the way so as to enable clear access to the decks. Mooring ropes are neatly coiled and hung on loops inside the cockpit lockers. Anything that applies only to the sybaritic harbour lifestyle is banished to inaccessible lockers or tied down tighter than a high court judge at an S&M parlour.

Harbour mode, by contrast, is based on the possibly rash assumption that disaster is less likely. In this mode comfort and convenience take precedence. It is assumed that electricity and water are likely to be available, and land-based exploration and shopping are primary activities.

On docking, a transformation occurs over an hour or so. Tables and cushions materialise from their secret hiding places. Homely rugs and lamps are placed strategically in the saloon and cockpit. Bicycles appear from the bowels of the boat and take up station on the pontoon. Books and newspapers scatter themselves on every surface as if by magic. Power leads and hoses snake between boat and shore. Towels and items of clothing manage to colonise any spaces unaccountably missed by the books and newspapers.

The reverse process usually takes considerably longer. We have a leaving checklist which we tick off like airline pilots before takeoff:

Computer screen restrained?—Check.

Liferaft unlocked?—Check.

Danbuoy extended & flag unfurled?—Check.

Man overboard equipment set & ready?—Check.

Hatches & windows secured?—Check.

Ventilators shut & turned?—Check.

Wind generator untied?—Check.

All cupboards closed?—Check.

Galley equipment restrained?—Check.

Cooker gimballed?—Check.

Electronics powered up & working?—Check

Anchor ball & light lowered & stowed?—Check.

Boarding ladders removed and tied?—Check.

Water tanks full & hose in & stowed?—Check.

Power lead disconnected, & stowed? [2] — Check.

Fenders removed & tied?—Check.

Cat ladders in? (Don't ask)—Check.

Engine checks complete?—Check.

Prayers said?—Check.

Clean knickers on?—Check.

Wills written & witnessed?—Check.

The threat of being stuck in St. Quay for another four days triggered a frenzy of activity. Boat contents flew in all directions as towels, cushions, rugs, lamps, books, bicycles and all the other previously mentioned paraphernalia of harbour life were hastily stuffed below. I was going to say 'stowed below' but that would have implied some degree of order and organisation. We completed what would normally have taken three hours in a frenetic half hour.

After this record-breaking preparation for sea, *Birvidik* shot out through the pier heads like a champagne cork at a bankers' bonus time, her crew nervously looking over the stern for the expected horde of irate, thwarted fishermen chasing behind. Luckily, we think they were still having Lunch.

Lunch in France is an institution which seems alien to British eyes but, once you get used to it, has a lot to recommend it. It also has knock-on effects on other aspects of life, such as shopping, of which more later.

---

[2] It's surprising how many people miss this one and sail jauntily from the pontoon trailing half a sparking lead through the water and shorting out the local substation. It's all terribly embarrassing.

In contrast to the British habit of grabbing a sandwich at the desk, the French take Lunch very seriously. So seriously, in fact, that we believe that whilst in France, one should always mentally capitalise the word. Nevertheless, the concept of a Lunch hour (twenty minutes in Britain) would be met with amazement by a Frenchman. Only an hour? It's usually at least two hours and we've seen as long as three and a half hours.

At around 12:30 a strange transformation occurs as streets gradually take on the aspect of a ghost town. People mysteriously disappear; shops which were bustling with activity one minute are closed, empty and dark the next time you turn round. I've tried to catch them at it by suddenly turning round unexpectedly but to no avail. They're open one second and desolate the next, but you can never actually catch them closing.

The only exceptions to this are, of course, restaurants which undergo the reverse metamorphosis. Getting a table between the hours of 12:30 and 2:30 is about as likely as getting a straight answer out of Tony Blair - It's damned near impossible, and if you think you **have** done it you've probably been conned into accepting something you didn't actually want and you'll still have to pay over the odds for it.

Before 12:15 and after 2:45 though, the kitchens are closed, so the knack of not dying of starvation in France is to get into the restaurant at 12:15 on the dot. Even then most of the tables are pre-booked.

As there are just fractionally more people in France than there are seats in restaurants, all of those not in restaurants take Lunch *en famille*. As the hapless and famished yottie wanders the empty streets in search of sustenance in any form, his senses are assailed by the smells of food and the sound of clinking glasses and animated conversation from the open windows of the houses he passes.

Bastards.

Round three to the stereotype.

Paimpol is at the Western end of a large expanse of mud

which, for about two hours either side of high tide, covers with just enough water to stop boats from bumping into the ground. Our unplanned early departure meant we arrived about three and a half hours before high water and so had to hang around twiddling our thumbs until there was enough depth of water to get to the lock. The incoming tide was carrying us swiftly into the shallows so we sniffed our way into about three metres of water and dropped anchor for the first time.

After Lunch and a sufficient rise of tide we upped anchor and negotiated the lock into Paimpol. Paimpol is an old working port which has slid into the present day with apparently effortless élan. It still has a sense of history and continuity but also an over-riding sense of fun. There always seems to be something musical, artistic or cultural going on, but without anyone seeming to take themselves too seriously. The old harbour has been modified into a marina and lies right at the heart of things. Even in May, when a lot of Brittany is still in a state of semi-hibernation, Paimpol was jumping.

The Celtic connection was very much in evidence. Pipers and fiddlers played jigs and reels, whilst across the road groups of large, bearded men in chunky-knit sweaters and denim caps sang something in Breton to the tune of 'What shall we do with the drunken sailor?'. Interspersed with these were various ensembles of assorted brass instruments - saxophones, trumpets, trombones, French horns and tubas - all being played with more enthusiasm than talent. Everyone was having a whale of a time, far too busy enjoying themselves to care an iota about whether they looked cool and sophisticated or not.

One point to the wishy-washy liberals.

Taking nearly four weeks to get the 150 or so miles from Jersey to L'Aberwra'ch is a bit excessive, even by our leisurely standards. This followed directly from our ignoring The Curse of Trebeurden, as a result of which we qualify perfectly for Einstein's definition of stupidity as 'Keeping on doing the same thing and expecting a different outcome'.

Five times we had been to Trebeurden, in July or August, and always the same thing would happen: We would arrive in beautiful weather, moor up and nip up to the restaurant at the top of the marina and have *moules frites* and a bottle of Muscadet al fresco. "This is nice" we would think "we'll stay here a couple of days and then move on to L'AberWrac'h". On the third day, just as we were preparing to leave, the weather would turn vile and stay that way for about ten days. We would then have to turn round and head back before we ran out of holiday. Perceptive readers will have an idea as to where this is going.

We arrived in beautiful weather, moored up and nipped up to the restaurant at the top of the marina for *moules frites* and a bottle of Muscadet al fresco. There were a couple of jobs to do, amongst them fixing the autopilot which had thrown a hissy fit leaving Paimpol. After a couple of intermittent teases it had packed in completely. We decided to stay for a couple of days of 'make do and mend'.

We didn't go to L'AberWrac'h on the third day, as the visibility was forecast to drop to under 500 metres and L'AberWrac'h is not the sort of approach one wants to make unless one knows exactly where one is – there are far too many sharp pointy hard things poking out of the sea in unexpected places. Monday brought a combination of force six to seven south westerly winds (right on the nose) and poor visibility. Things got progressively worse from then on, rising to force seven, then eight and culminating with the *piece de resistance* on the Saturday morning with a top end of force nine gusting top end of force ten.

This had the boat leaning over at 35 degrees, pushing the pontoon down into the water. The fenders squeaked and groaned as they were squashed almost flat and then chewed between the hull and the pontoon. Wind howled through the rigging and loose halyards clacked against masts, sounding as if the whole marina was overrun by demented castanet players with no sense of rhythm. Sails that weren't tightly wrapped unfurled in the wind with gunshot cracks and flogged themselves to tatters in minutes. Conversations in the saloon had to be carried out at the shout. Although we were firmly tied up in harbour it required concentration to move around the boat, even below. Cooking under these conditions required the co-ordination of a professional juggler and the nerves of a bomb disposal expert. The whole process is a gamble with boiling water and hot oil. If you come out of the other end with more or less the same amount of skin as you started with then you've won. In fact, cooking on a small boat is an activity best reserved for diehard adrenaline junkies with a well developed masochistic streak and a strong stomach, a point which will be addressed later.

By comparison, though, we had it easy. Two friends of ours, proper hairy sailors on a very tight budget, were anchored not far away throughout all of this. They had put up with it day and night for six days. Then, at the height of the storm, at three in the morning, their wind generator self destructed sending high speed debris clattering through the rigging. The sixty knot winds built up huge waves which broke over the bow in cascades of green water and had *Ocean Goose* snatching at her anchor chain. Their anchor snubber was a length of 32 millimetre diameter nylon rope with a breaking strain measured in tonnes. It snapped. The resulting snatch load was too much for their spade anchor, which had held valiantly throughout, and it lost its battle and dragged.

With superb seamanship they managed to reset the anchor, despite the already poor visibility being further obscured by flying spray. The next day they gave up and went into Morlaix, and that must have taken some doing under those conditions.

We had been giving them moral support by text messages. After the dragging we received a two word text – 'Truly frightening'. Are you there Graham and Katie? We salute you.

The next week continued very much in the same vein. Altogether we were stuck in Trebeurden for almost three weeks. This, however, gave us ample opportunity to experience another defining characteristic of French life, namely shopping.

Most men of our acquaintance only seem to enjoy shopping is if it is for something you can eat, drink, plug in or take apart in order to see how it used to work before you took it apart. In general, however, shopping in France is a far more agreeable and civilised experience than its equivalent in U.K. or Jersey (even for men). This is mainly because it is primarily about buying food. There are still many independent shops, specialising in specific areas, such as fishmongers, delicatessens, patisseries, bakers etc. There is also at least one market somewhere in the area every day of the week.

They do have supermarkets but even these seem less ruthlessly designed to use all the revelations of modern psychological research to surgically remove the contents of your bank account as efficiently and un-noticeably as possible than are their UK counterparts. (Yes, I know it's a split infinitive – don't be pedantic).

There are four aspects of French shopping, however, that need getting used to. The first, of course, is Lunch. It's damned nigh impossible to buy absolutely anything, anywhere in France between the hours of 12:30 and 15:00. It usually takes us until 11:45 to get ourselves organised, and then we have to walk the two miles uphill to where French shops are always situated (aspect 2). As a result we always arrive at Lunch time.

The universal French trick of always siting towns and villages, and therefore shops, on the highest point was, apparently, originally done to discourage attacks by pirates. The idea seemed to be that by the time the marauding hordes had climbed to the top of the hill they would have been too knackered for rape and pillage and would have had to buy a packet of Bensons and have a sit down to recover. This, with any luck, would have lasted until Lunchtime and by the time they got their breath back and picked up their cutlasses again everywhere would be shut.

In its modern incarnation it has led to our 'granny' shopping trolley coming into its own. One of the defining characteristics of being a boat bum is that, in common with pirates, one almost invariably arrives at sea level. It is always, therefore, about two miles uphill to the shops and two miles downhill back, fully laden. Whilst this is the right way round, it's still a bind carrying the four crates of beer, eight bottles of wine, three bottles of fizzy water, two slices of fish terrine and a baguette all the way back to the boat. We don't mind the quizzical and pitying looks we get. Have trolley, will shop – that's our motto. Anyway, we prefer 'interestingly eccentric' to 'sad gits'.

Aspect three of French shopping is that, although everywhere is blessed with a multitude of different food shops, there is a notable scarcity of others such as electrical shops, ironmongers, stationers and the like. There is one exception to this rule and that is hairdressers. If the French attitude to Lunch means that the word should always be capitalised, then the same must also be true of *'Coiffure'*. There are probably more hairdressers in France than there are restaurants, about three per capita at a rough guess. I reckon it must be an accepted principle that all able bodied adults are obliged to go to the hairdressers on an at least daily basis and must spread their custom around as many different establishments as is reasonably possible. Failure to do this almost certainly results in social and sexual ostracism and the subsequent removal of the individual's genes from the gene pool. Hairdressers therefore become a sexually selected characteristic of the environment.

The final aspect of French shopping is related to aspect three, and that is the difficulty of buying anything you might need other than food or a quick trim and blow-dry. Liz keeps a handwritten journal and I handwrite the ship's log every day at sea. Both were nearly full so we traipsed happily, innocently and confidently to the shops to buy replacements. We had even worked out the French if we got stuck.

Several cunningly hidden stationers later we were stymied. The French have lots of exercise books, but as a nation they seem to have trouble writing in a regular pattern - all their exercise books are marked out in little four millimetre squares. Either that or they're set out for double entry book-keeping or as address books. No straightforward lined books. Anywhere.

So, when we were approached by a helpful and unsuspecting assistant I tried my rusty French on her.

Assistante:"Bonjour M'sieu-Dame, est-ce-que je peut vous aider?"

Moi:"Oui, s'il vous plait, nous voudrons des cahiers"

A:"Bien sur M'sieu, les cahiers sont la-bas"

M:"Oui, je sais, mais nous voudrons des cahiers avec des lignes, pas des squares."

A:(surprised): "Avec des lignes? Pas des carres? Pourquoi?

M:"Oui avec des lignes. Pour ecrire un journal"

A:(Convinced we're mad): "Les cahiers avec des lignes? Les cahiers de ce genre n'existent pas."

M:"Ils bloody do existent. Nous avons loads sur le bateau, mais ils sont tous full up."

At this point she started to look slightly alarmed and began backing slowly toward the telephone so we decided to call it a day. We were tempted to go and pick up our lined books, go back and wave them in the window at her shouting *"Regardez! - Ils bleedin' do existent!"* But it was a long way up the hill again and anyway it was nearly Lunch.

We managed it to L'Aberwra'ch the next day. We left Trebeurden about 9 a.m., expecting half metre to one metre waves. What we got was two to three metre seas right on the beam, rolling us from fifty degrees one side to fifty degrees the other. This proved a good test of our stowage system, which failed in a spectacularly noisy fashion.

Despite our checklist we had forgotten to secure the computer screen which swung in wild arcs on its hinged arm. Luckily we noticed and rectified matters before it managed to pound itself to pieces on the grab rail. Then the lashings on the dive gear came loose and the tanks started banging around. Eight thousand litres of gas, compressed to 300 bar contains as much energy as about three quarters of a kilogram of TNT, roughly equivalent to three hand grenades. This is not what I wanted crashing from one side of the boat to the other, so I poked Liz out onto the aft deck on her hands and knees to effect a temporary restraint. The dinghy was swinging from side to side in its davits; the toaster took a successful suicidal dive off the galley, rapidly followed by a less successful attempt by the kettle, which was offered counselling and kept under 24 hour surveillance.

The aft cabin held out at first but finally succumbed. Drawers shot open and books flew. The cabin contents ended up in a jumbled heap in the floor, but the major disaster was the breakage of the full length mirror. How now was Liz to judge her final ensemble prior to the Commodore's Ball?

Nevertheless, getting into L'Aberwra'ch marked a psychological turning point. This was the furthest we had ever managed to get during our summer cruises, mainly as a result of The Curse of Trebeurden. Up until now there had been a subconscious feeling that this was just another summer cruise, going over familiar and well-trodden ground. At some point we expected a spoilsport voice to shout "OK – that's it. You've had your fun, now turn round and go back to work". No longer.

From here on, it was all new.

Southern Brittany - Camaret to Pornichet

June 1st 2006 – June 25th 2006.

Getting to Southern Brittany involves transiting the Chenal du Four to Audierne and then the Raz de Sein to Camaret. The Chenal du Four has a reputation for fog, which is a tad inconvenient as it involves tight confined pilotage between a plethora of rocks and reefs, all surrounded by strong tidal streams. It is a pussycat, however, by comparison with the ferocious reputation of the Raz de Sein.

The Raz is the rock-strewn passage between the Brittany coast and the Isle de Sein. At spring tides the current can run at up to seven knots and produce nasty overfalls which throw a yacht about like a numbered ball in a bingo hall. With any wind against the tide the sea becomes a maelstrom. Huge waves from Atlantic storms batter the lighthouses such as La Platte and La Vielle, breaking over their lights 33 metres above the rocks on which they stand. Photographers and artists have a field day.

Following our usual process, we had managed to time it so as to go through on a neap tide with the current behind us and with a benign forecast of very light following winds and a flat sea. We were still terrified.

As it turned out, our cowardice paid off. It was flat calm and *Birvidik* slid through at slack water like a thief in the night. There was so little wind that we didn't even bother to raise any sail. It was turning out to be one of those just-perfect days when, just approaching the anchorage at Audierne, the chartplotter (its bad connection fixed during the sojourn in Trebeurden) went down, closely followed by the radio coming out in sympathy. And they weren't even French.

This necessitated a sudden and unexpected reversion to traditional navigation. It also brought home just how much navigation has changed since the introduction of GPS. Although the first GPS satellite was launched in 1978, and degraded data were made available for civilian use in 1984, GPS didn't really take off in the non-commercial market until the mid to late nineties. Prior to that, everyone had to rely on the arcane intricacies of trad nav.

Modern sailors (and I definitely include ourselves in this) are a bunch of soft, southern big girls' blouses. Pampered by the comforts of technology we won't even contemplate going to sea if, for example, the bubble control on the Jacuzzi malfunctions.

When I first learnt to sail in the 1970s we blundered our way around the rock and current strewn Channel Islands with nothing more sophisticated than a lead weight on a length of marked string. The high tech versions had a depression in the bottom of the weight which was filled with tallow. When you pulled the lead-line up you could look at what was stuck in the tallow and tell the captain what sort of surface he was about to hit. As for position finding, big ships had Decca and loran-C. If we were lucky we would point a compass at a couple of dubiously identified marks, randomly scratch a triangle on the chart with a blunt pencil and confidently proclaim that we were somewhere in that triangle.

Probably.

Well, perhaps anyway.

If we were lucky.

Taking scale into account the said triangle could have accommodated most of the Channel Islands and adjacent coast of France. If we were unlucky, we had to rely on determining our Estimated Position. Doing this worked on the principle that a good 80% of the time we had a reasonable idea of where we had started from. All we then needed to know was which direction we were travelling in, how fast we were travelling through the water, in what direction and at what speed the water was travelling, and how much the wind was blowing us off course.

All of these were riddled with potential error. We were lucky if we could hold a course more accurately than five degrees either way. Speed through the water was calculated by throwing a piece of wood or a recalcitrant crew member off the bow and timing how long it took for him, her or it to disappear into the propeller. Tidal flow was interpolated from tidal diamonds on the chart. This, ironically, required you to know where you were so as to determine which tidal diamond to use, whereas the whole point of the exercise was to try and find out where you were in the first place. Finally, leeway was calculated by looking over the stern and guessing the angle between the boat's direction and its wake. Adding all these errors together you came up with what was dispiritingly known as a 'circle of uncertainty' which usually encompassed an area about the size of Belgium. You could then say with reasonable confidence that you might, just about, be somewhere in there.

GPS changed all that. Even the old style degraded signals gave you a position to within 100 metres, an undreamt of level of accuracy at the time. The kit I have at the time of writing is accurate to within two metres. That means that it can actually determine whereabouts on the boat I've mounted the antenna.

There are, however, two flies in this miraculous technological ointment.

The first is due to the fact that the electronic charts used in chartplotters are mostly based on charts drawn up in the nineteenth century. Latitude and longitude were determined using the positions of heavenly bodies, a sextant and a less accurate timepiece than you'll currently find in a posh Christmas cracker. The relative position of everything else was worked out using basic trigonometry. The upshot of all this is that although the relative positions of features to each other are usually reasonably accurate, their position on the chart can be a bit out. Well, quite a long way out actually. The worst we've come across was in the gulf of Patras. As we were approaching Trizonia harbour in a clearly marked channel, a glance at the chartplotter showed us, rather disconcertingly, as being nearly a kilometre to the north, causing havoc by sailing through the middle of downtown Glifadha at rush hour. Errors like this make relying on a chartplotter in thick fog, or at night, a somewhat risky undertaking.

This particular little glitch, though, is amenable to technological correction. More up to date charts are being produced which are based on Google Earth, whose lat and long positions are accurate down to the metre. In fact I've just installed a free program on my laptop which, with the help of a 25 quid USB GPS receiver, shows the boat position on Google Earth accurately enough to say which side of a finger pontoon we're on.

The second glitch, though, is the one that triggered this little aside. Electronic systems can, and do, break down. Aside from the usual weaknesses inherent in any technology, electronics has one big Achilles Heel, the bogeyman of the digital age, the Electro-Magnetic Pulse. EMPs are large, rapid changes in an electromagnetic field. They have a number of causes, including nuclear explosions (fortunately not too common, other than in the vicinity of North Korea) and storms both solar and thunder. When an EMP hits a conductor, be it a wire, metal guardrail, alternator winding, printed circuit board or intimate body piercing, it induces a huge electrical current in the said conductor. This can range from tens of amps to hundreds, thousands or even more. This can fry circuitry (and, in the case of intimate body piercings, genitalia) [3] very effectively. You don't actually need a direct lightning strike. Near will do.

There is a fix to this, but it has to be done well before the EMP arrives. The solution is to encase everything that might suffer from the EMP in a Faraday cage. This is a sort of electromagnetic bunker and can easily be constructed from fine wire mesh, metal coat hangers and duct tape. Failing that, you can try sticking them in the oven. The downside is that the electronic gizmos must be completely electrically isolated and therefore they won't work while they're in there. So you're still stuffed. However, the next time you're flying through a thunderstorm you'll be pleased to know that an airliner fuselage is one big Faraday cage. Well, most of the time.

Prudent sailors, and we are nothing if not prudent, always carry paper charts as a backup. We also note down our position every hour so that if everything goes pear-shaped we can work out an estimated position from not too long ago. We note positions every half hour if things look a bit iffy. We should also really keep practicing at trad nav as

---

[3] Such piercings caused problems in the early days of electrosurgery (or diathermy as it is sometimes, inaccurately, known). This technique uses radio frequency AC current to cut and cauterise tissue. The earlier versions returned the current to earth through a large pad attached to the patient. This usually caused no damage as the current was dissipated over a large area and so produced little heating effect. However, any metal objects attached to the patient could concentrate the current even to the point of arcing, leading to some nasty burns in delicate places. Of course, as the patient was unconscious at the time this often only became apparent after the operation. During the actual procedure the smell of overcooked steak was masked by the smoke from the cautery site

the skills atrophy with disuse.

The reliability of chartplotter and GPS had, of course, made me lazy. I scrabbled back to the old method. I identified landmarks, took bearings, sharpened pencils, scrutinized charts, drew lines and set a course for the anchorage, which was just off a concrete jetty. As we approached it became apparent that the jetty to which we were heading did not meet any of the defining characteristics of the one to which we should have been heading. It was the wrong length and angle, the water was too shallow, there were no mooring buoys or boats anchored there and it had reeds and poles sticking out of the water. Ninety degrees to our left (alright, Port, if you insist) was a jetty which did meet all the aforementioned characteristics, including the fact that anchored by it were lots of boats. Among them were *Aubin* and *Force Seven*, who had set off with us on the same passage. They were looking at us rather quizzically.

We attempted to look casual. *"Hello, just pottering in here. Thought we'd pop across and have a look at that very interesting example of French Marine Civil Engineering over there and now we'll come back and pick up a mooring buoy."* We might have carried this off had we not cocked up by missing the first pass. On the second attempt the mooring hook broke.

Perhaps it was just the psychological effect of being somewhere new, but South Brittany had a completely different feel to it compared with the north coast. The north seemed to have a sombre air, characterized by the steel-grey granite that made up much of the landscape and most of the buildings. This, and the blue-grey slate of the roofs, echoed the rain-laden clouds that scudded across the skies. Even the postcards on sale in the area had pictures of boats and harbours under lowering stratocumuli. You'd have thought they could have taken the photographs on one of the eight sunny days of the year.

Southern Brittany, by comparison, exuded summer cheer and lightened the spirits, epitomized by the pink granite and bright colours of the architecture. Or maybe it was just because the sun was shining. As the sun was shining, we decided to go for a walk.

There was good cause for this. There are many valid reasons for taking up the cruising lifestyle, but keeping fit and healthy isn't one of them; despite sailing having been an Olympic sport since the games' modern inception in 1896. This status is just as well for Britain as most of its 2012 medal tally came for sports that mainly involved sitting down. In fact, nearly two thirds of them came from bum-based sports such as sailing, cycling, rowing, canoeing and horse riding. (As an aside, why does the rider get the medal – shouldn't it really go to the horse?)

Cruising sailing, however, is a sport in about the same way that darts or snooker can be classed as sports - *i.e.* not at all, really. There are far more strenuous ways of travelling across water, such as the aforementioned rowing and swimming or even idly paddling a li-lo with one hand while sipping on a gin and tonic. There are very few proper sports that can be carried out while sitting down eating a Full English Breakfast.

There's a certain amount of physical effort involved in doing things like hauling on mooring and anchor lines as well as grinding winches and wrestling corks from bottles of Chablis, but it's not an activity that taxes or develops stamina. As a result, you can usually tell a cruising yottie by the rolls of spare tyre and the labored breathing that follows an attempt to struggle up the disabled access ramp to the local deli.

The lifestyle is far more sedentary than most people (including many of its adherents) realize. Keeping fit, and weight down, needs a conscious effort and so we try to factor in long walks wherever we can. This has the added bonus of giving a feel for the place, outside of the immediate harbour area.

The coast in Southern Brittany is a long stretch of cliffs interspersed by indented bays with sandy beaches. Along it runs a *randonée*, part of the network of French footpaths that meander across the country. This path took us past scattered WWII fortifications: watch towers, bunkers, submarine pens and gun emplacements. These great, oppressive, mottled grey concrete leviathans bore witness to the area's importance as a naval, especially submarine, base. It was from here that the Battle of the Atlantic was organised from the German side. One of these massive emplacements had been converted to a museum dedicated to the whole campaign.

It is only relatively recently that the image of the German submariner has evolved from the stereotypical tin fish full of sneaky, cowardly, goose-stepping Nazis creeping up on innocent shipping, hitting from behind and then running away. Films such as 'Das Boot' and 'The Sinking of the Laconia' show a much more complex and morally ambivalent history. These men, boys many of them, were far from cowards. They lived for months in terrible conditions and almost constant mortal danger. Dying in a submarine was a particularly unpleasant way to go, and die they did, in their hundreds. Buried away in the display was a small plaque giving the chances of being killed in WWII:

Allied Infantryman: 1 in 48

Royal Navy: 1 in 54

Allied Merchant Navy: 1 in 34

German Submariner: 4 in 5

Sobered and pensive, we returned to the boat, where I set about several diagnostic sorties into recalcitrant electronics. At first I hoped that the chartplotter would prove to be just a fuse, but no such luck. After just 35 hours use it looked as if we would have to send it back to Raymarine. Luckily, a blown fuse proved to be the reason the radio had failed. Unluckily, the root problem seemed to lie in the Navtex, which was built into the radio and still refused to work. Any attempt, so far, to cajole it into earning its passage resulted in a major sulk and it then, in a fit of spite, took the radio out with it

If you frequent yachting circles you will come across the phrase 'Shake-down cruise'. This is a sort of pre-cruise

cruise, the purpose of which is to trick all the little wrinkles and foibles hidden about the boat into showing themselves so that they can be rectified before the cruise proper begins. We really should have had one of those.

In its absence we had started to develop a level of paranoia usually only exhibited by long term amphetamine users. We were constantly on the alert for any unexpected sound; any hum, knock, whine or rattle. Eventually it got to the point where, if they weren't there, we'd imagine them.

Liz had recently triggered this by innocently enquiring mid passage "Should the engine be making that noise?"

"What noise?"

"I don't know – that noise."

I immediately became a man driven to the very edge of madness. Every sound, every vibration had me freezing, ears cocked and eyes swivelling. So, once the electronics had been given a good kicking, the overalls went on and all the engine covers came off. The engine bilge pump hose had come loose and took a while to sort, but everything else seemed OK. I prodded, poked and waggled everything thing that could be prodded, poked and waggled (and quite a few others that really couldn't, or shouldn't, be). Nothing.

Finally, in desperation, I dug out the remote underwater camera to check out the prop. Crouching on deck in bright sunlight with my head under towels, peering at a murky image on a minute screen, I looked a bit like a Victorian photographer, but without the birdie. Overall, everything looked OK. I wanted to put the engine in gear and run it against the mooring buoy to see how the prop shaft felt and looked under load, but Liz exercised her veto. She felt, quite reasonably in the circumstances, that the way things had gone so far we'd rip up the mooring buoy. We decided to treat it like a dodgy prostate and exercise watchful waiting.

The leg from Audierne to Loctudy followed our usual cowardly pattern of flat water and no wind. Not so from Loctudy to L'Orient. This was due to breaking our golden rule of not going out in anything over a forecast force four. The forecast was for a force five to six, from the NE. As we were heading SE this should have been ideal, giving us a good wind on the beam and a relatively smooth sea as there was no fetch from that direction. What we got was a six to seven from the SE - dead on the nose and with a long fetch to build up some seriously interesting waves.

It was not a pleasant trip, but it was quite educational. The waves were just the wrong length for *Birvidik* to ride. As she ran down one wave the bow met the oncoming one at the trough and ploughed into it, burying itself in green water and throwing great arcs of spray out each side. Buoyancy would then come into play, fortunately, and the bow would rise up and point at the sky, sending cascades of water back down the boat. This motion is very descriptively known as 'hobby-horsing' in boating circles.

The scuppers seemed permanently full of water. This caused me some consternation as I began to wonder whether the diesel filler caps would be watertight against a half metre head of water. Diesel engines resolutely refuse to run on salt water, more's the pity. I spent the entire trip nervously waiting for the engine to falter and die. Luckily, there was very little water in the tanks when I checked them on arrival.

After six hours of this we arrived, wet, bedraggled, cold and nauseous, at the entrance to the river Scorff. The trip upriver to L'Orient consisted of dodging various sizes of shipping and trying not to get run onto large metal buoys by the considerable ebb current. This led us to the Port du Commerce. Here, there seemed to be a festival of some form on and the place was heaving. We had to negotiate a flotilla of barely controlled dinghies zigzagging erratically across the entrance. Having squeezed through these we found the visitor pontoons full and were directed to raft up against one of those large, old wooden fishing boats of which France seems particularly full. We managed to hit that quite solidly, splitting our capping rail in the process. We had put the fenders at the correct height for a dinky little pontoon, not a thundering great hulk of wood that towered four metres above us.

We found ourselves in the middle of a competition. To

our port side we were assailed by an amplified selection of finger-in-the-ear and diddley-eye music, whilst on our starboard side (and unfortunately winning) was the French version of 'Slipknot'; like the original only louder, less talented, and less tuneful.

The next day, things musical continued to fail to improve. We were subjected to what appeared to be a contest in which all the local schools sent their pupils to sing French versions of those perennial French favourites 'What shall we do with the drunken sailor" and "Blow the man down" in batches one after the other. It was almost completely tuneless and out of time. In fact it was more 'shouting' than 'singing'. I suspect it was judged by a technician with a decibel meter rather than a musician.

L'Orient is interesting and lively, but hardly quietly rural. We were frequently treated to the soothing sounds of late-night drunken revellers stumbling, slurring, retching and urinating around the quays; so much so that we started to feel we were back in St. Helier marina. This was complemented by hammering and banging as the stalls and stages for the recently ended festival were dismantled.

In addition there appeared to be a very irate Frenchman on the quay. Whilst he and a couple of others were packing away their equipment from the festival, something about the packing of the van seemed not to have met with his unqualified approval. There was much shouting and yelling, and the sound of spanners, pots, pans, and furniture being thrown. A large saucepan arced gracefully into view from the quay ten metres above, bounced on the pontoon and splashed into the water by the boat. We paused briefly, looked at each other and carried on our conversation as if nothing had happened. A little later there was a crunch as a van reversed into a stack of trestle tables and sent them flying, followed by a screech of tyres and a stream of French invective. Shortly after there was an oath, a kick and another pan fell to a watery grave. We continued being terribly British whilst silently praying we didn't end up buried under an archaeological layer of industrial catering equipment.

We were also next to a very noisy ramp, which moonlighted as the local pissoir. Liz saw more willies here than she ever did at work. Mind you, with her having been mainly occupied with ear, nose and throat surgery that's probably not so surprising. For all their failings, they usually managed to get the patients onto the table the right way round.

It was a spring tide while we were there. The tidal range in L'Orient is considerably less than the twelve metre range in Jersey, but it is still a respectable four and a half metres on a big spring tide. The pontoons and ramps are designed to accommodate this. The pontoons float up and down on runners fixed into the harbour wall. The ramps are hinged at the top and the bottom slides along the pontoon as it rises and falls. At high water the ramp is almost parallel with the pontoon and as the tide rises the whole arrangement resembles the closing of a giant pair of nutcrackers. Just hold that image in your mind for a bit.

We found another use for the ramp. If you can't be bothered to actually fold away your folding bike, simply arrive back from your cycle ride at low water, place your bike out of the way under the ramp and settle down in the cockpit for a well-deserved cup of tea and a read. Wait for the pontoon to rise with the tide *et voilà!* - one compact bike.

Perhaps it was the creaking of the moving pontoon that triggered the synapses in my brain, but I glanced over to the ramp and the full implications hit me. I vaulted out of the cockpit, grabbed the first bike and yanked. Nothing happened; the ramp was stuck fast on the saddle. It was only compressed by about a centimetre, but it was stuck fast nevertheless. I resorted to the usual male response in these circumstances and applied more force, bracing my feet against the harbour wall. Veins bulged in my neck and my face went a delicate shade of purple. Still no luck, and the tide was still rising so the compressive force on the bikes was increasing by the minute. Having run out of intrinsic force-producing ability I employed the customary second male tactic in these circumstances and started searching frantically for a machine of some sort to enable me to apply even more force. "A huge lever – that's what I need" I thought, and started looking for a long enough length of scaffold pole left over from the shenanigans of the previous night. No luck. I was just about to rush over to a passing French van and ask if I could use his jack to try to lift the ramp from the pontoon when Liz's exasperated shouts finally penetrated my concentration: "Bob! Try letting the tyres down!" The woman's a genius.

Once Raymarine had come up trumps with a brand new chartplotter (which was pretty good of them, considering it was out of warranty), *Birvidik* set off downriver. After one night in Port Haliguen, we went on to the River Vilaine. La Vilaine is tidal for quite a way up; or rather it would have been if they hadn't built a large dam across it at Arzal.

The thing with rivers is that they're unbelievably untidy. They pick up all sorts of crud as they wander through the countryside and then just dump it when they get to the sea. The Vilaine flows through four of France's one hundred départments and seems to have managed to deposit a fair proportion of all four of them on the seabed in the approaches. At low tide the approach dries and you can't get nearer than about six miles from the lock without running aground. Under such circumstances the cowardly (and sensible) thing to do is approach on a rising tide. Then when you run aground on the sand bar the rising tide will lift you off and immediately carry you forward about ten metres so that you can run aground again. If you keep this somewhat erratic progress up for a few hours you'll eventually arrive at the lock. We had decided to employ this tactic and had timed our approach so as to reach the lock by about eight in the evening, on the end of the flood tide.

Approaching a new manoeuvring ground is always a bit of a sphincter-twitching experience for us, especially when it's going to get dark soon and the tide is turning to the ebb. The pilot book and charts give you some idea of what's going to come, but what it actually comes **as** is usually a surprise.

Our normal technique under these circumstances is to

peer anxiously in the general direction of where we think we should be going and try to get an idea of the layout. This is invariably a waste of time as we do this when we're about four miles off and any detail is completely indistinguishable at that distance, especially through haze, fog, rain and encroaching gloom.

This particular approach, though, had none of these impediments and we managed, with the aid of binoculars, to pick out the lock at a distance of about two miles. It looked full – absolutely packed out. This was just a teensy bit of a problem as the eight o'clock locking was the last one of the day. Failure to get into this would leave us two options; dry out in the river and fall over or turn round and rush six miles back out to sea on the falling tide. The latter would most likely result in us running aground and falling over anyway, and in a much more exposed position. So we headed on up toward the lock, anxiously scanning ahead with binoculars every 45 seconds. The lock still appeared full.

We worked slowly up the winding approaches, gingerly picking our way through the channel, trying to avoid the withies on either side, and fully expecting to run aground at any point. Not so the local boats who came zapping past us at full tilt and proceeded to pile into the lock ahead of us. The view through the binoculars looked increasingly less encouraging as French boat after French boat threw itself into the lock. Panicking, I shoved the throttle forward and raced them for it. If we ran aground then we ran aground – sod it.

The trouble with binoculars is that they compress perspective. Objects at a distance look much closer to each other than they really are. That's why telephoto lenses are useful for making crowds look larger and more closely packed than they really are. This is handy for the likes of demonstration organisers and the producers of programmes such as 'Today in Parliament'. Cynical MPs increase this effect with a technique they call 'doughnutting', whereby the few MPs actually present in the almost deserted chamber pack themselves round those scheduled to speak, thus making it look as if the chamber is actually packed out and everyone is doing their job properly. The broadcasters collude in this deception by zooming in.

When we got close enough to use the naked eye it became apparent that there was still room for us to squeeze in at the back, which we did with a sigh of relief. We tied up to the lock sides with fifteen minutes to go until the lock operated.

We thought we'd cut it fine, but still the French boats arrived in droves, pushing on the boats at the back of the lock, namely us, and gesticulating wildly, demanding that we move forward to let them in. Trying to do this resulted in the boats in front of us gesticulating equally wildly and demanding volubly that we bugger off backwards and leave them alone. We bounced to and fro in this game of nautical ping pong for about ten minutes until a loud klaxon (with a K) went off and for some unfathomable reason all the boats at the front of the lock moved forward about twenty metres and let everyone in.

As the lock gates closed they nudged the last few boats forward and jammed us all together cheek by jowl, rendering the intricate web of lines that seemed to bind each boat to every other one and to the lock side completely superfluous. They the sluices opened and we all rose in stately harmony, locked together like a giant jigsaw puzzle.

On the other side of the lock was a large, calm basin surrounded by rolling countryside and gently wooded slopes. On each side of the dam there was a marina nestled into the corner. No-one had to go more than about three hundred metres to find a berth.

So why, when they opened the upstream lock gates, did it look like the start of the Indianapolis 500? As soon as the water had stopped rising, engines were revved up, filling the lock with dense clouds of black smoke, dilute sulphuric acid and assorted carcinogens. Ropes were brought in from the lock sides and other boats' lines were hastily untied and thrown vaguely in the direction of whichever other boat appeared nearest. Even before the gates were opened boats were trying to force their way to the front which, given how tightly packed the boats were, was a geometric impossibility.

Among the assembled throng of boats was a bathtub-sized open motor boat with a little cuddy near the front. In this cuddy, crouched behind a wheel the size of a side plate, stood the Breton version of Albert Steptoe. He must have been about ninety. His milky eyes glared out from beneath the peak of a faded blue Breton cap. His face bore an expression of fierce concentration which was intensified by his sunken lips. He had obviously got to the age where the effort involved in putting in his false teeth far outweighed any concerns about outward appearance and social perceptions. His substantial wife stood on the tiny foredeck with a puzzled expression on her face, trying to make sense of the spider's web of ropes that had suddenly appeared as if by magic.

Despite the fact that the lock gates had not shown an iota of movement he revved his engine and slammed it into ahead. His wife, still entangled in a cat's cradle of ropes, was taken completely unawares by this development and lurched backwards as the boat surged forwards. We looked on aghast, waiting for her to fall into the churning lock and be drawn into his propeller, probably followed by an expensive splintering noise as he rammed into the boats ahead. Luckily, he had omitted to untie his stern line which brought him to an abrupt and unexpected halt, a turn of events which also took his wife by surprise. She had gamely managed to regain her balance after the unsuspected surge forwards, but this sudden reversal proved too much for her and she fell flat on her face on the foredeck. This seemed to have no effect whatsoever on Captain Chaos. Unable to work out why he wasn't moving he applied the standard Y chromosome response in such circumstances and gave it more revs.

The sternline groaned and creaked, but held. The cloud of carcinogens thickened and the chorus of particularly expressive Gallic exhortations reached a crescendo, accompanied by a Danse Macabre of arm waving and shrugs. Eventually, a crew member from the alongside boat, in an act of remarkable bravery (or stupidity), stepped across the churning gap between the two boats, put his hand on Chaos's throttle hand, gently pulled it back to the neutral position and pointed aft to the still attached sternline.

By this time the crowd of ghouls lining the locksides was four or five deep. Arzal is a beautiful area, but very quiet with only two restaurants and no shops, not even a hairdresser's. The main social activity and source of entertainment appears to be watching the antics of the boats in the lock and waiting for something to go wrong. It's rarely a long wait, but this must have been cup final day for them.

The second half opened with the lock gates. The logical thing to do here is to wait until the boats in front of you have gone and then gently exit the lock in a calm and relaxed fashion. *Mais non!* The French procedure is for everyone to hurtle forward simultaneously and attempt a sort of block manoeuvre so that the entire contents of the lock come out in one lump and then fragment in different directions like a charge of grape-shot.

This might just have come off had Captain Chaos not entered the volatile mix. He now appeared to be experiencing some problems with his throttle cum gear control and began kangarooing forwards and backwards, rebounding off the boats around him, which caused them to bagatelle into their neighbours in turn. It did, however, convince the boats at the front that it might be a good idea to get the Hell out of it PDQ. Into the recently vacated space shot Captain Chaos, heading straight for the lock wall. We closed our eyes, gritted our teeth and put our fingers in our ears. When the anticipated crunch failed to materialise we tentatively opened our eyes to the sight of Captain Chaos, by some arcane trick of Breton seamanship, exiting the lock sideways. Those of us that remained resumed breathing and eased our way out to find a mooring.

It's strange how the simplest little misadventures always seem so much more sinister when they happen in an unfamiliar setting. Foreign countries are, by their very nature, unfamiliar; as everyone who has been abroad on holiday will appreciate. There is a qualitative difference, though, between 'abroad' as experienced by a package tourist and 'abroad' as experienced by a cruiser, who tends to feel far more vulnerable. We're not talking holiday resorts here, where punters are cushioned by the familiar – made to feel at home, with the holiday rep as ersatz mum who will kiss things better and make sure they get home if things really go tits-up. The cruiser is much more psychologically aware of his greater dependence on his own resources and of their pathetic limitations. He is also far more sensitive to how much he doesn't know about the culture in which he finds himself.

While at Arzal we decided to take the bikes and make our way to La Roche Bernard, about five miles upriver. All went swimmingly until I turned round on the way back to find no Liz who, as it later transpired, had stopped to take a photograph and then wandered off down the wrong road at a crossroads.

I was worried as she had the beer supply in her panniers. I cycled up and down the stretch of road several times, but found no sign of her. I tried down the side roads where I was relieved to find no mangled bikes or pools of congealing blood, or even worse, spilled beer. I went back to where I had last noticed her absence and waited for half an hour - still no Liz. It was becoming more and more bizarre, as if she had suddenly and inexplicably dematerialised from the planet. With increasing sensations of panic and visions of road accidents and bloodthirsty Gallic Ted Bundys floating before me I pedalled frantically off to find help.

Soon afterwards a French family were sitting down to a civilised Lunch in their deserted country house, when they were disturbed by a frantic pounding on their door. On opening it they were confronted by a swivel-eyed English madman ranting away in 'O' level French and gesticulating wildly. When they finally twigged he wanted to use their telephone, *Pere de Famille* pointed in the direction of the hall with the poker he'd been hiding behind his back.

Unfortunately, I discovered that I couldn't reach Liz's mobile from a French phone and so in another flurry of mangled French (and to the relief of all the others present) hi-tailed it down the road on my bike.

Liz, meanwhile, was blithely cycling gently along what she was convinced was the correct route. This is understandable as all French countryside looks the same - rolls of hay in fields, deserted farmhouse on the left, half built deserted farmhouse further down on the right and lots of villages with familiar names, all beginning with 'Ker'.

She was heading for a village called 'Mazon' which seemed to trigger a few synapses in the spatial awareness section of her brain. This was due, I suspect, to the fact that it had been mentioned on signposts on the way out, but at no point had we actually passed through it. Perhaps it also registered by virtue of being one of the few that didn't begin with a 'K'.

Liz would like it noted here that I had the map and she was therefore at a disadvantage. I would like it noted that this was because I could read said map, and her having possession of it would not have made a jot of difference to her navigational progress.

By the time she got to Mazon, discovered her error and turned back, I was frantically pedalling back to the boat intending to call her mobile from mine. I arrived to find not only my mobile, but Liz's as well, nestling lovingly alongside it. So much for plan b. I jumped back on my bike and began pedalling vigorously back along the route, my legs pumping like pistons as I mentally worked out how I could report her missing to the Gendarmerie without bringing suspicion upon myself. Two minutes later I met her coming the other way. I was surprised at the amount of relief I felt. Only then did I realise just how irrationally frightened I had been.

From now on she always has to have her phone with her and some emergency money sewn into her knickers.

Biscay

If we were nervous at the prospect of going through the Raz de Sein we were quivering wrecks at the thought of crossing Biscay. The bay has a fearsome reputation for a number of very good reasons. Its geography ensures that it funnels all the predominantly westerly Atlantic storms, which can last for days on end, into its arms and then proceeds to heap them up on the shallowing seas created by the continental shelf. As a result the waves build to terrifying proportions. To add to all this, any ship caught in a westerly gale here is faced with hundreds of miles of lee shore with few harbours of refuge. Most of those harbours that do exist are extremely dangerous to enter in strong westerly winds and it's usually safer to stay out at sea if you can and take your chances there. Especially in the days of sail, being caught in a gale in Biscay was something greatly to be feared.

In these days of reliable diesel engines, the ability to beat to windward and vastly improved weather forecasts this is not so much the case, but it did not prevent us from viewing the prospect with increasing trepidation. We had made the mistake of conducting extensive research on Biscay prior to planning our crossing. This research seemed to consist mainly of reading articles in the yachting press describing capsizes, dismastings, men overboard and days on end of utter terror and exhaustion, all in lurid detail. As the date of the crossing approached, the atmosphere on *Birvidik* became quieter and more reflective, interspersed with the odd, give away episode of forced light-heartedness and gaiety or bouts of gallows humour.

We had done one overnighter before, as crew on a friend's boat, but never with me as skipper, never with the two of us as sole crew and never on our own boat. This would also be the first time we would be out of radio range and not in a position to run for cover if we hit a serious problem. Niggling doubts as to whether this whole enterprise had really been such a good idea began to surface.

We estimated that our crossing of 350 miles from Pornichet to Cedeira in North West Spain could take anything from two and a half to four days, depending on conditions. For most of that period we would be more than 24 hours from any port of refuge and effectively out of radio range. A reliable weather forecast became a *sine qua non* for this little jaunt.

We are spoilt these days. There was a time not long ago, well within the rapidly shortening memory span of many cruising today, when obtaining a weather forecast entailed hunching over in a lurching, smoky, oil lamp-illuminated cabin with your ear pressed against the speaker of a tinny transistor radio as the comforting tones of 'Sailing By' announced the 00:33 BBC shipping forecast. This dealt with 31 sea areas the size of Wales and upwards in three minutes and 300 words. To cope with these restrictions, a coded shorthand was employed which was incomprehensible to those not trained in its arcane eccentricities: *"Rockall, Malin, Hebrides, Bailey, Fair Isle, Faeroes, South East Iceland. Southerly 7 becoming south Easterly Gale 8 soon. Rough. Rain and sleet. Fair, becoming poor to very poor. And now the reports from coastal stations at 18:00 G.M.T. today...Tiree. Southerly 6. Rain. Good. 998 millibars, falling slowly..."*

The familiar format took on the air of a religious rite as nervous mariners awaited the pronouncements of the high priest of the BBC met office from the inner sanctum of Bush House. 'Going foreign' involved leaving this cosy sanctuary. Although radio 4 could be picked up on long wave, reception became progressively poorer and the forecasts progressively less relevant. The gallant English mariner then found himself in the discomforting position of being dependent on the dubious information emanating from Johnny Foreigner.

Given the traditional English incompetence in foreign

languages, it was really rather decent of our continental cousins to make a habit of giving forecasts in English as well as their own language. We have, however, met some ultra xenophobes who seem to be convinced that the English versions are made deliberately erroneous by vengeful continentals still smarting from Trafalgar and the Armada.

Continental marine forecasts usually consisted of a stream of static-scrambled, machine-gun French (or Spanish/Italian/Greek etc), followed by a further static-scrambled stream of fractured English in an impenetrable accent. If your boat was lucky enough to be equipped with an SSB radio the size of Norfolk along with the necessary highly expensive and power-hungry accoutrements, the predictions could occasionally be enhanced by the technological miracle of a weatherfax; this latter being a dirty grey sheet of A4 with some slightly dirtier greyer smudges on it. Some yachtsmen proclaimed that they could divine the forthcoming weather for up to three days from this rune. Personally we reckoned we used to have as much luck from consulting pine cones and strands of seaweed, augmented occasionally by inspecting the entrails of a recently slaughtered chicken or goat.

Weather forecasting has improved out of all recognition over the last twenty years, coinciding, and not coincidentally, with the explosion in available computing power. The number-crunching capacity of modern mainframes lies outside the boundaries of the human imagination, which evolved to deal with phenomena of a much more modest scale.

In essence, weather forecasting involves attempting to establish current weather conditions accurately, preferably over the whole planet, and then calculating how things will develop using mathematical models based on physical laws. There are two fundamental difficulties with this. The first is the measurement of initial conditions, namely how accurate they are, along with their resolution, or how close together the points from which you take your measurements are situated. Closer points give a fuller and more accurate starting picture which, given the somewhat depressing implications of chaos theory for weather forecasting, is highly desirable. This fuller picture, however, requires an awful lot more sums, leading us on to the second difficulty: actually doing the sums. It is not the difficulty of the mathematical operations; each could easily be done by anyone with 'A' level maths. Well, anyone who got 'A' level maths more than about twenty years ago, before it morphed into 'O' level maths with a spray job and four re-treads. The problem is doing them more quickly than the weather does them.

Even a short range forecast requires several billion calculations, something that would take 1500 mathematicians working in eight hour shifts about six weeks to do by hand. [4] The final result would be a month and a half out of date when it was eventually produced. The latest (2010) Met Office computer in the UK can do those calculations in one millionth of a second.

The upshot of all this is that forecasts are more accurate, more frequently updated and much easier to obtain than they have ever been. Forecasts for four days ahead are now more accurate than one day forecasts were 30 years ago. They are disseminated by VHF, SSB, satellite comms and the internet, and are updated at three hour intervals. Resolution has improved from sea areas larger than some countries to squares one kilometre by one kilometre.

Meteorologists, however, like social workers, can't win. They're damned if they do and damned if they don't. If they put an accurate assessment of the degree of uncertainty into the forecasts they are accused of being vague, and if they don't they are accused of being wrong. People, and yotties are among the worst offenders here, quite unrealistically expect long range, highly accurate forecasts with resolutions on the scale of a broom cupboard and all at no cost. Something along the lines of: *"At number 24 Acacia*

---

[4] All calculations in this book are of the back-of-the-envelope variety and should be taken with a large pinch of salt. If they're accurate to within an order of magnitude I'll be pleased. And surprised.

Crescent it will be overcast with light drizzle in the front garden until 10:45, whilst washing can safely be left on the line in the back garden until 12:50 when the drizzle will move 40 metres south, leaving the garage in hazy sunshine. The wind will be from the South, but not strong enough to blow the smoke from the bonfire at number 28 in through the kitchen window".

Not us. We want all that plus we're willing to pay for extras. We got hold of every free forecast we could, which all predicted light winds and calm seas for at least five days. We didn't believe a word of them. So we paid fifteen quid plus exorbitant mobile phone charges for a one to one conversation with a Met Office meteorologist in Exeter – money well spent. After he had very patiently calmed me down and soothed my fears, he assured me that there were no monsters or bogeymen out there and that Biscay was going to have very light winds and calm seas for the next five days, the only slight niggle being a two metre west-northwesterly swell. So we stocked up enough food and drink for two months and set off, hearts in our mouths, at 06:00.

It didn't look any different to setting out for France from St. Helier: a bit of land behind you and nothing but sea for the whole 180 degrees in front. The difference was psychological – from Jersey, you knew that there was land hiding over the horizon, just fifty miles away. Even if you held a random course anywhere in that sector you'd find land in short order. Here you knew that at best it was nearly 400 miles to your destination (that's four days at four knots remember), and if you really made a pig's ear of it you might not hit land for 4000 miles. Bill Cooper, in his and Laurel's excellent book 'Sell up and Sail' posits that there are two types of yachtsman: those who shit when they see land and those who shit when they can't see land. We fall into the latter category. Bill also goes on to say that there are some unfortunate souls who shit under both sets of circumstances, but that they rarely go to sea.

Go to sea we did, and like most long worried about experiences, the anticipation was far worse than the reality. The sea state and weather conditions were exactly as predicted – wind force two to three, fine on the bow and a slight sea with a two metre swell just aft of the starboard beam (coming from the right and just behind in English). We motor-sailed all the way, although the sails were more for steadying the boat and making us more visible than for providing any propulsive force.

The land dipped below the horizon behind us and for the first time we were really 'all at sea'. As we became used to things the occasional rushes of "*Oh my God – we're miles from anywhere with nothing but sea!*" became less frequent and we settled into a routine of watchkeeping, eating and snoozing. Then, as the day progressed, flashes of "*Oh my God – it's getting late and it'll be dark soon*" started.

About 9:30 the sun sank below the horizon and the sea and sky darkened to a purple hue. The stars were far more visible than we were used to and gave a surprising amount of light – enough, even before the moon rose, to see the horizon. This was one of the few times in our lives that we had been able to look at the stars without their being optically overwhelmed by man-made light sources. This must have been how every night looked to our forebears, before the invention of electric lighting. It was easy to imagine why they were so awestruck by it. In our light-polluted previous lives the night sky had usually appeared to be an expanse of black with a few dozen stars visible, only a few of those of any significant brightness.

What a difference in the middle of Biscay, far from the benefits of civilisation. With our eyes able to adjust fully to the darkness we could see the full glory of the night sky, ablaze with the light of thousands of pin-prick lights. The Milky Way was at last given the chance to demonstrate why it so deserves its name; its broad brush streaking across what looked like a quarter of the heavens.

I lay on my back looking up, mesmerised and awestruck. The nearest of these stars, was a tad over four light years away, an unimaginable distance. The fastest spacecraft we have ever produced managed a speed of 250,000 km per hour and that was with the help of the sun's gravity. That works out at seventy kilometres every second, or London to New York in a fraction over one minute. At that speed it would take 160 years to reach Alpha Centauri, the nearest star I could see.[5]

The faintest stars I could see under these circumstances were from the Andromeda Galaxy. The light then entering my eyes had left them 2 ½ million years ago. Our spacecraft would take four hundred thousand billion years to get there – fifty thousand times longer than the universe has been in existence. If, at the very same moment that I was looking up, any beings on planets around those stars had been looking up in our direction they would be looking at light that left Earth before humans evolved.[6]

Anyone lucky enough to be looking in the right direction on the night of the nineteenth March 2008 would have seen a bright flash of light for about forty seconds. The flash came from an exploding star, a supernova seven billion light years away. Our observer would have been looking back in time halfway to The Big Bang, well before The Sun, let alone The Earth, had appeared.

Perhaps Douglas Adams was right – if life will insist on existing in a Universe of this size, then the one thing it cannot afford to have is a sense of proportion.

My copy of the International Regulations for Preventing Collisions at Sea (the 'colregs', colloquially) runs to 30 pages of close type, including annexes. The easiest way to start up an argument amongst yotties is to invent some obscure and extremely unlikely scenario, usually involving highly improbable combinations of submarines, dinghy racing,

---

[5] Proxima Centauri is actually a smidgeon closer, but is too faint to see with the naked eye.

[6] Apparently, this last statement is actually unsupportable in modern physics but it sounds good. As far as I can work out (which isn't very far, in all honesty) the Special Theory of Relativity predicts that it is not possible to establish exact simultaneity in these conditions. The general idea holds true though.

poor visibility, hovercraft, disabled dredgers, trawlers, malfunctioning radar, overhead power lines, man overboard, engine failure and restricted channels, and then asking how the colregs would apply, especially (and this is the clincher) who would have right of way over whom and why. There are hours of fun in this. The best is to be had when in a yacht club bar full of men of a certain age, all wearing yachting caps and blazers festooned with club badge, gold braid and buttons, and all of whom have spent an inordinate proportion of their sad, empty lives learning every regulation by heart, thus leaving them little or no time to go out actually sailing.

Those regs less likely to be needed we leave to crib sheets available at the steering position. We have few enough operational brain cells left as it is, without cluttering them up with the likes of *'The forward anchor light prescribed in Rule 30(a)(i), when two are carried, shall be not less than 4.5 metres above the after one. On a vessel of 50 metres or more in length this forward anchor light shall be placed at a height of not less than 6 metres above the hull'*. As to right of way, we have a simple, easy to remember set of rules:

1. If it's bigger than us, it has right of way. (This includes all military and commercial shipping)

2. If it's faster than us, it has right of way. (This includes all small catamarans and almost all dinghies). If it's bigger and faster than us, execute a 180 degree turn and run away at full throttle.

3. If it's a charter boat, it has right of way (This is self preservation)

4. If it's not moving at all it has right of way (This includes buoys, harbour walls and lighthouses).

5. If in doubt, it has right of way.

In fact, the only time we do not concede right of way is if the helmsman of the other boat is clearly a man of a certain age, wearing a yachting cap and blazer festooned with club badge, gold braid and buttons. If such an opportunity presents itself we raise a confusing signal in the rigging, such as a laundry basket, a dog biscuit and International code flag 'Juliet' and then head straight for him. He will be the only one within a 500 mile radius who actually knows that Juliet means 'I am on fire and have a dangerous cargo; keep well clear of me'. It's just too good an opportunity to miss. Every time he gives way, we turn so as to put him back on a collision course. Puce is such a surreal, but strangely interesting colour for the human complexion.

There are, however, a few colregs which are essential to know by heart; mainly because if disaster strikes, failure to have followed them leads to your carrying the can at the subsequent board of enquiry. Prime amongst these is Rule 5: *'Every vessel shall at all times maintain a proper look-out by sight and hearing as well as by all available means appropriate in the prevailing circumstances and conditions so as to make a full appraisal of the situation and of the risk of collision.'*

On long passages, this is impossible for the single-hander. All of those single-handed sailing heroes of the English-speaking world, from Joshua Slocum through Francis Chichester, Alec Rose, Chay Blyth and Robin Knox-Johnson to Pete Goss and Ellen MacArthur have broken this most basic rule of seamanship on a daily basis throughout their voyages. You have to sleep sometime. For double-handers such as us it is difficult and tiring, but it gets easier as the number of crew increases. Following from that, it would be logical to expect large commercial ships with a lot of crew to be the ones that keep the best look-out. Economics and the free market have put the block on that idea.

The demand for (financial) efficiency and the ease with which a vessel can be registered in states which put more store by profit than they do by reputation or human life has resulted in massive ships being run through crowded waterways at high speed whilst manned by an often overtired, underpaid and underqualified skeleton crew.

Fishing boats can be as bad if not worse. We were once motoring in a crowded and restricted approach to a French port when a large fishing boat came steaming out towards us at full speed. Despite our being the stand-on vessel, we would willingly have given way if it had been possible to do so without endangering others around us. We just managed to squeeze out of its way. As it roared past, throwing boats on their sides in its wake, we could see that there was no-one at all on the bridge. It was on autopilot and full throttle, with all the crew on the deck sorting out the nets. I reported it to the harbour master, only to be met with a sympathetic, but ultimately dismissive, Gallic shrug. It's amazing how the French can make one shrug and a moue convey *"I appreciate that life is a crock of shit M'sieu, and I sympathise. This, however, happens to be your crock of shit and you're on your own"*.

In fact, the only ships that you can almost guarantee will be keeping a first class look-out are coastguards and warships, but they are excused colregs – they have a note from their mum, the Government.

In its roundabout way, this has been leading to our first night passage and the setting of watches. During the day we stand watches as and when circumstances and personal inclinations dictate. From 22:00 to 10:00 we stand watch three hours on and three hours off. This was, like most things on a boat, a compromise – in this case between being long enough to get a decent period of sleep when off watch and being short enough to enable you to stay awake when on watch.

Crossing Biscay is a fairly gentle introduction to night watches as it is very big and quite empty. Any boats in it are therefore spread very far apart. The likelihood of bumping into anything is comfortingly small. Apart from when we were within ten miles of the coasts our only contacts in two and a half days were hearing one ship on the radio and seeing one pair of fishing boats. This contrasts dramatically with the night crossing from Sardinia to Sicily, which was the marine equivalent of Friday night rush hour on the M25, but without the road markings, street lights or central reservation and with all the drivers being Italian males aged between eighteen and twenty five, running on pure testosterone.

Nevertheless, there have been instances where two sailing yachts, each unaware of the other's existence, have managed to collide at night in the middle of the Atlantic so some form of look out is indicated. Our system employed a digital kitchen timer. The reasoning went along these lines:

* We were doing about five knots

* Although some high speed ferries do over 25 knots, these are rare in Biscay, so let us assume any other ships have a maximum speed of fourteen to fifteen knots.

* The worst case scenario is for both us and the other ship to be heading directly toward each other with a closing speed of about twenty knots.

* Given our height of eye and the expected height of the lights on a high speed craft, we should be able to see them at a range of about seven miles.

* At a closing speed of twenty knots it would take around twenty minutes to hit us from seven miles away, so....

* If we take a really good look round every fifteen minutes we will have a five minute safety factor.

So we set the timer for fifteen minutes, have a really good look round, start the timer and snug down in the cockpit/make a cup of tea/read a book/fantasise about forcing all politicians to be obliged by law to stand on stage at the end of their party conferences and sing 'The Birdie Song' on live television (complete with actions).[7] We do this until the alarm goes off when we repeat the whole process.

About three in the morning on the first night, I was snugged down in the cockpit, drifting in and out of a light sleep when I awoke with a start. I wasn't sure what had woken me, but I was aware of a faint smell which I couldn't

---

[7] Actually, with regard to the last of these activities, I've just had the rather disappointing thought that Boris Johnson could probably carry that off. I'll have to think of a different humiliating fantasy.

pin down. The hairs on the back of my neck started to prickle. I stood up and looked around, eyes and ears straining – nothing. After a few minutes I was just settling down again when I could have sworn that I heard a single, loud, heavy breath right by my ear. I sprung upright in my seat, and just caught something out of the corner of my eye - a faint, ethereal glimmer, fleeting in the darkness. The smell was back again, stronger, slightly fishy or seaweedy.

I am a fully paid-up member of the 'The supernatural and paranormal are a load of old bollocks' society, but there is something about three o'clock in the morning. It is known as 'The hour of the wolf' in some cultures. Statistically there are more deaths in the early hours of the morning than would be expected by chance. I'm sure there are sound physiological reasons for this.

Despite my rational veneer, my hindbrain took over and the adrenaline started to kick in; hair standing up, rapid heartbeat, clammy skin, butterflies in the stomach and senses heightened. Suddenly, the sea erupted around the boat. Water splashed and slapped against the hull and into the cockpit. Silver iridescent streaks flew through the water on both sides and dark shapes spun up into the air. The explosions of heavy breathing were accompanied by a twitter of high pitched squeaks as a pod of about twenty dolphins cavorted, dived and barrelled around the boat.

As they sliced through the water the bioluminescence transformed them into streamlined wraiths leaving a trail of intertwining silver vortices behind them. The squeaks built, faded and built again almost as if following a score.

It is difficult not to be anthropomorphic about dolphins, especially after an experience such as that. They didn't seem to be fishing; they seemed to be doing whatever they were doing for the pure hell of it. This magical performance went on for a good half an hour until, as if on a single cue, they all suddenly turned right and disappeared off into the night and left the world to darkness and to me.

Apart from a couple of other visits from dolphins, the rest of the crossing was uneventful. Far from being an extended purgatory of terror and tiredness as we had feared, the major sensation throughout the trip was boredom, closely followed by irritation at the constant rolling. *Birvidik* rolls easily in a beam swell of the right frequency and this one was of exactly the right frequency.

To enable non sailors to get an idea of this, try the following thought experiment: Imagine a grumpy giant picking up your house, turning it on its side at 45 degrees and giving it a good shake, then turning it over the other way and repeating the process at fifteen second intervals for fifty hours. You'd soon nail down your teacups.

We did, however, make good time. Such good time, in fact, that we had to slow down in the end to avoid making landfall before it was light. At 10:30 in the morning, Spanish courtesy flag flying, we motored through the narrow entrance into Ria Cedeira. Biscay was under our belt and we were now in Galicia. All we wanted now was to anchor, shower and sleep.

Spain (Part 1 – Galicia)

On the map, France and Spain are close neighbours, contiguous along a 500 km border. As such one might expect, and possibly hope for, a degree of similarity. One would be disappointed.

That border, long though it may be, is based on a formidable physical feature, namely the Pyrenees. Before the advent of large scale mechanised civil engineering, the Pyrenees posed a daunting physical barrier, which severely limited travel and reduced the interplay between the two societies.

Separation is the primary requirement for the occurrence of evolution, whether genetic, cultural or linguistic. Luckily, genetic evolution, in humans at least, is a ball-achingly slow process and so the Spanish and the French have not, as yet, evolved into separate species. They remain physically and genetically capable of interbreeding and this phenomenon is not completely unknown.

I suspect, though, that it could possibly be a tad rarer than might be expected, given the reduction in the difficulties of travel which resulted from the unparalled improvements in transport infrastructure. This is because separation does not have to be geographical for evolution to occur. Among other things, it can also be temporal.

Cultural evolution is a considerably faster process than its genetic counterpart. Over the last five centuries or so, *La Vida Española* has become considerably different from *La Vie Francaise*.

This is observable in many aspects, but is perhaps most pronounced in the different ways in which the two societies structure their day. For many years we used to drive from St. Malo to the Algarve every Easter. Given the roads and my lily-livered driving technique, it was usually around nine in the evening by the time we approached the Spanish border. By this time, France was settling in for the night.

Bars and restaurants were closing, curtains were being drawn and lights were dying out across the countryside like the fading embers of the last starburst firework of the display. By 9:30, France was shut.

For the first time traveller this did not bode well for the prospects of obtaining food, drink and shelter. We, however, were old hands and knew that Spain was only a short drive away. As we crossed the border there were the same few lights scattered across the dark countryside. The difference was that here, the lights were popping on one by one, instead of snuffing out. Spain was just waking up.

By midnight on the Spanish side the party was in full swing, while a few kilometres away in Aquitaine all that could be heard was the gentle snuffling of the slumbering population. By six in the morning the French are waking bright-eyed and bushy-tailed, ready to put in a good morning's work before settling down to the serious business of Lunch. The Spanish, meanwhile, are just staggering, bleary eyed to their beds. There, they will snatch a couple of hours sleep before heading out to put in a few hours' work, after which they make their way home again for the serious business of a siesta. Over the course of a normal day the likelihood of both a French and Spanish national being simultaneously awake and in the same locality is infinitesimal.

Hence my suspicion that Franco-Spanish hanky panky might be rarer than expected. Mixed marriages, like murder, require motive, means and opportunity. As far as the French and the Spanish are concerned, the first two are as plentiful as they are in all human societies. The last mentioned, however, tends to be in short supply.

The Rias Altas

Ria de Cedeira to Ria de Camarinas

June 28th 2006 to July 16th 2006

In yachting circles this area of Spain is known just as 'The Rias' and it is an exquisite cruising ground. Rias are fjord-like flooded inlets, apparently reminiscent of the West coast of Scotland, but warmer. Not a great deal drier, though.

The scenery was strikingly dramatic, especially after Southern Brittany. Steep, craggy, wooded slopes fell precipitously down to the sea. Narrow gaps in these opened up to reveal wide expanses of sheltered water with endless creeks and bays crenellating the shores.

Those inlets North of Cape Finisterre are known as the 'Rias Altas' and those South of Finisterre are known as the 'Rias Baixas'. The spelling is a give-away. In Spanish it would be 'Bajas'. Like Brittany, Galicia has its own language, more akin to Portuguese than to Spanish. Also like Brittany it has a strong local tradition and a well established longing for autonomy. For such a small and sparsely populated area it also seems to have a propensity for producing dictators, with Fidel Castro having had Galician parents and Francisco Franco having been born in Ferrol. It is rather ironic then, that shortly after Galicia was granted autonomous status in 1931 it was Franco who, in 1937, annulled that statute and ordered the suppression of the Galician language.

Breeding ground for dictators notwithstanding, they do like a party. With their parties they love fireworks. I mean really love them. Not a *"Ooh they're nice, let's let them off two or three times a year and all go 'Oooh, Aaah' at them"* sort of love them. Oh no, the Spanish set off fireworks on a daily, nay hourly, basis. Any excuse will do - It's a fiesta (that makes if damned near weekly); next week's a fiesta; last week was a fiesta; it's someone's birthday somewhere in Andalusia; ooh look somebody's caught a sardine - anything.

Such frequency could, of course, breed a certain ennui

after the 200th time, so the Spanish have a cunning method of countering this. They don't use ordinary fireworks as such. In fact the visual element is completely missing. The country seems to have cornered the market in high explosive, appearing to have got hold of all and any of it that the Americans might have missed. A Spanish firework display announces itself with an ear-shattering crash followed by a shock wave that collapses lungs, liquefies spleens and makes your nose, eyes and ears bleed. Then they send in the heavy stuff. George W. Bush probably got the 'Shock & Awe' idea after attending a rather restrained Tupperware party in San Sebastian.

The real biggies though are the religious festivals. Every Spanish village worth its salt has an effigy of the Virgin Mary that secretes tears, blood, milk or some other bodily fluid at propitious moments and a reliquary containing some withered, mummified remnant that purports to be something like the left testicle of St. Bastard, the patron saint of Human Resources Consultants.

A classic example of these occurred in Muros. It was a real biggie, the Fiesta of the Virgin De Carmen. They really do seem to have an awful lot of virgins. Shame really that the whole virgin idea is based on a mistranslation from Aramaic via Hebrew into Greek. The original word just meant 'young woman'. Never mind.

We had anchored off the town for a good view. Graham and Katie on *Ocean Goose* poled up a little later as, being proper hairy sailors, they had sailed all the way. We had just enough time for the ritual exchange of insults when all hell was let loose as the Galician Fiesta Artillery (mortar section) fired off everything it had.

They use an interesting technique which demonstrates a rather different attitude to health and safety from that encountered in Britain. Their ordnance consisted of rockets twenty centimetres in diameter and about a metre and a half long, excluding stick. The bottom ninety centimetres of this was filled with propellant and the rest with high explosive. Apparently there is quite a cottage industry manufacturing these devices, although there is rumoured to be a developing shortage of cottages.

In the U.K. they would (if allowed at all, which is unlikely) have to be stuck in a two centimetre thick steel tube buttressed all round with sandbags and blast screening. The designated ignition operative would, after showing documentary evidence of having completed the requisite training and up to date refresher courses, be required to don full body armour and flash suit before lighting the thing with an eight foot match complete with built in safety shield. All spectators, of course, would have to be two kilometres away, housed in a secure bunker protected by four metres of reinforced concrete, and watch the show on a grainy monochrome CCTV relay.

Not the Spanish. Two guys stood on the quay, cigarettes in their mouths, in front of a pile of homemade RPGs, all of which were piled on their sides, pointing at the assembled onlookers. To fire them, they held the body of the rocket lightly between thumb and forefinger, rested the stick on the ground and pointed the whole ensemble skywards. With their free hand they took the cigarette from their mouth and lit the blue touch paper. With exquisite timing they deftly released thumb and forefinger just as the propellant started to lift the rocket and it soared gracefully through their fingers and into the sky before detonating and keeping the local glaziers in business until the next fiesta.

When, trembling, we raised our heads above the cockpit coamings and peered through the smoke we saw a procession of boats streaming out of the harbour, led by a flag and foliage bedecked fishing boat. On said boat was the Virgin Del Carmen. This was not a real virgin but a wooden representation. Either that or she was so heavily into opiates that even the combined artillery of the Spanish fiesta committee couldn't rouse her.

The trip round the ria was accompanied by a band. Well, alright, about 120 drummers and a couple of maniacs with trumpets. The trumpet playing was of such strident awfulness, uncontaminated by such concepts as being in tune or time, that I now have no further qualms about practising the saxophone anywhere in Spain.

Now, say what you like about Graham, but you can always rely on his enthusiastic embracing of local customs. He managed to achieve the impossible by using his foghorn to make an even more God-awful noise than the trumpeters. This served as a challenge to the other yotties in the anchorage and even, to my eternal shame, to me. The massed band of the International Brigade of Collision Avoidance Devices (Auditory Division) will be spoken about in hushed and reverential tones for generations to come in Muros. Mind you, there was a suspicion that the French yacht didn't have a foghorn and was doing something unspeakably French with a duck.

Suspecting (correctly) that the Spanish were only just starting to get the hang of things by late evening, we all went into town by dinghy at 10 p.m. The fair was the usual explosion of colour and noise. There were stalls selling all sorts of clothes and various other gaudy items, but mainly, and inexplicably, shoes.

Spanish street stalls sell a fairly restricted range of items, but the most popular are shoes. About every third stall sells shoes. Not just any shoes; no sensible brogues, no stout walking boots, or even overpriced counterfeit designer trainers. To earn a place on a Spanish street stall, a shoe must meet three very stringent criteria:

a) It must be gaudy. I mean really gaudy. It should be of a colour never found in nature, with a shiny voilé pattern sufficient, in bright sunlight, to trigger a migraine at a range of twenty-five metres.

b) It must be pointy. Preferably honed with a pencil sharpener and requiring orthopaedic surgery to get any normal foot into it.

c) It must be alone. Pairs of shoes have no place on a Spanish street stall.

All the shoes are piled in a large and random heap on the stall, with no attempt to sort them by size, colour or type.

If my colloquial Spanish were better I could test my theory that they are, in fact, arranged alphabetically.

Attempting to buy shoes from a stall seems to involve rummaging through the pile, casting rejects left, right and over the shoulder. Upon selecting the desired shoe, one then waves it under the nose of the stall holder who looks at it quizzically as if trying to ascertain the purpose of this strange item. He then rummages frantically through his pile trying to find the mate of the proffered footwear, almost invariably without success. He then shrugs and returns the shoe to the prospective customer who tosses it back on the pile. We're still trying to work out how this form of 'commerce' actually makes any money.

The first stop from Cedeira though, was not Muros, but A Coruna. Liz's description of the trip was "Grey and miserable with a nausea-inducing swell", so we won't dwell on it. A Coruna, however, more than made up for this. The whole ambience was breathtaking. The centrepiece was one of those impressive plazas that the Spanish do so well. Dominating it was an imposing building with towers, the roofs of which were covered with bronze. This was the town hall. The square in front of it was completely paved, and set around the edges were small cafes and bars. Off the main plaza were numerous narrow streets crammed with restaurants, whose tables and chairs spilled out onto the street. There were throngs of people here and the atmosphere was electric. It was so exhilarating, in fact, that we decided to go out later that evening for a typical tapas. This led to what was to become known in family folklore as the infamous 'Night of the Black Todger'. It's not what you think.

We went to one of the bars that had been really crowded with locals when we passed earlier in the day. It was down a narrow street with tables set outside under genuine XVII century arched columns. As it was only 9:30 in the evening all the locals were just starting to get ready to go out and there were plenty of tables, so we sat down and were presented with the menus by a waiter who must have been all of fifteen; a lovely bloke, keen, amicable and efficient without so much as a hint of adolescent surliness.

I ordered a beer (successfully) but the poor lad was completely flummoxed (as are most Spanish waiters) by Liz's order of a vodka and soda. So he brought her a large glass of shandy. After much gesticulating and saying 'vodka' in every intonation and accent we could think of, he went away and returned with a bottle of Smirnoff. Mind you, he'd hedged his bets on the soda bit and brought a tray full of assorted of mixers for Liz to choose from.

We studied the menu and decided our choices were limited by two factors; our piscovegetarianism and the fact that we'd left the English/Spanish dictionary behind. So we worked out a choice of tortilla, salad, cod croquettes and *empanada* (little tuna pies). The waiter returned and looked questioningly at us, pad and pencil poised expectantly.

I don't speak Spanish. In fact, the only language I speak with even the slightest degree of fluency is Portuguese, and then only at the level of an eight year old. "Well," I thought, "They can't be all that different" and so I ordered by speaking in Portuguese with what I hoped was a Spanish accent, supplemented by pointing and grunting. This was greeted with a torrent of fractured Spanish at about 560 wpm and an apologetic shrug. After trying Portuguese in another range of accents including Serbo-Croat, Chechen and a throat infection, we worked out that tortilla was off, as were the empanadas. Spanish restaurants seem strangely reluctant to serve tortilla in the evening. "*E.U. Public dining (relevance to time of day) standardisation directive 2002/597 9(d)*" I suspect.

This severely limited our options. Our communication with the waiter was about on the level of two year olds, so even if we'd managed to get across that we wanted to know what something was, we wouldn't have understood the answer. We therefore resorted to the Marxist philosophy (Groucho tendency) of "Here are my principles. If you don't like them, I have some others". We decided to order something that looked like we might be able to eat it and then see if we could work out what it was when it arrived. And then eat it regardless.

So we ordered what we suspected to be tuna salad and cod croquettes, followed by *queso provolone al horno* which looked like it might be cheese cooked in an oven, and *fabada casera* which was in with a chance of being beans in some guise or other.

We were then handed the impressive wine list - four pages of wines none of which either of us had ever heard of. So we went for one of our other ploys which is 'Choose a type of wine you know, and order the second or third most expensive'. This worked perfectly, except for the fact that they didn't have any of the one we chose. Or choices numbers two to six. Or, in fact, any of the Ribeiro wines except the five euro ones, which would probably have cost about sixty centimos (forty two pence), a litre in the supermarket and should really have been marketed as pan scourer. In the end, using Portuguese as a tonal language, like Thai, seemed to get across the message "Well, what have you got then that's white and doesn't taste like Ajax?" So he pointed at two of them and we chose one purely at random.

The wine arrived, and this was a winner. 'As Laxas', Albarino, since you ask, and very good it was too. Then the food arrived.

First on the table was the mixed salad with tuna; excellent, if a bit on the large size. This was followed by the bacalao croquettes, which were exquisite. Hot on the heels of the cod croquettes was the queso provolone al horno which was, indeed, cheese and spices cooked in an oven. Then came the fabada casera, which the waiter deposited on the table in pride of place. He removed the lid with a flourish and smiled expectantly at us. We stared at it. Then we stared at the waiter, whose smile was beginning to falter. We smiled, nodded encouragingly, and stared back at the fabada.

It was, indeed, beans. Beans in a savoury gravy, baked in an oven. Beans in a savoury gravy, baked in an oven, along with various parts of the anatomy of a pig of which few people are aware or would, in all honesty, want to be aware.

And the black todger. It sat squatting on the beans as if daring you to eat it. It was cylindrical, about four centimetres in diameter and eight centimetres long. It wasn't black pudding, it was far too black. The skin was resistant to abrasion, sharp edges and most corrosive liquids and had the tensile strength of twelve millimetre stainless steel rigging wire.

In contrast the filling had the texture of - well, how can I put this. I wouldn't have been surprised if they had just cut out a section of large intestine and cooked it without cleaning or even emptying it. It managed to be sticky and crumbly at the same time which isn't easy.

Bravely, we tried a small amount each. We have just discussed said taste, and have come to the conclusion that it was truly indescribable, and that's definitely not as in 'sublime'. Among the terms rejected as being nowhere near man enough for the job were 'vile', 'rancid', 'disgusting', 'cloyingly organic', 'toxic waste', 'emetic', and 'dogshit'.

We ate the rest of the meal with gusto, pausing occasionally to toy with the beans and try to make some inroads into the fabada. Unfortunately, although the beans were very pleasant, the crumbly nature of The Black Todger's filling ensured it spread throughout the dish and contaminated everything in it. It also managed to coat the cutlery, all the other crockery and the table cloth. It seemed to have some sort of instinctive dispersal program. Everything became contaminated with it, including several passers-by. If it ever learns to reproduce we're all in deep trouble.

Cruising has, with considerable justification, been defined as 'repairing boats in exotic places'. Whilst in A Coruna, we decided, in a vain (and continuing) attempt to get our own access to weather forecasts, to try and buy a Navtex, as the one built into the radio was kaput. A very helpful man in the somewhat Olde Worlde chandlers said that yes, he had heard of thees theeng called 'navtex' and he was pretty sure there was one in Barcelona. Or possibly Alicante. Or Seville maybe. After several garbled phone calls in Spanish, including one in strangled Spanglish between me and The Man in Barcelona, we were assured that it would be in A Coruna by the next day, and that we could get it a special price if we paid cash and not by credit card.

Sure enough, we got a phone call the next day to say that it had arrived. Poor, trusting fool that I am, I went round several cash machines with several different cards withdrew the required number of Euros, hopped on my bike and pedalled off to get my new toy.

On my return, I excitedly started drilling holes and poking wires through them, followed by screwing lots of other bits in other places. I powered it up and switched on. I take it that by now you are ahead of me. As the shops were shut, we realised that it would have to be tomorrow before we took it back, and at that point the crass idiocy of paying large amounts of money in cash in a foreign country became blindingly apparent.

I spent most of the night memorising what I hoped was the Spanish for "What do you mean I can't have a refund? Give me my money back you thieving, conniving bastard" (*¿Qué quiere decir que no puedo tener un reembolso? Dame mi dinero que robar, connivencia bastarda*, since you ask). The next morning I trotted off on my bike, fully expecting to find that all the people in the chandlers had suddenly forgotten what limited English they seemed to have had the day before. Much to my relief (but, it must be admitted, coloured with a little disappointment that I wouldn't be able to use my newly acquired linguistic skills) they were most apologetic and gave me my money back without quibble. So, all was well, but still no weather forecasts.

It is striking how, once on a boat, even the simplest of everyday tasks become more complex, convoluted and problematic. Take, for example, the mundane, everyday activity of filling up with fuel. In normal life this merely involves climbing into your car, driving the short distance to your local filling station, popping in about 60 litres of petrol and then handing over your life savings and half your current pension pot. An innocent might have thought that refueling a boat would be the same. An innocent would be wrong.

Birvidik carries 1600 litres of fuel, which is a lot for a sailing boat and frequently comes as a surprise to fuel dock attendants. You have to use a fuel dock, despite their being about as common as cocktail bars in ISIS [8] controlled desert. You **could** make 80 round trips to the local petrol station with a couple of 10 litre jerry cans but it would be extremely tedious. So we discarded this option and decided to top up the fuel tanks to replace that which we had used motoring across Biscay. This was an interesting manoeuvre, the fuel berth being nowhere near the position shown in the pilot.

For a start, there was so little water depth in it that we could only get in (and out) for 45 minutes either side of high tide. Doing this entailed leaving the marina, going round the castle to the old and now very dilapidated marina, picking our way through crumbling pontoons and old dinghies, executing a sharp right turn so as to avoid the large unexpected (and uncharted) rock sticking out from the rough stone quay, and then slamming the anchors on before we ploughed into the stone steps. Then we had to rapidly grab hold of the multitude of ropes being thrown at us by the agitated pump operative who was working under the pressure of knowing that he had an hour and a half to fuel up the queue of boats behind us if he wasn't to end up with one of them perched inelegantly on the debris covered rocks that formed the base of his pontoon.

Little did he know of *Birvidik*'s Tardis-like fuel tanks, or of the two 20 litre auxiliary tanks we had strapped on deck. Twenty five minutes later, after giving him eight hundred Euros in exchange for the eight hundred litres of diesel, he waved us goodbye with a sigh of relief as we repeated the inward manoeuvre, but this time backwards. He was lucky we were just topping them up.

Returning to the marina we moored up again opposite

---

[8] or IS, ISIL, Daesh, SCISM or whatever the bunch of murdering, medieval-minded, misogynistic thugs are called this week.

a large customs launch moored to port of the marina entrance, on the decks of which strolled well-armed uniformed officers, all highly polished to within an inch of their lives. They had truncheons, handcuffs and an impressive array of firearms. It was all very scary and intimidating but, in the three days we were there, that's where they stayed - in the marina. They may not get out much, but if any of those nasty drug runners were to come into the marina for a quick wash and brush up then by God they'd be in trouble.

Our last day in La Coruna did not quite go according to Liz's plan, which had involved something along the lines of finishing the jobs to get the boat set for the next day, then a bit of shopping, followed by a touch of sunbathing, and finishing off by taking the tram around the city or walking through a couple of the beautiful parks and pausing for a civilised coffee.

She started successfully enough by bundling me into a clothes shop and refusing to let me out of the changing cubicle until I had successfully tried on (and agreed to wear) a complete summer wardrobe for only £80. Given the many comments I continually receive on my sartorial elegance, I considered this totally unnecessary.

Back on board Liz casually mentioned that she thought she could smell diesel (c.f. "Should the engine make that noise"). We both had a sniff around, but came to the conclusion that we were being over sensitive. Boats always smell of diesel.

That was until a bit later when I was digging around for something in the cockpit locker and found it five centimetres deep with diesel. That was the rest of the day virtually taken care of. Three buckets of diesel later it transpired that the tank breather pipe had come adrift and every time the boat rolled a squirt of diesel shot out of the stub of the pipe and into the locker. It could have been worse. Imagine if we'd gone through the next couple of trips (descriptions coming up) with that size of hole in the diesel tank.

The Rias Baixas

Ria Muros to Bayona

July 16th 2006 to August 5th 2006

Having survived the rigours of the Fiesta de la Virgen del Carmen, we moved on to the little marina of Portosin, chosen because it was a good spot from which to visit Santiago de la Compostela and after all that stressful cruising we thought we deserved a holiday.

What we did on our holidays by Bob Newbury, aged 57 and a 1/4:

We went on the bus to Santiago de Compostela. It was nice. There are lots of buildings and churches and things. And squares and arches. We stayed in a hotel. It was cheap but good. It was nice. Then we went to see the Cathedral. It was big. The organ was very very loud. We ate dinner in the street. It was raciones. These are like big tapas. They were nice. We stayed up very late and listened to music in the square. It was nice. Then we went drinking. It was nice too. The next day we came home by bus. We feel like shit. We can't keep up with the Spanish.

Santiago is the final destination of El Camino de Santiago, the network of pilgrimage routes that converge on it from all across Spain; indeed from all over Europe. The main pilgrimage route is the *Camino Francés*, the 780 kilometre stretch from St Jean Pied de Port to Santiago.[9]

This tradition has been going on since medieval times, when its completion earned the pilgrim a plenary indulgence. This was a sort of spiritual get out of jail free card, which let the him off doing time in purgatory for his

---

[9] The Chieftains' 1996 album 'Pilgrimage to Santiago' explores the links between Celtic music and the music of this area of Spain. It's well worth a listen if you can get hold of it).

back catalogue of sins. Or, of course, you could just buy one, a bit like the heavenly version of being a political party donor.

Usually, the pilgrims carry little with them, which makes sense if you're walking nearly 500 miles across Northern Spain in June. The better off have been known to send their assembled creature comforts on ahead by car so that their Christian Dior outfits and chilled Truffle Martinis are waiting for them when they arrive at the Hotel Flash Ponce de Leon, prior to being whisked up to a penthouse suite by the concierge. Traditionally, though, a pilgrim carries three items, a staff, a gourd and a scallop shell; the gourd to store liquid, the scallop (the symbol of St. James) as a food bowl and scoop, and the staff for fending off packs of indigent New Age Hippies offering to read his aura for five euros.

Many of the modern pilgrims also carry with them the incoherent metaphysical blatherings of the likes of Shirley MacLaine and Paulo Coelho. Perhaps the quality of Ms MacLaine's insights and the value we can ascribe to them can be judged from the online blurb for her 2001 book 'The Camino: A Journey of the Spirit' (Pocket Books), which was published, appropriately enough, on April 1st. After a paragraph that places her and her fellow pilgrims in company with Saint Francis of Assisi, Charlemagne, Dante and Chaucer it asserts:

"For Shirley, the Camino was both an intense spiritual and physical challenge. A woman in her sixth decade completing such a grueling trip on foot ..." Then, with an apparently straight face, it says *"even more astounding was the route she took spiritually... through past lives to the very origin of the universe."*

Reason notwithstanding, the torment continues unabated: *"Immensely gifted with intelligence,[and] curiosity, ... Shirley MacLaine is truly an American treasure."* This stringent critical analysis segued into the revelation that by *"Balancing and negotiating the revelations inspired by the mysterious energy of the*

Camino, she endured her exhausting journey to Compostela until it gradually gave way to a far more universal voyage: that of the soul."

Wading through even more of this sycophantic drivel we learn that *"Through a range of astonishing and liberating visions and revelations, Shirley saw into the meaning of the cosmos, including the secrets of the ancient civilizations of Atlantis and Lemuria, insights into human genesis, the essence of gender and sexuality, and the true path to higher love."*

The hagiography concludes with the exquisite modesty of: *"With rich insight, humility, and her trademark grace, Shirley MacLaine gently leads us on a sacred adventure toward an inexpressibly transcendent climax. The Camino promises readers the journey of a thousand lifetimes."*

Savour this moment. My being speechless is a rare occurrence.

"With rich insight and humility, and her trademark grace?" It's beyond bloody parody. *"Through a range of astonishing and liberating visions and revelations"* Had she not checked the provenance of her Salmon Stuffed Portobello Mushrooms? [10] They can be iffy things, fungi

If only I'd read these books before we arrived. If only we'd turned up on foot carrying a stick, a gourd and a scallop shell instead of by bus carrying a couple of cheese sandwiches, a pacamac and a digital camera. I could have negotiated a revelation or two, proved Fermat's Last Theorem and reconciled quantum mechanics and general relativity before I'd got past the halfway mark. Either that or discovered that the next Dalai Lama was scheduled to be the reincarnation of Elvis and would be born in a lockup under the Holborn Viaduct with a couple of Roswell aliens acting as midwives. With any luck I could have had a transcendent climax. Haven't had one of those since I came off the hallucinogens.

---

[10] Taken from a cookbook by Shirley MacLaine. They're actually very tasty, if a bit of a faff to prepare.

In the interests of balance I did attempt to read 'Camino', mainly to try to ensure a calm and measured judgement instead of my usual splenetic, opinionated, apoplectic spluttering. It didn't work. By chewing off a couple of fingers I managed to get through the bit about the high frequency energy of the ley lines increasing the rate of vibration of the etheric and dense matter that made up my brain (page five). Banging my head repeatedly on a winch distracted me from the snippet informing us that her homoeopath and acupuncturist had informed her that earplugs obstructed the meridians to the kidney (page eleven). However, by the time I reached page twelve I was confronted with the assertion that the road and her (her, note, not its) energy would provide all needs and that she (MacLaine) would be having philosophical discussions with a stick and the ground. At this my pre-frontal cortex was beginning to liquefy and dribble out of my nose so, reluctantly, I had to admit defeat and retire hurt.

The city itself, though, is impressive. The outskirts are like any other city, but when you get to the centre it is overwhelming. The whole of the old town is a labyrinth of narrow streets opening up into squares of all shapes and sizes. The squares are lined with cafes and usually have a monument or fountain in the centre.

The town has evolved rather than been planned and so it is quirky, idiosyncratic and endlessly fascinating. The medieval coexists with later periods and the modern day. You wander through streets lined with twelfth century arches and through alleyways between buildings where two people pass with difficulty. It is easy to get the impression of what it must have been like to live in those times.

Everywhere you pass you come across churches, monasteries, convents, university buildings and the like. Wherever you look up there are ornate religious images topping the buildings. On street corners and the walls of the squares you suddenly find yourself leaning against a baroque carving that is hundreds of years old. Despite all this, it is not a museum piece. People live and work here. And party. My how they party.

We arrived about mid-day on the 21st June, along with several thousand pilgrims. More pilgrims continued to arrive thick and fast, the arrival rate increasing as the feast of St. James (25th July) approached. On that day thousands of people pack into the Praza de Obradoira and file through the Cathedral.

Ah yes, the cathedral. I am rarely lost for words, as is apparent to most who have met me, but I cannot even begin to describe the place. Photographs do not do it justice, it is awe inspiring. The huge vaulted naves are covered in intricate statuary and reliefs, and the whole thing is dominated by a massive gilded altar which covers the (purported) remains of St. James. To add to the effect the gigantic organ was blasting out devotional music. When it pulled out all the stops and let the bass really reverberate it pressed all the buttons in the psyche. The Catholic Church certainly knows a thing or two about manipulating emotions. Mind you, with two thousand years of practice combined with the tricks they assimilated from the previous procession of assorted priests, shamans, witch doctors and snake-oil salesmen, that is to be expected.

Recent research has put forward an intriguing possible mechanism for this. There is a building body of evidence that religious, spiritual or other paranormal experiences are associated with unusual activity in the temporal and parietal lobes of the brain. Separate studies have indicated that this could be associated with infrasound.

The human ear can hear sounds ranging from very deep bass at around twenty hertz to a very high pitched whistle at about twenty two kilohertz (a hertz is one sound wave per second). It is not equally sensitive across the whole range though. Sounds of two to four kilohertz are perceived as louder than other frequency sounds of the same intensity. These frequencies are those used in alarm calls in humans. The human scream falls within this range, as do babies' cries, which is why they drive you demented in restaurants and aeroplanes. You just can't switch them off. It's also for that very reason that most alarms are pitched at around three kilohertz.

Outside of this peak range, sensitivity falls off, at an increasing rate as it gets towards the outer limits of hearing. Sounds above the upper limit are not heard, although such ultrasound can be heard by other animals. Hence the 'silent' dog whistle. As an aside, this upper limit falls off rapidly with age and exposure to loud noises. I've just tested mine and my upper limit is around fourteen kilohertz. Most consonants are in the higher frequency range whereas vowels are much lower, which explains why I have great difficulty understanding people in noisy environments. A commonly heard phrase (well, commonly heard for me, that is) such as 'You clumsy arse – you're standing on my foot!' comes out as 'oo umee ah – oar a-ing o i u' which is exactly the wrong way round for aiding comprehension. Rmvng th vwls bt kpng th cnsnnts mks thngs mch lss dffclt t ndrstnd.

At the other end of the scale, sounds become inaudible below about nineteen hertz, although ones just below this can sometimes be felt. Think of the vibration you feel in your chest when the bass drum of a marching band goes by or the sensation you get just before your ears start to bleed when your daughter's obnoxious new boyfriend turns up the bloody great subwoofer he's just installed in his rebuilt canary yellow Ford Capri. Other animals, usually big buggers such as whales and elephants, can sense infrasound. This is very useful as it can be used to communicate over immense distances. Low frequency sounds carry far better than higher ones. You'll have noticed this when your neighbour turns up his stereo and starts playing air guitar to his Santana back catalogue. All you can hear through the walls is the bass. Carlos Santana's exquisite guitar work has been attenuated by the five millimetres of plasterboard that the tightwad developer put in when he divided the place up into flats.

However, to get back to the point. In 1998 an electrical engineer called Vic Tandy saw a ghost. In one respect this was to be expected as he was working alone, at night, in a building that was reputed to be haunted. In all other respects, it was not to be expected as Tandy was a level headed practical sort who didn't believe in ghosts. Nevertheless, he began to experience the classic effects of raised adrenaline – elevated heartbeat, goose bumps, butterflies in the stomach, hair on the neck standing up etc, and he developed the uncomfortable feeling that he was being watched. Out of the corner of his eye he saw a murky grey shape slowly take on what appeared to be human form. When he looked straight at it, though, it disappeared.

Tandy had no explanation for this, but by serendipity he was an avid fencer and the next day he happened to bring his foil into the lab to repair it. He clamped it in the vice and it began to vibrate. Rather than run round in circles screaming 'Save me it's a poltergeist!' he moved the arrangement around the lab and identified null points where the vibration stopped and others where it was stronger. He worked out that it was vibrating at about eighteen hertz and deduced that it was resonating in sympathy with an infrasonic wave. He eventually tracked it down to the air conditioning unit. When he switched that off the vibration stopped. He speculated that infrasonic waves might be responsible for quite a number of supernatural experiences. Interestingly, human eyeballs resonate at around eighteen hertz. This, combined with the human brain's well documented urge to find patterns in sensory data, could explain the murky grey shape.

This idea was picked up by Professor Richard Wiseman of the University of Hertfordshire and Sarah Angliss, a musician and engineer. They set up an ingenious large scale experiment in which two free concerts were given during which the auditorium was flooded with infrasound at different points of the performance. (For those nerds wanting to know how the infrasound was generated, it was a seven metre long sewage pipe with a low frequency speaker in the middle). The audience was asked to fill in questionnaires at set points in the performance to measure their emotional response to the music. These points were selected to contain instances with and without the infrasound. A more detailed description of this and associated experiments can be found in Professor Wiseman's fascinating book 'Quirkology'.

The results were striking. There was a statistically significant increase in unusual responses during the periods with added infrasound. These included:

'shivering on my wrist, odd feeling in stomach',

'increased heart rate, ears fluttering, anxious',

'Like being in a jet before it takes off',

'a sudden memory of an emotional loss'

and (my favourite)

'pre-orgasmic tension in body and arms, but not legs'.

Further to this, a number of church and cathedral organs contain very large pipes which produce almost pure infrasound at around sixteen to seventeen hertz. Professor Wiseman reports one pipe manufacturer as saying that such pipes were either a very expensive way of creating a small draught or a cost-effective way of helping the congregation find God.

Of course, the psychological effects experienced in the cathedral were not solely due to infrasound. That is one part of a combination of visual, auditory and olfactory stimuli combined with the hypnotic effect of ritual; all potentiated by the expectations inculcated by cultural history. Being able to rationalise it doesn't stop it working though. It is a very strange sensation.

Another strange sensation was the affront I felt at the behaviour of some of the other visitors. It's right that such a part of mankind's history, culture and heritage should be open to all, but it is still a place of devotion for those who do believe. Despite my derision for organised religion and any belief in the supernatural, a little respect for other people's sensitivities is only fitting.

It was good that almost the entire cathedral was open to the public, believers and non-believers alike. Given that there were people in there praying, it seemed to me that the few requests made (in almost every language) regarding behaviour were quite reasonable: No headgear, no flash photography, no video recording and suitably lowered voices. There was also one small area set aside where people could sit or kneel and contemplate the Eucharist. It was asked that no photographs be taken in that area. These were complied with by most, but there were a significant number of people with the ubiquitous baseball caps on back to front shouting and laughing, flash photographs going off all the time, and video cameras running.

Some were very intrusive with their cameras, to the point of coming right into the personal space of those praying in order to photograph them. Others walked around those in the area set aside for prayer and contemplation, and one moron even stuck his video camera in and waved it around whilst speaking a commentary over it. Bloody appallingly crass, arrogant and insensitive.

OK, rant over, I feel better now.

In a vain (and foolhardy) attempt to keep up with the Spanish partying we retired to the hotel for a couple of hours' sleep in preparation for the evening. Throughout the fortnight there were a whole range of musical and artistic events, all free and mostly in public squares or one of the churches or colleges. We were a day late for Flamenco dancer Joachim Cortes and a day early for the saxophonist Maceo Parker.

We went out at 9 p.m., wandered the streets for a bit and then ate at one of the street cafes. By our normal bedtime we were just starting the main course. Just before midnight we finished eating and made our way through the crowded streets to the Praza de Quintana, where there was a Galician group followed by a Mozambiquan band. It was mobbed.

It was still mobbed at 2:30 - 3:00 a.m. when we wandered on to a bar for a final drink. How do the Spanish do it? By my reckoning, if you add up the time spent eating, drinking and working, they only have time for about four hours sleep in every 24.

Hints for non-Spanish speakers.

Go and dig out your old Spanish/English dictionary. You know, the one you got for that disastrous fortnight in Lloret de Mar in 1974. Got it? Good.

Now look up *'supermercado'*. It says 'supermarket' doesn't it. Well cross that out. Insert 'dingy, cramped little corner shop with an idiosyncratic stock list', because that is what you will find behind every façade that has 'Supermercado' plastered across it in foot high letters. Before entering one of these emporia you should be aware that the chances of finding what you want are very slim. To improve the odds from about 0.0001 to 0.0007, you should ensure that you are fitted with night vision goggles. The second thing of which you should be aware is that the stock list for one of these establishments is surreal. In the depths of the stygian blackness you will find row upon row of dusty wooden shelves, stacked closely together with just about enough room between them for two undernourished stick insects to pass each other. These shelves are mostly empty, but occasionally you will come across such bizarre offerings as votive candles, watering cans, car deodorisers and those naff little water filled Christmas scenes that become enveloped in flurries of artificial snow when you shake them. What you are most unlikely to find is food, apart from crisps and tins of unidentifiable parts of equally unidentifiable sea creatures.

We've come to the conclusion that the Spanish don't cook at home, as it is virtually impossible to buy the ingredients. Given the ludicrously cheap tapas and raciones places, this is hardly surprising. On top of which, where would they get the time with all that partying? The mystery that we have set ourselves the task of solving, though, is where do the tapas bars buy their ingredients?

There was a slight hitch before we left Portosin, in that my dental bridge finally gave up the ghost after a valiant fight against superior forces. This left me looking like a villain from a spaghetti western, which did nothing for my already intrinsically fragile self confidence. So, without much hope of success, we went to the marina office to see if they could point us in the direction of a halfway competent dentist. Carmel, the receptionist was as charming and efficient as ever, phoning her sister to get the name of a recommended dentist, and offering to ring the dentist and make an appointment. It was Spanish hours so we had to come back at about 5 p.m. to see if she had had any success.

At 5.30 we returned to find that Carmel had made an appointment for 7 p.m. with a dentist in Noia, about 5 km away. She then rang and arranged a taxi, giving him instructions on where to drop me, right outside the dentist. What a diamond. The dentist said he could carry out a temporary repair, which took him about 25 minutes. When I offered to pay he refused, saying it was only a temporary repair and he couldn't possibly charge me for that. By 8:15 I was back, all fixed and no charge. How about that for service.

This was only one of countless examples of the friendliness, helpfulness and hospitality we encountered in every country through which we have travelled. It is a tribute to my stubborn intransigence that I have managed to retain my cynical and generally curmudgeonly outlook despite so much evidence to the contrary.

Carmel was so exceptional, though, that we wrote a letter to the managing director of the marina to say how impressed we were with the marina and especially with Carmel. It was pleasing to get an email from her six months later saying that she had been promoted and given a permanent position partially, she was sure, as a result of that letter.

The anchorages in the Ria de Arosa brought home the scale of the problem posed by forest fires in Spain and Portugal. Despite its higher rainfall compared with the rest of Spain, Galicia has a high incidence of summer forest fires. Although the area has only sixteen percent of Spain's forests, it has twenty five percent of Spain's forest fires. Untended eucalyptus trees are rich in highly flammable resin. Once these forests are alight they are almost impossible to extinguish.

Between eighty and ninety percent of the fires are

considered to have been started deliberately. Dark rumours in bars and cafes variously blamed livestock farmers who wanted to clear the land for grazing and developers who wished to build on rural land. The 'Countryside Law' in force at that time prevented the development of large areas of rural land. There was, however, a get-out clause, stipulating that land ravaged by fire changed status to 'urbanisable'. They could never have guessed what effect that would have. *"Well bugger me – we insert a clause that enables huge profits to be made if a bush fire 'accidentally' starts and all of a sudden fires break out all over the place. Who could have foreseen that?"* Obviously drafted by the incompetent, the naïve or the bought. You choose. This law has been changed recently to prevent building for 30 years after a fire, which should put a stop to many of the scams. Some also suspect that fire-fighters themselves, trying to earn extra money, play a significant part as arsonists.

The that summer was the worst for a long time. Over 100 fires raged in the first two weeks of August. More than 80 000 hectares of countryside, equivalent to the entire county of Nottinghamshire, were burned to a cinder along with all the wildlife that couldn't outrun the flames. An estimated eleven people were killed by the fires, including two women who were trapped by flames when their car broke down. Palls of smoke hung over town and country alike, drifting as far as Madrid, 500 kilometres away. The sun struggled weakly through the smoke to give a pallid, lilac hue to the sky. Dust and soot drifted down and settled in layers over everything that didn't move - roads, pavements, buildings, tables, statues, boats. Even moving didn't offer complete protection; clothing turned a speckled grey and dogs and cats slunk around like the before pictures in a Head & Shoulders ad, the long-suffering look on their faces daring onlookers to laugh at them.

The nightly entertainment on board *Birvidik*, after hosing yet another layer of soot off the decks, was to sit at anchor with a pre-dinner drink, watching the fire fighting planes picking up their loads of water to dump on the surrounding fire-ravaged hillsides. The skill of the pilots was breathtaking. They flew down the narrow corridor between the steep hillsides, banked steeply into a 180 degree turn at the end and came down to skim the water between the moored boats. As the scoop touched the water at about 90 miles an hour the pilot has to simultaneously counter the sudden drag which tended to tip the nose down, and the sharply reduced airspeed, putting it at risk of stalling. Then they powered up and flew off, climbing as hard as they could to clear the hillsides before heading for the fires to dump, in ten seconds, the 5500 litres, (5 ½ tonnes) of water they had picked up. I wonder if the fire-fighters on the ground supplement their families' diets by scooping up wood-barbecued fish with rather surprised expressions on their faces.

Forecast bad weather persuaded us into a marina. We chose Sanjenjo, which has a glossy, full colour brochure. Spain, I strongly suspect, does not have a Trades Description Act. Within the brochure were the following claims:

Claim: Weather forecast.

Reality: 2 day old tatty, faded fax of a synoptic.

Claim: Telephone & fax.

Reality: Where?

Claim: Wi-Fi internet on pontoons.

Reality: Blank looks from office staff.

Claim: Showers, toilets & launderette.

Reality: If there, cunningly hidden. Shrugs from office staff on asking.

Claim: Restricted access.

Reality: Waist high gates left open.

Claim: 24 hour surveillance.

Reality: Security guard dozing in café.

To top things off, a loud blast of what purported to be music drew our attention to a large stage, complete with a gigantic bank of speakers the end of the pontoon. The whole set up was reminiscent of a 1960s tower block conceived in the 'brutalist' school of architecture. After various sound checks at about 120 dB we were treated to Spanish heavy metal, a cacophony compared to which British heavy metal is Mozart incarnate. They managed to achieve a signal to noise ratio of about -20dB and therefore attained the holy grail of grunge – almost completely music-free distortion. We retired, sour-faced; grumbling about missed sleep and ruined cocoa.

To top it all, it was the most expensive marina we had yet to come across - forty euros a night. It was all pose and front, and no substance.

This is possibly because it's the favoured playground of the Spanish equivalent of Sloane Rangers or whatever the overprivileged, self-absorbed air-heads are known as these days. There is certainly no shortage of expensive, flash 'designer' bars, clubs and lounges whose (What is the plural of 'ethos' – 'Ethoses' 'Ethoi' Ethe?) and customers take the concept of 'shallow' to new depths.

Given the truncated and contradictory weather forecasts we'd managed to scrabble together, we were uncertain as to whether to go further up to the shelter of the Ria, or to head across to Bayona. The only certainty was that we were going to get the hell out of Sanjenjo. We decided to poke our noses out in the general direction of Bayona and see what transpired. We could always turn round and run away. In the end we did go to Bayona, passing between the mainland and the Islas Cies. The trip was very atmospheric and quite surreal with mists and strange patches of sea, rolling then smooth, interspersed with large areas of white froth. Spooky. There was a three to four metre or so swell out of the lee of the islands, but it was well spaced (about ten seconds) and so not a real problem.

Bayona surpassed even A Coruna; another fantastic, vibrant Spanish city. The usual crowded small streets were thronged with tapas and raciones restaurants and the city has two additional attractions: a castle, which has been converted into a Parador, and a thundering great statue of the Virgin Mary on top of an equally thundering great hill. The entrance fee for each was 1 euro. In fact, the entrance fee for anything in Spain seems to be one euro. Probably an EU directive, *'Public monuments and heritage sites accessibility charge concordance directive 2006/417/(a)'* . The British Government, though, has probably negotiated a derogation which allows them to charge an individual up to two percent of GNP for the privilege of walking out of his front gate.

We looked around the castle, which was stunning. Everywhere we turned there were views crying out to be photographed; purple Bougainvillaea scrambling up grey stone arches; glimpses of blue seas and tree clad hills across battlements. Throngs of wealthy people, ever so trendy in an awfully restrained and refined fashion, sat eating on the terrace, effortlessly oozing confidence and class. I looked down at my baggy t-shirt, paint-spattered shorts and tatty sandals and slunk away, feeling like a tutu-clad hippo in the middle of the Bolshoi Corps de Ballet.

Having climbed to the dizzy heights of the top of the castle, we turned a corner and saw the even higher Virgin of the Rock, a fifty metre statue on top of a 300 metre hill. "I want to go up there." said Liz. I didn't. "OK dear." said I. We trekked our way up the hill, paid the obligatory euro each and were allowed in through a narrow door in the bottom of the statue. Once through, we entered a dim tunnel little wider than my shoulders which wound up a spiral staircase. Not much good if you suffer from claustrophobia. Just to add to the general merriment, there were plaques set into the walls at intervals carrying such cheering messages as "Holy Mary, Mother of God, pray for us now in this, the hour of our death." [11]

Never mind, we thought, we'll be out soon. And we were - straight into a little concrete boat, just about waist height and just about big enough for the two of us and maybe

---

[11] I've since got a better translation where it reads , "pray for us now in this **and** the hour of our death.", so not quite so depressing overall.

an anorexic gerbil. This boat was held delicately in the Virgin's right hand fifty metres up in the air above a straight drop.

I don't do heights. Being more than a few metres off the ground induces a state of catatonic terror in me. Thought processes freeze and race alternately. My brain questions the structural integrity of whatever it is that is temporarily preventing me from tumbling, flailing, to my doom.

This is a bit of a limitation to the cruising yottie. If there is one characteristic by which sailing yachts are defined, it is their masts, which tend to be noticeable by their height. *Birvidik* is a ketch and so the sail area is spread between two masts. As a result, the main mast tends to be quite a bit shorter than would be the case with a single-masted rig such as a sloop. Nevertheless, the top is still twelve metres off the bloody deck. This is more than enough to reduce me to a quivering jelly. My instinctive response to potential maintenance and repairs at the top of the mast is therefore to put my fingers in my ears and go "La la la la" as loudly as I can. Unfortunately, this is not a practical solution.

Most yacht masts are subject to massive lateral forces in even moderate winds. In strong winds they don't bear thinking about. Dismasting is one of the Yottie's worst nightmares and, to be fair, yacht designers generally do their best to make it less likely. Usually, they do this by tying the top of the mast to various points all round the deck using high tensile steel wires. It's not, however, a 'fit and forget' system, much as I would like it to be.

Rigging wire is strong, but elastic. This is a good thing in that the stretch in the wires absorbs the sudden changes in load and prevents transitory but unsustainable forces.

This is all very well, but it means that the mast and its fittings flex and move.[12] This produces prime conditions for

---

[12]This phenomenon is also employed in other load-bearing structures such as aeroplane wings. If you look out of the window from an overwing seat during flight you will see it flexing and moving up and down by up to a metre or so. Don't worry – it's meant to do this. The time to worry is if it doesn't flex. Then the wings will fall off at the first sign of

work-hardening, or metal fatigue as it is commonly known. Such a possibility, combined with the dreaded crevice corrosion leads to the necessity of inspecting the top of the mast at regular intervals to verify its structural integrity. On top of this yacht builders love to put gadgets such as radio antennae, navigation lights, wind instruments and radar scanners up masts, all of which have an irritating ability to go wrong. Combining all these factors leads to my having to go up and down like a Russian exchange rate.

Many sailors, better men (and women) than I am, view this prospect with equanimity, even excited anticipation. They sprawl, limply relaxed in the bosun's chair, swinging insouciantly from side to side while their crewmates haul them up to the masthead where they happily effect the most complex repairs whilst singing away to their heart's content. Some don't even bother with a bosun's chair. I have seen them shin up sheer 15 metre masts and then balance precariously on a couple of protruding grub screws while using both hands to free a solidly seized 25mm fitting. Mind you, most of these arboreal gymnasts are either Antipodean or South African and therefore lack the imagination, self awareness and sensitivity exhibited by most normal human beings. As a result they are genetically incapable of fear.

This does not make them brave, merely fearless. I, on the other hand, am brave. I still go up the mast, despite being reduced to a quivering jelly at the prospect. That is not to say that I do it any more often than is absolutely and unavoidably necessary, nor that I swing my way up bare masts like a free-range gibbon.

You can tell at a distance when I am about to ascend the mast on *Birvidik*. It looks as if I'm making a solo attempt on the north face of The Eiger. I have more kit than Edmund Hilary had in 1953. The whole operation is planned like a military operation, with as many fall-back scenarios and

---

turbulence. In fact, the test-to-destruction wingflex limit of a 787 is over 7.6 metres.

safety-critical redundancy factors as a moonshot.

First of all, I set up two halyards. One to serve as a hoisting line and the other, tightened until it plays top C, to act as a safety line. These have been especially selected to be able to withstand shock loads equivalent to those likely to have been produced had Cyril Smith taken up bungee-jumping. Next in line is the bosun's chair, which is a reinforced canvas bucket with a rigid seat built into it. Attached to the bosun's chair is a professional climbing harness complete with shoulder, waist, thigh and crotch straps. These are tightened until I look as if I've been kicked in the nuts by a zebra. The harness also has a friction grip carabiner with a breaking strain measured in tonnes. This is clipped onto the safety line. The hoisting line is then attached to the harness by a quadruple bowline. The other end is wound round the main winch and I begin my ascent.

Did I mention that we also have mast steps? This is just as well, as Liz would never be able to lift my fully-equipped bulk unaided, even with a winch. Ashen faced, I climb the steps, keeping my eyes fixedly forwards and upwards, never daring to look down. That way lies madness, loss of nerve and public humiliation.

All the way up, my fevered imagination is working overtime. Despite all my precautions I am convinced that some vital component is about to fail catastrophically and send me plummeting to the deck, bouncing painfully off mast fittings and cross trees before hitting the deck in a plausible facsimile of a plastic bag full of overripe tomatoes. Was that rope tied properly? Has the sheave at the top been corroded and weakened? Will the hoisting line slip out of Liz's fingers and jump the winch?

When I finally reach the top I wrap both arms round the masthead and cling on in white-knuckled desperation. As I hang there, teeth clenched and eyes screwed shut, I call down to Liz for her to tie off the hoisting line. For the sake of the assembled watchers and my already dubious status amongst my peers, I try to do this in a controlled, calm and measured tone of voice. That is the intention. What actually comes out is a querulous, high pitched squeak modulated by hyperventilation and hysterical low wailing. It is at this point that I usually realise that, in my panic and confusion, I have left the tools behind and need to send down a bag on a string to collect them.

All that needs to be done now is to carry out whatever essential job drove me to undertake this madness in the first place. This, almost invariably, requires two hands. I am well aware of this, but it still doesn't stop me from trying to carry out complex operations with my teeth while still clinging fiercely to the mast with both arms. This, without exception, is unsuccessful but I try it every time nevertheless. Once I have finally abandoned myself to my fate and used both hands to do the job, all that then needs to be done is for me to disengage the friction carabiner and for Liz to lower me gently back down. On reaching sea level I abandon all pretence of self control, and self respect for that matter, and throw myself prostrate on the deck, sobbing uncontrollably.

When a semblance of sanity returns, I pick myself up and divest myself of my climbing apparel. Ignoring the pitying and embarrassed looks from my watching contemporaries I gather my wits, go below in as dignified a manner as I can manage, and pour myself a stiff drink.

That's it – all over.

Until the next time.

Portugal

Portugal often seems to have a bit of an inferiority complex. It shouldn't, really, considering what it has achieved in terms of opening up and discovering new worlds, in addition to running one of the largest empires in history. This isn't bad at all for a country with a population half that of Burkina Faso, accounting for barely over 1% of the world's population and a land area only a whisker more than Serbia's. It certainly punches above its weight.

The Portuguese seem to have a nagging underlying anxiety about being seen as playing second fiddle to anyone, especially to their former colony, Brazil or to their overwhelmingly larger neighbour, Spain. Shame then, that Spain just managed to pip it to the post to claim the record as the last remaining Fascist dictatorship in Europe. Portugal finally revolted against Caetano on the 25th April 1974, and so Franco held the record until he died on the 20th November 1975. They could take some consolation from the fact that this gave them nineteen months during which they could stand along the Portuguese side of the River Guardiana waving insulting banners about *El Caudillo*, much to the irritation of the Guardia Civil on the Spanish side. The Spanish authorities responded to this *lèse-majesté* by closing the borders.

As Portugal's only land borders are with Spain, this was a bit of a pain on two counts. Firstly, it brought all land based trade to a grinding halt. More importantly, though, it caused severe inconvenience to us as we were trying to get from Seville to the Algarve on a motorcycle at the time.

Since then, Portugal has changed dramatically. Up until the revolution, the Salazar and Caetano regimes had adopted a somewhat isolationist approach – not quite up there with Albania's Enver Hoxha but working on it. It had similar effects too. Like Albania, Portugal had remained a backward, agricultural society, highly hierarchical and grossly underdeveloped compared with its neighbours. That says something, considering its only direct neighbour was Spain which wasn't exactly at the cutting edge of European industrial and social development.

Infrastructure was primitive. The primary means of transport was the donkey and one of the biggest industries was the canning of sardines, in which the fiddly bits of the process were still done by hand. Even by the 1980s there was only one motorway in the entire country. This almost (but not quite) connected the two major cities of Lisbon and Porto.

Although its economy is still a basket case, Portugal has entered the modern age with vigour. It now has all the hallmarks of a developed western nation: free elections, lesser inequality, greater disposable income, freedom of speech, extensive road networks, greater consumer choice, widespread car ownership and an apparently insatiable demand for consumer electronics.

There has, of course, been a price to pay. Swathes of countryside are disappearing under tarmac and mortar. The village and family support networks have been significantly eroded. Villages themselves are atrophying as the young and skilled move to the cities. Being a wishy-washy liberal, I'll stick with saying that whether it has all been worth it overall remains open to debate. [13]

---

[13] Of course it has been bloody worth it, unless you're an unrepentant deposed dictator looking back nostalgically to the good old days. Either that, or one of those irritatingly crass and insensitive North London middle class twats who want areas to remain trapped in twee poverty and oppression so that they can regale and impress their co-dinnerpartistas with tales of how they found this *'lovely little village, Darling. So authentic. Untainted by coarse commercial and tourist influences, don't you know. Just a boutique hotel, of course. You absolutely must go there. Next year we're going to Chile – we found this gorgeous little collection of hovels there – just like it was when Pinochet was in charge.'*

The West Coast

Viana de Castello to Lagos

August 5th 2006 to September 24th 2006

End of the first season

We lived and worked in The Algarve for five years in the early 1980s, and so returning to Portugal had something of the feeling of a homecoming about it. It was also a pleasure, after the linguistic desert of Spain, to be able to converse with people again, albeit at the level of an eight year old.

There was, however, one fly in the ointment that had been nagging at me for some time as we approached Portugal and that was the country's reputation for bureaucracy. We had experienced this at first hand during our previous time there. This was a hangover from the dictatorships of Salazar and Caetano. Under the *Ancien Régime* it was reputed that the entire country and its not inconsiderable overseas possessions had effectively been carved up by seven extended families who handed down privilege and influence from generation to generation.

Unfortunately, genetics being the lottery that it is, each generation contained its expected allocation of inbred halfwits who were not only patently incapable of running a large agricultural fiefdom along with 15 percent of a minor empire, but weren't even to be trusted with administering some petty, fly-blown backwater in Mozambique or Angola. Something, obviously, had to be done with them, preferably not at the expense of the families involved, so they came up with a solution that is breathtakingly Machiavellian in its elegance and simple complexity.

They created a bureaucracy whose sole raison d'etre was to make life as difficult as possible for ordinary Joe Public, or '*Ze Povinho* as he is known in Portugal. Every activity or status of ordinary life, for every individual, had to be recorded, classified, stamped and, most importantly, authorised – preferably in the most obscure, labyrinthine, awkward and inconvenient manner possible. Obviously such a mammoth undertaking would require an army of bureaucrats to administer it. Fortunately, as the job description for these positions was simply to blindly follow the rules without at any time engaging the brain, they now had the perfect dumping ground for the aforementioned idiot-sons of the seven families. To be fair here, it must be admitted that by the middle of the 20th century Portuguese bureaucracy had been dragged kicking and screaming into the 19th century and these positions were opened up to the idiot-daughters as well. And the best bit was that all of this was paid for by taxes on the poor bastards who had to put up with this crap all their poor, nasty, brutish and short lives. I'm sure that Salazar would have liked to have made them solitary as well to get the full Hobbesian set, but that might have affected the tax base in the long run.

It also had adverse effects on the bureaucrats themselves. Much as they tried to suppress it, deep down they knew that they didn't really have a proper job. They knew that the mass of the population regarded them as parasites, about on a par with pubic lice but without the same level of passion and pleasure associated with their acquisition. The insecurity engendered by this knowledge manifested itself in their characteristic attitude to those unfortunate enough to be compelled to seek their services. With a very few notable exceptions they displayed a level of bombastic, arrogant superiority coupled with a deliberate, bloody-minded and highly inventive obstructiveness that bordered on the psychopathic.

The system was so alien to the eyes of Northern Europeans that their reaction when they first confronted with it was denial, promptly followed by confusion then shocked disbelief. Hot on the heels of disbelief came apoplectic indignation leading after a decent interval to resignation, rueful amusement and, finally, acceptance.

A favourite bar game for ex-pats was a competition to

top the previous speaker's tale of bureaucratically induced tedium. This could go on for hours. One example (my own as it happens) will have to suffice to give a flavour of how it was even in the early 1980s, already seven years after the revolution. The whole business was obviously deeply ingrained in the Portuguese psyche.

Early on in our time in Praia da Luz I let it be known in the bar that I needed a motorcycle licence.

"Ooh no – you'll have trouble with that" muttered the assembled Corporal Frasers into their drinks.

"Nonsense" I replied. "It's just a matter of doing your research and being prepared."

I did my research and planned the project with an attention to detail worthy of Operation Overlord. I already had a British heavy motorcycle licence. Research indicated that I could convert this to a Portuguese one. Step one was to get a translation of my existing licence. This had to be carried out (for a fee, naturally) by an authorised translator. The nearest one lived fifteen miles away. Then it needed to be notarised (for another fee) by a notary who lived eight miles away in the opposite direction. After that I had to go to the town hall to apply for the licence. I spent about a week ensuring that I arrived at the town hall fully equipped.

I knew I had to bring my Brit licence and the notarised translation. On top of that, I also knew that it is impossible to do any form of official business in Portugal without special, official, crested paper called *papel selado*. This, of course, could not be bought just anywhere. You had to trek to a special government office secreted away down a back street, which was only open for short and spectacularly inconvenient periods. In addition you needed stamps. Not ordinary, buy at a post office, newsagents or from a machine type stamps. Not simple, everyday stick on your postcards type stamps. Oh no. These were *selos fiscais*; special, official, government-business type stamps which could only be bought from another special, well hidden office over the other side of town, which was open at different, but equally inconvenient times. These stamps are available in a number of different denominations, so I decided to stock up on fifty centimo stamps so that I could put together any of the likely amounts requested, with a couple of twenty five and ten centimo ones as insurance.

I had been told that this was all that was needed, but decided to throw in my passport, and residence permit as a backup. Then I chucked in my birth and marriage certificates just in case. I drew the line at my first aid and cycling proficiency certificates.

An earlier reconnaissance had identified the correct department for driving licences and had also revealed a further idiosyncrasy of Portuguese bureaucracy: There were no pre-printed blank forms for all the various applications. Instead there were hundreds of different exemplar pro-formae pinned to the walls. I asked advice from the staff but was met with dismissive shrugs. Luckily a passing agricultural labourer took pity on me and explained the system in perfect BBC English.

Rather than be given a blank form which you then had to fill in, you had to first identify the particular form required from the pro-formae on the wall. Then you had to laboriously copy the form onto a sheet of papel selado, filling in the blanks as you went. Portuguese spelling, grammar, syntax and punctuation were all closely scrutinised when you finally got to the head of the queue with your completed form. Any errors were pounced upon with glee and you were sent off to start again on another sheet and return to the back of the queue. Crossings out and corrections were not permitted and they had anticipated the invention of tippex by several centuries by making papel selado a pretty blue colour which made correction fluid stand out like a Barry Manilow T-shirt at an Iron Maiden gig.

How, I asked my friendly advisor, did this system work in the years before the revolution when the majority of the population were illiterate? He smiled. You had to get it written out (for yet another fee, of course) by an authorised scribe, who was frequently a close relative of one of the jobsworths behind the counter or even an off duty jobsworth making a bit more on the side.

The town hall closed for an extended lunch at 1:30 so I arrived, fully laden, including several back-up sheets of papel selado, at 9:30. I identified the required form, unpinned it from the wall and took it to the minuscule writing shelf to copy. At this point the three clerks behind the counter, who had up to then studiously ignored my hypocritical pleasantries and acknowledgements, all shouted and waved their arms, indicating that the examples should not be removed from the wall. Had I taken the trouble to look round I would have seen that all the other supplicants for official absolution were holding their pieces of papel selado against the wall with one elbow whilst simultaneously squinting at the pro-forma and copying it down with the other hand. I followed suit.

Dear Mr President of the Camera I copied laboriously (in Portuguese). *My surname is....., My date of birth is ..... My Christian name is..... My father's name is.... My mother's maiden name is.... I live at..... I went to school at ..... my fiscal number is.....* This went on for paragraphs, demanding increasingly obscure and irrelevant pieces of information before finally ending with *please can I have a motor cycle licence?* I was becoming increasingly concerned about some of the information they were asking for as, even if I could work out what it was they wanted I still didn't know the answer myself. Then I had one of those light-bulb moments. If I didn't know it then it was a dead certainty that they didn't either, and so I could just make it up. My mood lightened considerably.

Mother's maiden name? – Amelia Stormvogel-Undercarriage.

Father's occupation? - Leotard adjuster. I had to get the Portuguese bits right though, which I did after three screwed up sheets of my expensive papel selado had joined the myriad others in the bin.

Marshalling my resources, I joined the queue. I was beginning to feel quietly confident. When I got to the front I began to believe that Portuguese bureaucrats had received special training in sniffing out a smug air, no matter how well suppressed. He looked at me with ill disguised suspicion.

Qual quiser? He asked brusquely. Among the defining characteristics of the Portuguese civil servant were a complete lack of civility or service and a refusal to speak any foreign language. These were people supposedly drawn from the most highly educated stratum of society. A lot of tertiary education was carried out in English. Most ordinary Portuguese in Lagos spoke English. Many also spoke French and German. It wasn't just that their livelihoods depended on it. That morning I had had a long conversation in English with a guy employed by the local council as a gardener. Not here though. It's our country – speak our language was their attitude.

"Fair enough" I thought. *"Queria uma licenca para conduzir uma motocycletta".* He looked disappointed. *"Papel Selado?"* I handed it over. He scrutinised it minutely. Unable to find any fault with it he thrust his hand out *"Licenca Inglesa?"* I handed it over. He remained stone-faced. *"Traduzido da licenca Inglesa em Portugues?"* Keeping as straight a face as possible I handed the translation over. His face lit up. *"Nao e notarizado"* he said exultantly. I pointed out the notary's stamp and turned it over to show the notarisation on the back. The beginnings of a scowl were forming on his face. I suspect that the beginnings of a self-satisfied grin were forming, probably unwisely, on mine.

He was beginning to get desperate and so started to go off script. *"Passaporte?"* I slapped it in his open palm perhaps a little too smugly. *"Residencia?"* I whacked my residence permit on the counter probably a little too triumphantly. You could see the thought in his face – "OK sunshine, if you want to play it that way." His look blackened. *"Certificado de nascimento?"* he demanded, in a tone of voice that actually read as 'checkmate'. We were beginning to get quite an audience by now and this was not helping his humour. It was now a matter of pride and honour. I handed over my birth certificate and was just congratulating myself when I realised that I had got too cocky for my own good. If he bothered to cross reference my birth certificate with my carefully copied papel selado he would see that my mother's maiden name was certainly not Amelia Stormvogel-Undercarriage. I held my breath. Luckily, the Sheerness Registrar of Births and Deaths in 1949 had a beautiful copperplate hand which made it very difficult for a non-native English speaker to read. He missed it.

He took all the paperwork and retired to a desk behind him. A subdued ripple of approval went through the assembled customers behind me. I couldn't help a little smile and nod at them. I felt like a folk hero, the William Tell of the Algarve. He arranged all my papers in order and went into an adjoining room, returning with a large ledger about the size of a medium suitcase. He then (and this is no exaggeration) blew the dust off the ledger, opened it and proceeded, painstakingly and at a snail's pace, to copy into the ledger everything I had written on my *papel selado*. This took about twenty minutes. He was making sure that not only would I be seriously inconvenienced by my display of *lèse-majesté*, but that all the others in the queue would suffer in this reprisal. I smiled apologetically at those I had inconvenienced but they all seemed to think it had been worth it.

Eventually, he returned to the counter with my papel selado. "*Selo fiscal*" he asked. I was sure I could sense and air of resignation and defeat in his voice and almost felt sorry for him. Almost.

"*Qual valor?*" I asked, smacking a handful of assorted stamps on the counter perhaps a little too smugly than was really warranted. "*Um Escudo*" he said dejectedly. I handed over two fifty centimo stamps and his face lit up. "*Nao. Nem dois selos de cinquenta centimos, mas um selo de um escudo so!*" A low groan spread through the crowd. I turned and asked if anyone was willing to give me a single one escudo stamp in return for two fifty centimo ones. My nemesis glared a warning at them. They shuffled and looked at their shoes. None was willing to incur his wrath; they had all been waiting too long in this queue already.

I slunk out to buy a one escudo stamp. By the time I got back the town Hall had closed for the day. When I returned the next day the clerk pointed out that the date on my papel selado was now incorrect and I would have to start the whole process over again.

I finally got my licence about a month later.

In the light of this, you can understand that I looked on our forthcoming clearing in to Portugal with some trepidation. The possibilities for bureaucratic harassment were just too numerous. Most worrying was our VAT status. We had no official receipt to show that *Birvidik*, and all the gear on her, were VAT paid. She was classified as VAT exempt because she was built before 1985 and was in the EU on the night of the 31st December 1992. We had papers confirming this, but these were in English. We also had a bill of sale showing that we had bought her in the UK and therefore any VAT concerns should be the responsibility of UK customs. None of these would be of any use at all if we met up with a particularly stroppy official. I was worried that we could have a VAT bill for up to twenty grand slapped on us and the boat impounded until the matter was sorted out to official satisfaction.

As it turned out my fears were groundless. The officials were either uninterested or friendly and helpful. No one wanted to see any of the wheelbarrow load of documents that I carted round to all and sundry. It seemed that the Portuguese bureaucratic machine had undergone a total character change in the intervening 20 years. The culture of arrogant obstructiveness had withered and died. Strangely enough, in a perverse sort of way I rather missed it.

Unlike the Rias, the west coast of Portugal is not a cruiser's paradise. There are few, if any, decent anchorages and night stops have to be made mostly in man made harbours and river mouths, many of which are difficult or dangerous to enter if the prevailing onshore swell builds up to any degree. They also tend to be a good day's sail apart. Or a good and uncomfortable day's motoring if you happen to be going

North against the prevailing winds. Some boats going north make a huge detour out to sea and back. This adds hundreds of miles to the route, but it's still better than plugging the wind and sea. Luckily, we were going south.

The first stop in Portugal was Viana do Castello, where we went upriver and moored in a very small and very hot marina – forty degrees Celsius and not a breath of wind. We were directed to moor alongside the fuel berth. The town is extremely pretty, but we were by then getting church, cathedral and quaint narrow street overload. Nevertheless, we saw a temple on top of a ruddy great hill/mountain and decided that this was a challenge. In fact, it was a challenge to be overcome by going on a funicular railway, so we set off to find it.

One of the problems with quaint, winding, labyrinthine narrow streets is trying to find your way around. In Viana do Castello this is further complicated by the fact that the town seems to be neatly bisected by a combination of railway lines and a multilane motorway. It took us a couple of hours of walking round in circles until we discovered that the only way across this no man's land was via the railway station, which acted as a sort of Checkpoint Charlie between the two communities. So we crossed the great divide and strode triumphantly to the funicular railway to find it closed for renovation.

Given the heat we decided to leave the 550 metre climb until early the next day and retired hurt to the boat, staggering blinking out a couple of hours later, just in time for a drink at the local bar, which overlooked the bridge designed by Gustav Eiffel. Liz was at pains to point out that this did not count as 'taking her to Paris', something I had rashly promised to do on our honeymoon 25 years earlier but had somehow never quite got around to actually doing.

The next morning a queue of boats at the fuel berth served as an alarm clock and we climbed all 2000 feet to the temple of Santa Lucia, at which we paid another one euro entry fee (I told you it was an EU directive) to climb another 200 feet to the top of the temple through the mandatory narrow spiral staircase.

Back on terra firma, several men with old bellows cameras offered to take your photograph with the temple in the background. After Liz had nagged me for about twenty minutes I gave in and went along with this. The process was fascinating. The camera had the big cloth over the back as used by Victorian photographers. The photograph was taken in a similar fashion, by removing and replacing the lens cap and estimating exposure time by eye – no light meters here. Exposure was made directly onto paper which was developed into a negative image in small tanks under the camera while being shielded from the light by the cloth. The negative image was then placed on a board in front of the camera and re-photographed.

The next stop, Leixoes, has nothing of note and the town wasn't worth a visit, but it was useful as a staging post at which to leave the boat while we went to Oporto, and were we glad we did. Oporto is an intertwining network of steps and irregularly shaped red roofed houses interspersed with modern office blocks and a plethora of building sites and road works. The least changed part is the collection of areas running down to the river (another damned great climb - how far have we climbed in total this trip?). These stairways were very atmospheric, with modernity only appearing once in the form of the local junkie shooting up in the narrow, stepped street. It would have made a great photograph, but I chickened out.

We took a river boat trip which was well worth doing. The pilot says *"A word of warning. It is well known that the river Douro carries most of Oporto's raw sewage to the sea, and several crew have been taken ill after handling ropes that had been in the water."* This did not seem to bother the local populace, who (it being another stinking hot day and sixty miles from the sea) used the banks of the river as a beach. Families swam off the slips and the local children amused themselves and passing tourists by throwing themselves off the great cast iron bridge that spanned the river.

Liz achieved the impossible by getting me onto a city tour. Generally, I politely decline proposals to take such tours. In my experience they were often little more than attempts to sell me stuff I didn't want. This one, however, included a visit to a port cellar, which was a striking experience. There were thousands of great barrels of wine and port, some dating back to 1867 and the smell permeated the place. You felt as if you were breathing port. The explanatory talk was a little rushed as the guy giving it, who must have been all of 23, had to give it in Portuguese and then repeat it in French, English, Spanish and Italian. To cap it all he was obviously fluent in all of these as he had conversations with each of the nationalities. Flash git.

At the end there was a tasting. We were expecting a half thimble full of a couple of ports. What we got was a fair sized glass of four different ports. It worked. I staggered across to the shop bought a bottle. It stayed in the cupboard for months and then we gave it away.

The internet is a wonderful thing, but sometimes it makes things worse. Weather forecasts are a case in point. In the proto-scientific days, post hanging seaweed but pre-internet, it was quite simple. You turned on the radio or looked in the marina office, got the weather forecast, made a decision and then usually regretted it, whatever decision you made.

Nowadays, you go to a local internet café, and look up the U.K. met office site and dutifully note down the forecast. Then to be on the safe side you look up in turn MeteoFrance, The Spanish and Portuguese met office forecasts, DWD (German), Wind Guru, Swell finder (who wants to actually find the stuff?) and OnPassage.com.

You then compare said forecasts and find that they all disagree with each other and that none of them agree with the actual weather you can see out of the window. This data overload induces a type of catatonic state which can, in predisposed individuals, become almost permanent and no further sailing is undertaken. Ever.

I appreciate that here I am displaying precisely the unreasonable expectations of which I complained in my previous apologia for meteorologists, but you shouldn't be reading this book if you're looking for consistency.

None of the forecasts had made any mention of the force 6-7 winds we were experiencing every morning up until about noon. So I had a think and said to Liz "It's probably a local phenomenon; possibly a katabatic wind flow funnelled down the river by the high valley sides. We'll leave early tomorrow and it'll probably ease right off once we're away from the estuary." Wrong. On all counts.

Once outside the harbour we ended up doing 7.5 knots under sail, with main and genoa both reefed to half. This caused some degree of nervousness at first, especially as the wind was gusty, going down to about a force six and then hitting you with an eight. This, combined with the wind-induced waves running in at about sixty degrees to the two metre NW swell, made for a somewhat erratic motion including rolls of more than forty degrees off the vertical.

Just as we were starting to get the hang of it, the wind started to ease. Then ease more. Then drop completely. So we put the engine on and started to potter on. At which point, the wind picked up again so we switched the engine off. At which point etc etc. It continued playing this endlessly hilarious game for about an hour and a half and then got bored and settled down to a very convenient force 4 - 5 on the beam. Perfect sailing conditions. We left the autopilot to it and sat and lounged on deck in the sun. This idyll was only broken once when the GPS alarm sounded to let us know that it hadn't the slightest idea where we were. It turned out that this was because Liz was sitting on the antenna. (Liz would like to point out that aforementioned antenna is a small plastic mushroom, not a large metal spike). We now know that Liz's backside is completely impervious to electromagnetic radiation. So we continued as before. Even when we turned onto a run with genoa only we were making five knots.

At this point, I started getting delusions of competence and decided that we would not only go into Aveiro rather than the easier Figueira de Foz further on, but also that we would sail in rather than use the engine. The Atlantic Spain & Portugal Pilot has this to say about Aveiro: "*There are strong tidal streams and the entrance can be dangerous on the ebb ... In September 1999 a yacht was lost while attempting to enter at night in a 3m swell.*" This is accompanied by an aerial photograph of the entrance showing a considerable amount of broken water, even though it was taken an hour before high water on a calm day with median tides.

Reality hit when we turned the corner of the breakwater to find broken water to our left, sinister looking current flows to our right and a large freighter harried by an armada of small motor boats heading down the middle towards us. The engine came on a bit sharpish.

Then there was the current. On the way in, supposedly approaching slack water, we were pottering along at about four knots through the water when I thought "That buoy's going past a bit swiftly", looked at the speed over ground and saw we were doing nine and a half knots, meaning there was five and a half knots of current near slack water – what's it like at half tide? We had, of course, decided to do this on a high spring tide with a coefficient of 115.

We anchored that night in the Baia de Sao Jacinto, just to port after the entrance. The next day, my delusions of competence returned and I decided it would be fun to navigate up the narrow, busy, shallow channels to the town of Aveiro itself, six miles inland. To further complicate matters, the information we had was (a) scanty and (b) conflicting. We had different times and depths for high tide, exacerbated by conflicting reports as to whether the yacht club pontoon existed at all. There was further disagreement as to whether we could use it, even if it did exist, and if it didn't, whether we could go through the lock to the town itself. In a flush of unjustified optimism we decided to give it a go anyway.

Late in the afternoon we weighed anchor and shot out of the entrance. The current turned us sharp left and we headed off upriver at about five knots. We were working on the assumption that the current would ease as we worked our way further upriver, with the tide turning and the water having a choice of different routes.

The area was hauntingly attractive; very low lying, with shallow channels meandering through salt pans, dykes and the odd scenic cement works - a complete contrast to the rias further North.

The first part of the channel, the Canal Principal de Navegaçao, was easy to follow. It was well buoyed but, even had it not been, all that was needed was to keep the commercial docks close to starboard. About three miles up things got a little trickier. The main channel took a sharp left and lost much of its buoyage. The landscape underwent a transformation. The water spread out into wide lagoons and salt pans, irregularly dissected by low earth and stone dykes. Interspersed on the dykes were tiny huts, occupied by the *saleiros* (salt gatherers) when they were working the salt pans. Ramshackle wooden landing stages and causeways dotted the landscape. The whole prospect developed an austere, surreal and ethereal beauty. The buoyage and the GPS enabled us to keep to the channel, with a least depth of about four metres, but it would have been very easy to have drifted a small distance off the channel into a shallow lagoon and run aground. Not a very inviting prospect at high water on a big spring tide.

The pilot (2000 version) said we could lock through into the Canal des Pyrimides, but the almanac (2006) made no mention of this. In contrast, the almanac said we could moor alongside the yacht club pontoon just outside the lock whereas the pilot was strangely silent on this matter, not even mentioning its existence. To starboard we identified the lock's holding pontoon, which was fully occupied by two very decrepit looking, uninhabited French boats. To port was what we thought must be the yacht club pontoon. We turned to have a closer look. As we did so we were deflected by a considerable turbulence which we took to be the outflow from the lock sluices.

The area did not look very inviting. A crumbling

concrete jetty rested on piles that had rotted away to reveal the reinforcing rods that ran down into them. On top of the jetty were a range of derelict industrial buildings, all with every window broken. Graffiti covered much of the walls. Newspaper blew across the gravel and dirt roadways, and corrugated iron hung loosely from the walls and creaked in the wind. It reminded us of a scene from a post nuclear-holocaust horror movie. We half expected to see horribly irradiated flesh-eating zombies lurching towards us from the darker recesses of the buildings. There was, however, a modern pontoon with a security gate, water and electricity.

Thinking that we'd made a horrible mistake we considered returning to the anchorage, but decided to moor here and see if we could get into the city itself via the lock. We picked our way slowly up channel, carrying a current of around four and a half knots and with great relief found that this was, indeed, the yacht club pontoon. There still looked to be a bit of current, but as we were so far upstream we put that down to flow from the lock. So we had a choice, moor into wind or into current. Into current, we decided.

It was a good choice. It turned out there was a current of seven to eight knots running along the pontoon. We can only do eight to nine knots under motor at full power. Liz leapt gamely ashore with the midship spring and attempted to tighten it round a cleat on the pontoon. The current then gained control of the boat and pushed it back and sideways, tearing the rope through Liz's fingers. A slight rope burn ensued. Bravely she stuck to her appointed task and got a turn round the cleat. A chap from the yacht club took the hastily thrown bow line. Liz took the hastily thrown stern line. By a combination of strenuous heaving on their part and exhausting waggling of the throttle and wheel on my part *Birvidik* gradually came to rest alongside the pontoon. It was a good job we chose to come in the way we did or we'd have taken out half the other yachts on the pontoon.

A conversation in a mixture of broken English and broken Portuguese established that the pontoon belonged to AVELA, the local yacht club, and that we were welcome to moor here for as long as we liked, water and electricity included. Our inquiry about payment was met with a shrug, and a suggested 10 euros per night – not bad for a 42 foot boat. We expressed some disquiet about security. He was adamant that there was no problem, but said that we'd need a magnetic key to get onto the pontoon. It was six p.m. on a Friday. The yacht club in the old disused fishermen's wharf building opposite was only open, he told us, on Saturdays and Sundays. We resigned ourselves to being marooned on the pontoon until the next day.

"Not to worry, though", he said "I'll phone the President of the club on my mobile and get him to bring you a key", which he duly did. Twenty minutes later the President drove up, accompanied by his wife and son. A few minutes behind him followed the club secretary. They beckoned me into the clubhouse to get the key.

Getting the key took about 35 seconds. Getting out of the clubhouse took an hour and a half, a long animated (if fractured) conversation, a tour of the club facilities (all of which were put at our disposal free of charge) and a considerable number of beers, for which no payment would be accepted. Offers of payment for mooring were waved away as matters of minor importance to be sorted out later. I tottered back to the boat clutching the key and singing the praises of Portuguese hospitality.

The next morning the folding bikes came out and we set off to explore the area. The immediate vicinity still retained its dilapidated appearance, but in the morning light it looked much more benign. There were no sullen hoodies skulking in doorways, nor any emaciated junkies shooting up in corners; just rows of friendly, if not particularly successful, anglers.

It was only a five minute ride into the centre of the city, which was absolutely stunning - a cross between Amsterdam and Venice with a distinctly Portuguese twist. Canals ran through the city, crossed by ornate and flower bedecked bridges. Old buildings lined the canals, many built on arches to allow the water to flow through. In contrast, opposite these were modern shopping centres which still managed to fit into the general character of the town. Nestling in amongst all this were tranquil sixteenth Century squares lined with cafes and restaurants and, of course, the tiny fifteenth Century cathedral that made Aveiro a city.

The whole city had a vibrant and friendly atmosphere. Most of the visitors (it just seemed a place that had 'visitors' rather than 'tourists') were Portuguese or Spanish. Apart from each other we heard no English spoken at all. Fado music played softly from the music shops and restaurants. We stopped off for lunch at a restaurant in a square by the fish market, where we ordered *dorada*, a sort of golden bream. Within minutes of our ordering the chef nipped over to the market, bought the fish and brought them back and cooked them. They don't come much fresher than that.

In the main canal were many colourful open boats, somewhat reminiscent of gondolas. These were not a tacky crib from Venice, but were *moliceiros*, boats that had traditionally been used to collect seaweed for use as fertiliser. The advent of chemical fertilisers had made them redundant but they had been re-employed, probably much more profitably, taking visitors on tours around the shallow lagoon. The local knowledge of their operators, combined with their draft of less than fifty centimetres fully laden, enabled them to visit even the most inaccessible parts of the lagoon. Well, we had to have a go, didn't we? They draw a lot less than *Birvidik* and they know where they're going.

The next day we went to the internet café to check the met. Uncharacteristically, all the forecasts seemed to agree. What they agreed on was that one of those 'unseasonal depressions' that seem to follow us about had worked out where we were and diverted South East toward Northern Iberia. This meant that the usually 'firmly established' Northerlies had been replaced by a 'very unusual for this time of year, Squire' West to South Westerly force five to eight for the next three to four days.

Quote from the pilot for our next port, Figuera de Foz: "In strong onshore winds" (i.e. West to South West) it can be dangerous. A British yacht was lost in 1997 and waves were breaking all the way across the gap when visited in 1999."

Given that our current position was well sheltered, close to an attractive city with all facilities and, most importantly, dead cheap we decided to hole up here until the unseasonal depression buggered off back where it belonged (i.e. over Britain).

In the interim, a visit to Coimbra was planned. This involved taking the little local train, the *Comboio Regional*. Buy your tickets in advance and the 120 km round trip costs just £1.50 each. Pleased with our forethought and planning we set off the next morning, tickets clutched in our sweaty little hands, to catch the 9:03 to Coimbra.

Things did not go exactly according to plan.

We arrived at the station in plenty of time, discovered which platform we wanted and waited dutifully for the train. At 08:50 a train pulled up gently to platform 4 as anticipated, but the little sign on the front telling you where it was going seemed to have blown a fuse. Undaunted, I asked a nearby station employee if the train went to Coimbra, and was assured that indeed it did. Just to make sure, I asked if we needed to be in any particular part of the train. We've had this before where the front part of the train goes to the assigned destination whilst the last two carriages wander off across the country on a frolic of their own. "Did we already have tickets?" he asked (only in Portuguese). "Yes" we replied triumphantly. "Sit wherever you like then" he said, so we did.

The first inkling that things might not quite be completely as they should have been appeared when a woman and her three children arrived, looking pointedly at the numbers on her tickets and at the seat numbers above us. We consulted our tickets, but there were no seat numbers to be found. Despite our offers to move she wandered off mumbling and sat further down the carriage.

The second inkling manifested itself when the announcement "next stop is Coimbra B" came over the loudspeaker. Whilst heartening in itself, the fact that we'd only been travelling for eighteen minutes when the timetable clearly stated that the journey took an hour was somewhat confusing. By now we realised that we'd got on an intercity express instead of the local chuffer that stopped at every town, village, hamlet and isolated farmhouse on route. It pulled in to Coimbra B a mere nineteen minutes after leaving Aveiro. Coimbra A, which was our stop, could only be a few minutes away, and we'd be in the city forty minutes early. Smug with our good fortune, we stayed put as the train pulled out of Coimbra B.

Twenty minutes at 200 kph later it became apparent that either (a) Coimbra was an inordinately large city, or (b) we were now halfway to Lisbon. Given the total absence of buildings over the last twenty minutes or so our money was on (b), and we resolved to get off at the next stop and get a train in the opposite direction.

A quarter of an hour later our chance arrived when we pulled in to Pombal, which was almost halfway to Lisbon. The good news was that the journey back to Coimbra only cost us £1:20 each. The bad news was that it was a local chuffer and took an hour and twenty minutes. So we finally alighted in Coimbra only two and a half hours after we set off and one and a half hours later than we would have done had we got the correct train originally.

Coimbra is the most culturally significant city in Portugal. It was the capital from 1139 to 1256. It has one of the world's oldest universities dating from 1290, with illustrious buildings and surroundings to match. The university is in the old town, crowning the Alcacova hill which overlooks the deep slopes down to the Mondego River. The Portuguese equivalent of Received Standard English is 'Coimbra Portuguese'. Everywhere you look there were the usual abundance of old houses, chapels, monasteries, convents, churches and cathedrals, all intertwined with narrow streets winding down steep steps to the river.

We wandered round the university, trying to get enthusiastic over the wonders of a seat of learning still operational amongst squares and statuary, some of which was unchanged since before 1066, but it was no good – we'd had enough. It was all starting to blur into a kaleidoscope of red roofs, squares, sculpture, gilded altars, baroque columns, fountains and monuments; La Coruna, Santiago de Compostela, Bayona, Viana do Castello, Oporto and Coimbra all intermingled and recombined in our addled brains. We were jaded with the wonders of the past. We just couldn't face one more magnificent example of the beauties of our cultural heritage. We were overexposed - cultured out.

So we had a cup of coffee and caught the train back, deciding we needed to introduce a bit of variety; more rambling nature walks, cycle rides through the countryside, bit of music, scrabble evenings, beetle drives, old re-runs of Australian soap operas; anything but another bloody medieval bas-relief.

Back at the boat, we spent a couple of hours navigating our way through a Portuguese dictionary and wrote out a letter of thanks, which we dropped off at the Yacht club. The next morning Paulo (the President) and Alfredo, the Secretary, called by the boat to thank us for the letter and to tell us that Paulo would like to invite us to the club the next day for a *caldeirada* evening. Caldeirada is a kind of fish stew writ large, and Paulo had arranged for about thirty members of the yacht club to come and join us.

When we entered, the club had been transformed. A long table ran the length of the room, laid out as if for a formal dinner. Paulo greeted us, poured us a drink and introduced us to the assembled members. Some spoke very good English, but in most cases conversations were carried out in the usual mixture of broken English and broken Portuguese. As the evening progressed, conversation became more animated despite the language difficulties and the freely flowing wine (or perhaps because of the freely flowing wine).

Paulo had cooked the caldeirada and served it from a huge cauldron in the centre of the table. Our bowls were filled with an exquisite, fragrant mixture, containing what appeared to be every species of fish known to man. This was mopped up with boiled potatoes and huge chunks of bread, and washed down with even more of the local wine, of which they were justifiably proud.

From our conversations we pieced together the story of the area and the club. The crumbling jetty had, until a few years ago, been the fishermen's wharf. The building in which the club stood had been a net storage and repair depot. When the fishermen were relocated to a brand new facility much nearer the river mouth, it was intended to develop the area with a marina, waterside homes, restaurant and the like. Unfortunately the local *camera* (council/town hall) had spent all its money on a football stadium for the European Cup and consequently the redevelopment had stalled. So, no nice new marina development, but look on the bright side - they did have a large white elephant of a football stadium that was used about once a month and lost money hand over fist. The club was now trying to set up a consortium to undertake the development, a mammoth task.

We were now starting to feel slightly embarrassed by the hospitality shown us, and decided to reciprocate by inviting members of the club on board for drinks the next day. We also raised the small matter of mooring fees, only for it to be waved away again as not worthy of attention at the moment. In the end, we only managed to pay them by putting cash in an envelope and posting it through the clubhouse door just before we left.

We were prepared for the next evening. We'd bought wine, more beer, nibbles etc and tidied up the boat in anticipation, expecting about three or four visitors. A total of about twelve turned up, all clutching bottles of wine and beer. We ended the evening with more drink on board than we had at the start. The few desultory bowls of crisps and nuts lasted about eight minutes. *Nao faz mal* (not to worry), said Paulo, and nipped off into the clubhouse. About twenty minutes later he returned with a huge bowl of *Pimentos de Padrao,* small, not too hot, green chilli peppers seared in a pan and dressed with sea salt (plenty of it around) and balsamic vinegar. The man definitely liked to cook, and he was very good at it.

We had decided to move on the next day as the weather forecast was promising. Paulo presented us with a club burgee and a commemorative medallion, and Alfredo explained the best time, tide and course for leaving. Everyone then chipped in with advice on harbours and marinas on the way south. For days we had been racking our brains trying to work out how we could show our thanks for their overwhelming hospitality. In the end we printed out and framed a series of photographs of the surroundings and of some of the members of the club, which we suggested could be hung in the clubhouse. We handed them over at the end of the evening. They were either genuinely pleased with them, or damned good actors.

We slipped our mooring at 0600 the next morning. The advice from Alfredo about tides was spot on. Although it was half tide, there was virtually no current as we pulled away from the pontoon, and no sound other than the quiet chug of the engine, the lapping of the water and the haunting calls of the egrets floating across from the lagoon. The watery light from the early morning sun as it penetrated and cleared the mist highlighted the austere beauty of the place. We had been eight days in Aveiro, each of them providing everlasting memories of a fascinating and unique place. As we turned into the main canal and Aveiro receded into the haze behind us our thoughts dwelt thankfully on the priceless experiences we had had and the hospitality we had been privileged to receive.

And to think – had it not been for an unscheduled stop, purely on a whim, we could so easily have missed out on something truly unforgettable.

In the end, we gave Figueira de Foz a miss and went on to Nazare. Even at our leisurely pace there's not enough time to stop everywhere. After an eleven hour trip accompanied by the ever present swell, we came into Nazare harbour and realised we'd left the mainsail up. This resulted in much frantic winching and grunting to get it in before we berthed. Hopefully all the onlookers thought we were a real pair of hairy sailors and always sailed into tight harbours as a matter of course.

As it was quite late when we arrived, we just sorted out the paperwork, had dinner and went to bed. We were rudely awakened at five in the morning by a British catamaran rafting up to us. It wasn't the noise of the boat that woke us, rather the Captain's voice bellowing out to his wife on the helm "Stop! Stop! For Christ's sake stop!" So we lay there and gritted our teeth, waiting for the crash and the bowsprit poking through the hull into the aft cabin. Luckily this never materialised. We never really got back to sleep though.

The next day, full of anticipation and excitement, we got the bikes out and cycled into Nazare. I appreciate that a Sunday in August may not have been the best of times to visit a seaside town not far from a capital city, but Nazare really left us cold. The front was packed with people, as was the beach, with the added bonus of regimented rows of tents covering any of the beach that was not already covered with people or umbrellas. This, though, we could probably have lived with, given the time of year. What did it for us was the unadulterated tackiness of the place. No useful establishments like delicatessens, hardware stores, little regional restaurants etc. Every three metres there was either a junk fast food joint, a stall selling crap souvenirs (nodding dogs a speciality) or..er..nope - that was it. The whole place made the most tatty and downmarket of fading British holiday resorts look like icons of cosmopolitan sophistication by comparison.

We went through the back streets and took the funicular railway up to the top. Away from the front you could see glimpses of what a lovely place this must once have been. Every so often a part of the beautiful old town broke gasping for breath through the surface slick of commercialised junk, but it's doomed. We really couldn't see how people could want to holiday here or buy any of the rubbish on offer; but it was heaving and all the aforementioned businesses were doing a roaring trade. It was all quite depressing really. I was even looking back fondly at the endless Baroque bas-reliefs. Still, as P.T. Barnum once said "Nobody ever went broke underestimating the public." However, we decided we'd had enough and set off for Peniche the next day.

I'm seriously considering joining a self-help group for incurable appalling snobs. I don't think it'll do any good though. I'm too far gone.

The leg to Peniche was an interesting little trip, it being the only part of the coast which requires a SW course, and the 3 metre swell being from the usual NW. Now *Birvidik* is a lovely boat, and I won't hear a word said against her, but when hit on the beam by a large swell with a time period of about eight seconds she does a very good impersonation of a pendulum, swinging about forty degrees to the left, holding it there for about a second, then swinging forty degrees to the right and repeating the whole process every eight seconds or so. Our stowage system had improved, but it was still far from perfect. Things soon started to fly about, so we decided to put a couple of zigzags into the course to ease the motion. This was successful to a degree, but it's a compromise between the easier motion and the extra distance you have to travel.

Peniche is much more appealing to our refined and cultured sensitivities. It's a picturesque town where life and work centres on the harbour; very much a working port, with a large fishing fleet and various ferries going regularly to the nearby Ilhas Berlingas. The harbour does have one slight drawback. Visiting yachts are moored on the outer pontoon in a corner of the harbour near the entrance.

Quote from the pilot book: "*The normally easy-going Portuguese seem to undergo a complete character change when they get behind a wheel, and drive like maniacs.*"

This, very accurate, observation referred to motor cars but it holds true for ship's wheels as well. As you approach the harbour there is a sign saying 'maximum speed 3 knots' in metre high letters. Visiting yotties meekly comply, crawl into the harbour and moor up on the pontoon. Once tied up, they hear a rumbling, roaring noise, look up and see a 25 metre, fifty ton ferry or fishing boat hammering past them at a distance of about five metres and a speed of about twenty knots. Such boats are displacement boats; they don't plane (much as the skippers try to make them). As a result, the boat is continually pushing fifty tons of water out of its way as it hacks toward the entrance, dodging other boats, canoeists and pontoons on the way.

Birvidik is quite a heavy boat and rides the resultant bow wave quite well. Aforementioned visiting yotties with lighter boats (i.e. most of them) are somewhat alarmed to see their pride and joy trying to climb up on the pontoon. If there were two or three boats rafted together the carnage that would result doesn't bear thinking about.

At the root of the quay lies a sixteenth century fort, built on the orders of Dom Joao IV as protection against threats from the sea. It now looks like a toy fort scaled up. Its bright yellow walls are surrounded by palm trees and neatly trimmed grass and each corner is crowned by a small octagonal, domed turret cantilevered out over the dry moat. Pay your euro entrance fee, though, and walk through the opened portcullis and it takes on a very different mien.

Under the Salazar dictatorship it was a prison for political dissidents, run by the feared secret police, the PIDE. The centre of the fort is a large, bleak, flagstoned square overlooked by slab-like three story mottled grey concrete blockhouses, each broken only by rows of barred windows looking forbiddingly down. Skeletal watchtowers rise starkly from each corner. In the centre is the cover to the large rainwater cistern, from which was drawn the cold water for the prisoners' weekly bath.

Within the buildings lie rows of tiny, stark cells linked by narrow corridors. Each section of seven or eight cells was partitioned from the next by triple gates. Only one of the three was allowed to be opened at any one time. Prisoners were banged up for 21 hours a day, the other three being occupied by meals (no talking allowed without prior permission from a warder), exercise (ditto) and the weekly bath. Even so twelve people managed to escape over a twenty year period, including Alvaro Cunhal, the leader of the Portuguese Communist Party, commonly referred to as 'The Fox'.

After short diversions to the Ilhas Berlingas and the beautifully preserved town of Obidos we left Peniche on the 29th August, with a weather forecast of NE four to fives. What we got was NW seven to eight. Mainly eight. This was the first time we'd ever been out in a full gale, but we, and the boat, acquitted ourselves satisfactorily. Mind you, it was an easy point of sailing for the conditions with the wind off our port quarter. We made eight knots under the genoa alone.

As we came round the cape into Cascais, the wind dropped away to nothing and we anticipated a nice easy moor on the reception pontoon. 'Done this sort of thing loads of times before.' we thought, "Piece of piss'. Does the Greek concept of 'hubris' mean anything to you?

As we were circling in the bay to line up the approach the wind suddenly gusted up to 30 knots and stayed there. It was coming off the pontoon at an angle, so we decided to approach into wind and at an angle and ferry-glide in.

As we approached the pontoon the wind increased to forty-plus knots. What I had failed to notice at first was that it had also veered by over ninety degrees and was now dead astern. This soon became apparent when we surged forwards toward the pontoon and my bursts astern failed to slow her down significantly. We were now doing three knots as we came near the pontoon. I changed plan and decided to go ahead, steering away from the pontoon and around the rapidly closing catamaran on the end. Liz was by now crouched ready to jump outside the wheelhouse, rope in hand and totally focussed on getting the line ashore. I shouted to her to stay on as we were going to abort the approach, but she couldn't hear me above the by now screaming wind, and jumped.

At this I changed back to plan 'A' and started to give reverse power, which caused the transmission to shudder worryingly. I hoped that if Liz could get the heavy line round a cleat and surge it we might get away with a few dents and a scorched rope. That was assuming the cleat stayed attached to the pontoon. If it didn't we were likely to plough into the catamaran, taking a chunk of the pontoon with us.

Liz is meticulous in setting up ropes before mooring, with everything laid up correctly and ready to go. This time, for some unknown reason, she had run the line over the guard rail rather than under it and through the fairlead. She instantly realised that the rail couldn't take the forces involved and rapidly unhooked it and re-attached it correctly whilst running alongside the boat. She had little time to get it round the last available cleat on the pontoon, but managed to throw a loop round it. In her hurry, though, the rope had whipped round all four fingers of her right hand and the force from the boat pulled it down onto the cleat.

She called out to me, her voice tight with tension "Bob! It's got my fingers!" She watched in fascinated horror as the rope, tensioned by 16 tons of boat travelling at three knots, crushed her fingers down to a fraction of their normal thickness, as she waited for them to pop off, one after the other.

When I heard her call I visualised the same thing and was filled with dread and a sense of helplessness, not knowing what I could possibly do to help her. I just instinctively did everything I could think of. I pulled the throttle as far astern as it would go. Simultaneously I swung the wheel over hard to starboard and gave full power to starboard on the bowthrusters. At this point it felt as if the boat was going to shake itself to pieces beneath me.

Whether these actions were enough, or whether we had the luck for them to coincide with a momentary reduction in windspeed we'll never know, but Liz managed to release the rope and free her fingers. Her little finger and ring finger were broken, with the former hanging loosely out at right angles from her hand. There were flaps of tissue hanging from her index and second fingers and deep abrasions across the backs of all four. But at least she still had them all.

By this time one of the marina staff had sprinted onto the pontoon and taken a bow line. The boat swung round head to wind and stopped short, with her stern resting against the catamaran. He turned to Liz and indicated that she should take the midship line and help him pull the boat forwards, clear of the catamaran. She held up her hand and waggled her finger at him, at which he went slightly grey and decided he could pull the boat in on his own. A few seconds later two others arrived to help and we effected a quick and dirty moor. I jumped off and ran to Liz's side. She had reduced the fracture herself by pulling the finger out and twisting it back into position, but the adrenaline was beginning to wear off and she was now starting to go into shock.

While all this was happening the marina office had called a taxi to take us to Cascais Hospital. Four hours, two X-rays and a further reduction of fracture (without anaesthetic) later we were back on the boat. Five weeks later the splint came off and she could start the process of getting flexibility back into her hand. Bad as it was, we both knew that it could have been much worse. If she hadn't been able to free the rope she would certainly have lost all four fingers.

We decided to stay put and consider our options. We were only 120 miles from Lagos, where we intended to overwinter. Liz's ability to crew was severely limited by her injury and we were worried that, once at sea, she might stumble and knock the damaged hand. So I went to the marina office to sort out a berth in the marina proper. I was told by the very helpful woman in the office that it would be no problem for them to give me a hand to move *Birvidik*. Just let them know and the guy would be standing on the dock ready.

We walked over to the allocated berth to check it out and found a full set of mooring lines already on the pontoon, so we laid them out ready to grab and went back to the boat, notifying the marina office on the way. "Yes Sir, he'll be there right away. Don't worry; he's done this sort of thing hundreds of times before". Reassured, we cast off, with Liz casting a tragic figure in the bow, and made our way round to the berth.

On arriving at the berth we found that not only had

the promised help failed to materialise, but someone had been along in the intervening ten minutes and removed all the lines we had so carefully laid out. Luckily, the conditions were very benign and I managed to hop ashore with our lines and tie us up.

Then the phone rang. I looked at the screen and saw it was my younger brother Steve's number. This was not a good sign. We get on fine together but we're not close. We never ring each other up just for a chat. I answered with a sinking feeling in the pit of my stomach. Barbara, Steve's wife spoke.

"Your dad's seriously ill. He's been in hospital for five days."

"Seriously ill as in what?" I asked.

"Seriously ill as in dying."

The rest of the day faded into a blur of activity. We sorted out flights back to the UK via Lisbon and arranged for a delivery skipper to take *Birvidik* the next 120 miles to our winter berth in Lagos. A couple of hastily packed bags were slung onto a trolley and we handed our home and everything we possessed over to the delivery skipper.

"Look after her – she's all we've got" I said rather pathetically. We turned and pushed the trolleys to the nearby hotel into which we had booked. We felt strangely guilty, as if we had betrayed and abandoned her.

We arrived at Heathrow late the following night, having decided it would be better to overnight there and hire a car the next morning. Unfortunately, we also arrived in the middle of a baggage handlers' dispute compounded by bad weather and a security alert. As a result, all hotel rooms had been booked for stranded passengers and out-of-hours crew. After many dispiriting phone calls we managed to secure what was possibly the last available room in Southern England; in a very middle of the road three star hotel an exorbitant taxi ride away from the airport. They quoted £200 for the night, excluding breakfast – take it or leave it. We took it.

Reg died at 5 o'clock that morning. We missed him by a few hours.

After calling in to see Steve and Barbara, we met my youngest brother, Roger, and drove on to Reg's house, where we would be staying. It was an odd and unsettling experience. 'Thames Avenue' sounds a good, solid, respectable, middle class sort of street. It was actually a working class council estate, but built in the optimism of the immediate post war period. Social housing was expected to be civilised in that land fit for heroes, not the soul destroying, spirit - sapping brutalism of the high-tech slums of the 1960s and 70s. The estate mostly comprised red brick semi-detached houses, each with a reasonable back garden and a small front garden. Large open grass areas lay within a couple of minutes' walk of all the houses and well tended garden areas were scattered throughout. The local primary school was a few minutes' walk away. In our early days there, only one person in the street owned a car and no-one had a telephone. Important calls were made from the many strategically placed phone boxes.

Throughout the 1970s the character changed, mainly as a result of the 'right to buy' legislation which obliged councils to sell off their housing stock to existing tenants at a ludicrously low price. My father opposed this legislation vigorously but, once it was in force, he took advantage of it and bought the house for £3 000. With the blind certainty of youth I took him to task for betraying his strong socialist principles.

My mother, on the other hand, was horror struck. Debt was anathema to her, the first step on the desperate slide to the Bailiff's knock. Eviction was not an uncommon occurrence in her formative years and she had told me of how unexpected events, such as sudden unemployment or unexpected medical bills could shatter lives and families almost overnight. She contracted diphtheria as a child and my grandparents were saved from the bailiffs only by the good offices of a sympathetic doctor.

The advent of the welfare state, especially the NHS, in 1948 greatly lessened these horrors, but did not eliminate them altogether. Even I could remember being ushered past such scenes as a young child. Those few belongings that had been left, usually beds, tools and anything not worth selling, were piled randomly on the pavement with the family stood disconsolately around them, at a loss as to what to do or where to go. No-one spoke and no-one made eye contact. Although everyone knew that there but for the grace of God went they, it was understood that any expression of public sympathy would only deepen the shame and humiliation.

I had lived in the house from the age of three until I went to University. My parents continued there until my mother died in 1985 and my father had stayed on, living there for a total of 55 years. In his latter years he had released most of the equity and it would now have to be sold. I walked through and saw the place with new eyes and old feelings. Although I had left over 40 years before, '18 Thames' had always been a fixture in my subconscious. Wherever I had lived, Manchester, Brighton, Jersey, Leeds, Portugal, New Zealand or (as now) everywhere and nowhere '18 Thames' had always been a psychological anchor, a homeland of the mind. Now it was no more. A door had closed.

What surprised me was how small it was compared with my memories. I entered by 'the back door' (it was actually at the side), which was the main entrance. Friends, tradesmen and visitors all used it. This was standard practice throughout the estate. It was known and expected. The glazed front door was used only for visits from luminaries such as the doctor or the clergyman. This was because important visitors were entertained in The Front Room, which was off the narrow hallway behind the front door. This room had the best furniture, the best wallpaper and the best carpet (the only carpet in the early days). The bay windows had the most expensive curtains in the house. It was always kept in pristine condition and from my childhood perspective it always had the air of a museum about it. This room represented about a quarter of the accommodation of the house and about one third of the contents by value, and it was hardly ever used. The only exception was Christmas when the drinks cabinet was stocked and family and friends were entertained there, always being handed a glass of sherry on arrival.

Standing in the tiny kitchen it seemed impossible that my mother had done the weekly wash for a family of five in 'the copper', a large metal drum with a gas ring under it, pounding the wash with a wooden dolly and draining the water via the tap on the side. There didn't seem room for such a large device in this tiny room, but my memory was looking through a child's eyes and the copper was probably as much smaller in reality as the kitchen itself was.

Looking around the house it came home to me how divorced I had become from my roots. I had grown up in an homogenous white working class environment; solid labour to the core. My father was the youngest of eleven children, nine of whom survived past infancy. His father was a semi-skilled seaman in the dockyard. My mother was born into a family only one generation out of the slums of the East End of London. This was my tribe. We believed in working class solidarity, the brotherhood of Trades Unions. We believed in the value of education as a means of hauling ourselves out of poverty. We considered the Tories to be the devil incarnate. One of the first co-operative societies in Britain was founded here. Working men's clubs abounded and many still survive to this day.

We were also casually racist, although without any real malice. There was just an automatic assumption that we were superior to all other races. I suspect this resulted from a hangover of the attitudes of the Empire and a manifestation of the 'Kick the cat' syndrome from those already at the bottom of the pile. We were not actively misogynistic, but there was a tendency to be patronising and dismissive toward women. Our worst ire was reserved for homosexuals, real or imagined, who were pilloried mercilessly. Lesbians were safe as they didn't even appear on our radar. Our imaginations were unable to encompass even the possibility of such activity.

To his eternal credit, my father had renounced most of these negative aspects of our tribal culture long before I had, and he had done so when it was much more difficult. He alone among the extended Newbury clan had lost any trace of the distinct Sheppey accent and was punctilious about using correct English, both spoken and written. I was a world-weary 24 year old when I first heard him say 'fuck' and it stopped me dead in my tracks.

Three days after Reg's funeral I said goodbye to Barbara and my brothers and closed the door to '18 Thames' behind me for the last time. Some remnants of my first tribal loyalty remain. I am still unreconstructed old labour. I still believe in equality of opportunity and making it as difficult as possible for the rich, the powerful and the influential to maximise their self interest by screwing the less fortunate; but I am no longer a member of my first tribe. In fact, I had not been a member for many years. It just wasn't until that moment that I fully realised it. I still think the Tories are the devil incarnate though.

We drove to Heathrow, flew to Lisbon and took a train to Lagos. We were back on *Birvidik*. We were back home.

Lagos

September 25th 2006 to April 14th 2007

The first winter

If you look at the dates above you will see another reason it took us three years to get to Turkey. In common with a lot of cruising yotties we don't go anywhere in the winter. It's perfectly feasible to sail in the winter, indeed some do, but most find somewhere to hole up and snug down for about five to six months.

Just as a boat has to be a compromise between conflicting priorities, so does the wintering hole. Ideally, it should be very well sheltered with secure and solid moorings. It should experience a pleasant winter climate. It should have reliable electricity and water supplies available at the pontoon, along with broadband Wi-Fi internet access. It should be close to or within a reasonable sized town which is not solely tourist based and therefore remains active throughout the winter. The town should provide all usual retail facilities as well as the artisans the yottie is likely to need. There should be a variety of cultural and social activities available. It should be secure enough to discourage opportunist thieves without feeling like Stalag Luft Three. It should have enough overwintering yotties to ensure a reasonably full social life without being over regimented and cliquey. There should be hauling out facilities and a secure and well serviced hardstanding area. On top of all that, it should be dirt cheap.

That's not much to ask, is it?

Lagos met all of those with the exception of the last one. It cost us 1400 euros for six months, including electricity and water. But it was worth it. It was also somewhere we knew. We had lived in nearby Praia da Luz for five years in the early 1980s and so we spoke some of the language and knew the area. Quite a few friends from that time still lived there, as did Liz's father, brother and sister. Not exactly a wildly adventurous choice for our first winter, then.

There was a large and active liveaboard community, mostly English, but with significant numbers of American, Canadian, French, Dutch, German, Italian, Irish, Finnish and Swedish. Luckily, the lingua franca for yotties is English and so a German will converse with a Swede in English, which is very convenient for the, shamefully mainly monoglot, Anglophone contingent.

Put a group of yotties, especially British yotties, together anywhere and they will find some excuse to form a club, association or interest / activity group. They then spend an extraordinary amount of time drawing up a ludicrously complex set of rules, the primary purpose of which appears to be to prevent as many people as possible from joining.

Actually it is unfair to single out yotties here, for what we are describing is a universal human characteristic, although far more pronounced in those who possess a Y chromosome. Golf clubs are prime examples, given as they are to fighting a valiant rearguard action to continue excluding the 52% of the population who are unencumbered by said chromosome. Though why anyone, irrespective of sex or sexual orientation, should want to join a golf club remains outside my comprehension.

I suspect that the root of this behaviour is the perceived need for a sense of exclusivity, the feeling that by being a member of this particular group one is in some way special. What's the point of joining a club if the world and his dog are members?

So the next stage is to undergo a series of schisms, splitting into smaller and smaller sub-sects, a bit like the Church of Scotland or almost any Revolutionary Popular Liberation Movement *"If there's one thing I hate more than The Judean People's Front it's the People's Front of Judea"*. This process continues until the original club eventually consists of 47 distinct units, each comprising a maximum of three individuals, with all units constantly at each others' throats.

I was going to extend this analysis to Islam but:

a) I'm too much of a coward,

b) I always thought Sunni & Shia recorded 'I got you, Babe', and

c) It's too complicated. The Church of Scotland ended up with a mere nine sects. With Islam I lost count (and the will to live) at twenty.

We had our first contact with this phenomenon within minutes of arriving at Lagos. We were still tidying the mooring lines when up to the boat marched an unusually neatly attired yottie. He was wearing immaculately pressed chinos, a blindingly white polo shirt and he was carrying a clipboard.

"I say," he said in slightly plummy, clipped tones "Would you like to sign this petition?" I waited, expecting a further explanation of the purpose of the petition. None was forthcoming.

"I don't know" I said, eventually, "What's it about?"

This rather flummoxed him, as if it were a totally novel concept that someone should actually want to have the origins, purpose and target of a petition explained to him before putting his name to it. After an awkward silence, his powers of speech returned.

"Oh, er, yes, well. It's to the marina management. We want them to make the singer in that bar up there turn his volume down. Or preferably stop altogether. Will you sign it?"

"That's a bit difficult." I said. "We've only just arrived and I've never heard him. He might be quite good and play at a restrained volume."

"Oh no - that's not the case at all. He's very loud and coarse. Goes on until the early hours of the morning. Gets drunk and sings Irish songs, you know the sort of thing".

I assured him that I didn't know the sort of thing, that we had not had an opportunity to judge for ourselves and it would be somewhat unfair to put someone's livelihood at risk on the basis of hearsay. This took him aback somewhat. He looked at us quizzically and suspiciously as if we'd got into the marina, and indeed yachting in general, under false pretences.

"Can't you just sign it anyway?"

"Sorry, no."

"What about your wife then?"

"What do you think?"

He gave me the sort of look that suggested he was memorising my face and boat name so he could be sure he blackballed me if I ever had the effrontery to attempt to join any club that he had any say in. Then he turned on his heel and walked off without a further word.

It wasn't long before we were approached by a representative of the opposing camp, who suggested we frequent the bar in question, if only for no other reason than to cock a snook at the 'poncy tossers organising the petition'. We had some sympathy with his overtures.

Thus were we introduced to the dubious delights of

what is known throughout the yachting community as 'Pontoon Politics'. It has reared its head at every place we have overwintered, although its severity has ranged from mere petty sniping and backbiting through organised campaigns of social ostracism and character assassination to covert sabotage and, *in extremis*, open warfare. Lefkas, our current marina at the time of writing, is probably the least affected. Mind you, I have to say that or they'll all start picking on me and I'll be kicked out of the embroidery group.

Any difference of opinion or belief; any lapse in manners or behaviour, however minor; any perceived slight, real or imagined, will serve as the trigger to initiate a schism and the establishment of yet another sect. At the same time any new arrival is assiduously courted by representatives of all the established groups, eager to assert their numerical superiority over their rivals. The problem is, of course, that success in this area directly compromises the purity of the original group and so provokes yet another secession.

So it goes on. Groundhog day follows groundhog day follows groundhog day until there are so many overlapping groups that to fully describe the situation would require a three-dimensional Venn diagram of such fiendish complexity that even Stephen Hawking's mighty prefrontal cortex would start dribbling out of his nostrils should he be rash enough to attempt its construction.

Oh - and by the way, the Poncy Tossers were right about the singer.

We were spared the worst excesses of pontoon politics by a stroke of serendipity. Among our friends in nearby Praia da Luz were Jan and Adrian, owners and administrators of a vast property empire. Well, a block of holiday apartments and a slack handful of villas. As luck would have it they needed someone to look after the business and their cat, Ginger, while they went skiing and traipsing across the few exotic places on the planet that they hadn't yet got round to. In return for taking on this onerous task we were given the use of their spacious 3 bedroom villa right in the middle of Luz, plus a hire car for the duration.

We moved into the villa on December 23rd. When we first moved onto the boat in Jersey we compressed the contents of a two bedroom house into a space 12 metres by 3 ½ metres by two metres – slightly less volume than an average suburban living room. It is impossible for someone who hasn't actually done it to appreciate just how much stuff can be squeezed into a boat. Every minute nook and cranny is utilised and the whole process turns into a four dimensional jigsaw puzzle. Four dimensions because you have to take time into account as well. Things not only have to be stowed so as to maximise the use of space, but they have to stowed in an order that allows you to easily get at frequently wanted items, or those that you might need quickly in an emergency. This is a constant work in progress as more and more previously unused spaces are found and more and more items are added to the inventory. The final give-away is the raised waterline. *Birvidik*'s has been raised by about ten centimetres to make up for all the extra weight she carries and this is by no means unusual for cruising boats. The water displaced by her sitting ten centimetres deeper in the water translates as an extra three tonnes stuffed in somewhere.

On moving into the villa the phenomenon occurs in reverse. Carloads of possessions quietly expanded back to their original volume during the transfer from boat to car to villa. This only involved the personal and domestic items. All those of a boaty nature remained on board. It still took us all day to get moved in.

Returning to the land-based life took a little getting used to. For a start, we were frozen. A space as small as a boat takes very little to heat up. Not so Algarvian villas. These are beautifully designed for their primary purpose, which is housing holidaymakers during the hot summer months. They have large, airy rooms, all linked by arched openings to form a spacious, interconnected, open-plan living space. Large French windows open onto balconies overlooking the swimming pool and the beach, giving views over the calm, azure sea lapping on the silken, sun baked sand.

These villas are lovely and cool in the summer but a bitch to heat in the winter. The villa had lain empty for a couple of months and the cold had permeated the entire structure of the building. This made the whole place a huge heat sink.

We switched on the electric heaters. They valiantly threw out bucket loads of BTUs, which the villa absorbed without so much as a blink of an eye or a degree rise in temperature. We switched on the oil filled radiators. The villa just laughed. We brought in the heavy artillery – a trio of three kilowatt blow heaters. These were strategically placed and cranked up to maximum. Street lights dimmed outside and the nearby sub-station started buzzing and gave off a dull red glow. The air in the immediate vicinity of the heaters rose by a fraction of a degree. There was a loud click from the power distribution box under the stairs, the lights went out and the heaters fell silent.

Three resets of the RCD later we came to the conclusion that any attempt to raise the temperature electrically was doomed to failure.

A feature of Algarvian villas not previously mentioned is that they all have beautiful fireplaces. These are usually highly ornate, bay-fronted and large enough to house an entire flange of baboons. They are also, in most cases, purely ornamental. Indeed, most are not even equipped with a grate. This one, though, had a large wrought iron grate and the scorch marks around the lining and up the chimney indicated that it had, in the past, been functional. I was despatched to forage for firewood and returned, considerably warmer than when I left, laden with logs, pine cones and kindling. Surrendering myself to my atavistic urges I entered 'Man Make Fire' mode, stacked the fireplace to overflowing and lit the blue touchpaper.

After a faltering start it caught and the flames spread, giving off a heart-warming glow and a body-warming blast of heat. Smiles of smug anticipation spread across our faces. The flames burned higher, licking up the chimney and heating the brickwork which started to act as a radiant heater. The room was now beginning to approach a temperature capable of sustaining life.

It may be a truism that there's no smoke without fire, but the converse is also true. It transpired that it had not so much been Man Make Fire as Man Make Smoke, and lots of it. Every three seconds or so a large cloud would roll out from under the lintel of the hearth and float up to the ceiling. At first we just assumed that this would stop once the fire really caught and the convective updraft through the chimney pulled air in from the room.

No such luck.

We stood around for a while, coughing and eyes streaming, making hopeful comments such as "I think it's getting better – I can see the kitchen now" and "Ooh look! Isn't that the dining table?" We were only fooling ourselves. By the time the room had warmed up enough for us to remove gloves and overcoats we were reduced to crawling on our bellies commando-style along the floor with wet rags over our faces. We headed towards the French windows where we met the cat, similarly attired, coming the other way.

In the end we had to give up and open all the doors and windows. The smoke was carried out by the icy through-draught, as was all our hard-won heat. Back to square one. Luckily, perseverance paid off and we discovered that by stacking the wood high right at the back of the hearth we could get the smoke output down, and the ambient temperature up, to liveable levels.

The winter sojourn usually incorporates another little ritual of the cruising life, the haul out. Boats are complicated artefacts. OK, not quite as complicated as aeroplanes, but they're getting close. Cruising boats, especially, have to combine the characteristics and services of a house with those of a sea-going vessel. As houses rarely float or sail well and vessels smaller than the QE2 rarely have utility rooms and garden sheds this presents some difficulty. The resulting compromise is then expected to operate in a harsh marine environment so it is no surprise that the maintenance requirements of a cruising yacht are rather high. You need to deal with all the things that go wrong in a house plus all of those that go wrong with the saily/boaty/floaty bits.

We deal with it by having a running 'snag list'. Whenever a problem, or potential problem, arises it is added to the list and given a priority ranging from 'Aaargh!' to 'Might get done before dementia sets in, but don't bank on it.' Important maintenance is carried out as it arises whereas the lesser snags wait until the winter or such time as I'm feeling particularly conscientious and energetic; which isn't often.

Some of this maintenance, however, is below the waterline. Antifoul wears off. Weed, barnacles and the dreaded coral worm build up on the hull, propeller, instrument transducers and bowthrusters. Sacrificial anodes gallantly sacrifice themselves and need replacing. Propeller shaft seals and seacocks wear and begin to seep. Chunks of fibreglass go missing when you hit things.

Some of this can be done in the water. Fouling can be removed with the aid of a mask, fins and snorkel or, better still, scuba gear. Through-hull fittings, though, are another kettle of fish altogether. There are some intrepid souls (or raving bloody lunatics as we prefer to call them) who have repaired or serviced through hull fittings while still in the water. This usually involves stuffing holes from the outside with plastic bags and tapered wooden plugs and then removing the fitting from inside the boat. At this point, and despite the plugs and plastic, a metre high fountain erupts inside the boat. Seeing this is a humbling and frightening experience. It is usually followed by a frantic stuffing of the hole with anything that comes to hand: socks, T shirt, towels, cat, small Dutch boy. You have to stem the flow very quickly. A typical skin fitting can be about eight centimetres across. At a depth of just 30 centimetres below the waterline a hole this size will let three tonnes of water into the boat every minute. Any delay and at best you'll have an awful lot of cleaning up to do. At worst the boat will go down in very short order. In the unlikely event of success the reverse has to be carried out to put everything back.

This is not for us. We have the boat lifted every winter lay up – usually in the spring. This is always a nervous time. We haven't driven the thing for several months. The propeller and bowthrusters are usually so fouled that they work poorly if at all. Then you have to steer the thing backwards into a lifting bay only fractionally wider than the boat in what is invariably a thirty knot crosswind. This is always done in front of the usual crowd of ghouls for whom the high point in their otherwise pointless and sad lives is to watch others flounder about making big dents in their pride and joy. The first time you use a yard for lift-out is even more nerve-racking as you don't have any idea of their competence or conscientiousness. It's not that uncommon for the lifting strops not to be sited correctly, resulting in the boat slipping out and falling. At best this is a couple of feet into the water, at worst several feet onto concrete. The latter is likely to result in a complete write-off and a seriously pissed off insurance company.

Lift outs have been made much easier by the invention of the travel hoist. This is a magnificent, if hardly elegant, piece of engineering. Its basic design suggests that it was knocked up in giant Lego by a bored eight year old on a wet Sunday afternoon in Norfolk. The structure is simplicity itself, a cuboid frame with one of the top spars missing. At the bottom of each of the four pillars is an independent, 360 degree steerable wheel. Spanning two of the top spars are a series of heavy nylon straps, attached to hooks suspended from wire hawsers wound through pulley systems. The whole thing is powered by a gigantic diesel and riddled with hydraulic piping. The driver stands in a small cage, confronted by a forest of levers and an array of dials and gauges that makes the instrumentation in a 747 cockpit look like an elevator call button.

As lift out approaches he uses five levers to steer the leviathan forward so that it straddles the lifting bay. He has a clearance of about five centimetres each side for this. Using another six or so levers he lowers the nylon straps into the water, to a depth below the draft of the boat. At this point, after much shouting and gesticulation, we back nervously into the lifting bay. A further four levers then guide the nylon straps forwards and backwards until they are lined up at the correct lifting positions. This last point is critical. Wrongly positioned lifting straps can cause untold horrors. Apart from dropping the thing, there is always the possibility of getting a strap under a transducer. This then takes the full weight of the boat on a small area and can pop the transducer through the hull. Getting a strop under the propeller shaft will certainly bend the shaft, if not tear the fitting out of the hull. A severely bent shaft, if not noticed at the time, will certainly be noticed when you go back in the water and put the engine in gear. A rhythmic thumping sound will be immediately followed by a crunching and tearing noise. This has two possible causes, neither of them particularly desirable. Either way it will be the sound of something ripping away from the hull. It could be the stuffing box, where the prop shaft goes through the hull, or the engine mounts where the engine is bolted onto the hull. If you're really unlucky it will be both. It's best avoided. Very good yards, such as Marmaris Yat Marin take a belt and braces approach. They have an underwater camera and they send a couple of divers down, just to check.

Once the strops are in position the driver then lifts them, balancing the lift between the different strops to keep the boat level. As we have a cut away forefoot there is always the possibility that the forward strop will slip off and let the boat dive headfirst downwards. We tie the strops together, just to be on the safe side. Once the boat is high enough to clear the ground and the odd feral cat, the hoist trundles slowly through the yard, picking a zigzag course between obstacles. Eventually the boat is propped up in a space approximately one and a half centimetres wider than the hoist.

Daunting though this is, it is a huge improvement on previous methods. Immediately prior to the invention of the travel hoist, cranes were used. These had the unfortunate quality of acting like enormous pendulums, the boat describing graceful arcs across the yard and smashing its way through cars, buildings or other boats like a gigantic demolition ball.

Even before the general use of cranes, unbelievably large weights were moved by that simplest of machines, the inclined plane. In its most basic form this was a simple wedge. Well, to be more accurate it was an awful lot of simple wedges. Large ships, weighing hundreds of thousands of tons, were lifted from their construction supports onto launching trolleys in this way. Gangs of five hundred or more men were arrayed on either side of the ship, each armed with a steel wedge and a large sledgehammer. They positioned the wedges and waited. The foreman signalled with a whistle, which he blew at regular, rhythmic intervals. On each blast the men would strike their wedges simultaneously, driving them in a fraction of an inch with each blow. Slowly, but inexorably, the massive ship would rise with each blast until it was high enough to be chocked onto the launching sled. Now that must have been something to watch.

Lift out time is usually marked by a sudden and dramatic fall in bank balance. The lift out and splash back in alone costs about £500. Then there are usually extra charges for rental of yard space, cradle hire, chocking fees, and pressure wash. Antifoul itself is eye-wateringly expensive. It costs us around £300 to put two coats on Birvidik. On top of this, there is usually the additional cost of alternative accommodation. Living on the boat while it's on the hard is not a relaxing experience. For a start, you have to negotiate scaffolding or a steep ladder every time you get on or off. In addition you can't use the toilets or shower on board and the sinks have to empty into containers which you then have to cart away to empty at frequent intervals. Nightly ablutions are a pain. Urine goes into a bucket whilst anything even less savoury requires you to clamber down the ladder and stumble across a cold, wet, dark, windswept yard at three in the morning. Every morning sees slop-out parade as a crocodile of bleary-eyed yotties converge on the toilet block carrying buckets of cold, stale urine.

You do, however, regain your fitness after the long winter lay-off. The legs are given a good workout by scaling the ladder thirty or so times a day. Upper body muscle tone and bulk are dealt with by rubbing off and re-applying the antifoul and rubbing down the topsides and then polishing them. A lot of this is done while perched precariously on a suspect ladder or trying to maintain your balance on a rickety, ramshackle scaffold, which leads us on to the average yottie's single minded refusal to attempt even a tenuous grasp on reality.

"It's a wonderfully healthy lifestyle", he crows with tedious regularity. No it bloody isn't. Think about it. Most cruisers are of, let us say, somewhat mature years. We're not actually designed to live this long in the first place. As far as evolution is concerned our job is to reach sexual maturity, reproduce like rabbits, stay healthy long enough to bring the brats up and then get out of the bloody way, preferably by shuffling off and dying somewhere.

Following that design spec the human body starts to come apart at the seams from about 35 onwards. By the time it gets to average cruiser age bits are failing or falling off it with alarming regularity. Just as the yottie starts the cruising life the insults and frailties to which the flesh is heir start to snowball. We're lucky, we started earlier than most.

To compound this, the yottie and his usually long-suffering spouse take up a lifestyle where flexibility, stamina, strength, balance and endurance are all at a premium. They live in a confined space which has the unnerving habit of suddenly throwing itself about at all angles and often find themselves in situations which require all the previously mentioned desiderata as well as the application of large forces in limited spaces.

Despite all this, our yottie stubbornly refuses to accept that he is anything other than in his prime and that his vast experience in the University of Life, combined with the sagacity of maturity more than makes up for the miniscule deterioration in physical and mental attributes that may, just possibly, have occurred during this extended learning curve. As anyone with an iota of sense would appreciate, this attitude, combined with the abovementioned circumstances, frequently results in tears before bedtime. Mr & Mrs Yottie throw themselves wholeheartedly into physical activity. The gym is patronised fully. Yoga and Pilates classes are enthusiastically attended. Long walks up the sides of mountains are undertaken. Bicycles are ridden with gusto and a total disregard for foreign roads and drivers. There has, inevitably, been a cornucopia of resulting medical catastrophes; hernias (no names, no pack drill), torn tendons and ligaments, frozen shoulders, dodgy knees, pulled muscles, crumbling teeth and haemorrhoids to name but a few.

Things are even further exacerbated during haul out. During this time the boat is no longer in the water but balanced precariously on its keel. Frequently, the only thing stopping it from crashing over on its side and causing a financial meltdown in the marine insurance sector is a ramshackle, Heath-Robinson arrangement of splintered, gnarled branches. These are jammed between the concrete and the hull by a series of rough wooden wedges which the marina staff enthusiastically knock into place with the aid of a 10 lb lump hammer. The whole rickety edifice is then, purportedly, held together by a random web of bits of old plank, supposedly acting as cross struts, held in with four inch nails.

Being on the hard, as this is known, has the advantage that the boat rarely starts throwing itself about at awkward angles. If it does, you're certainly in deep trouble and probably in Japan. Among its many disadvantages is the fact that you are working on uneven, unstable scaffolding about three metres above a very hard concrete floor. In positions such as this it has great survival value to be able to retain at least a rough idea of your physical circumstances in the short term memory. It is unfortunate then that short term memory is one of the first faculties to atrophy once past one's prime. It is staggering (literally) how many yotties completely forget that they're working on a narrow plank three metres up and blithely step back to admire their handiwork, or shuffle sideways off the end. Having made this rather fundamental error they then find themselves in need of another fast-fading couple of attributes, quick reactions and balance.

These are frequently found wanting.

It is no surprise then that the majority of accidents and medical misfortunes that occur to yotties take place during haul out. We personally know a long list of people who have suffered haul out injuries including two broken ankles, one broken wrist, one broken pelvis, one broken back, one severely crushed finger which almost resulted in amputation, two strokes, several hernias and a suspected heart attack. Oh – and burns associated with an explosion in a power boat. Apparently it's not a good idea to switch on a vacuum cleaner when the interior of the boat you are about to vacuum is filled with acetone fumes. Luckily no-one was seriously injured when the deck popped up and the funnel toppled over like a giant statue of Buddha after a run-in with the Taliban.

We could have put all these down to coincidence and an unusual statistical blip, except for the fact that one of the marinas we were in whilst in Turkey already had two wheelchairs and several sets of crutches permanently available. On top of this there was an ambulance permanently stationed on site. This, cunningly, was attached to the local private hospital so that at the first sign of disaster the injured are whisked off there before their tight-fisted next of kin can arrange to get them into the local State hospital.

There must have been a sufficient history of accidents and medical emergencies to suggest it would be cost effective to keep an expensive ambulance and somewhat less expensive driver on site 24/7. I'd have loved to have seen their business plan when they asked for the loan to buy the ambulance. "It's unethical and time consuming to go out and cause accidents so we've set up in partnership with the marina. They give the yotties enough rope and we swoop in and pick up the pieces (and wallets)."

Just in case the yotties prove themselves too incompetent to take full advantage of the opportunities to kill and maim themselves, many marinas generously help things along with the service pods. These are the boxes from which the boats can draw water and electricity (always a good mix). When we were hauled out in Marmaris we were directed to a box that looked as though it had come off second in an altercation with the 300 tonne travel hoist. It leant over at a drunken angle, three legs bent and one missing altogether. The door was missing except for a few splintered edges still attached to the hinges. Assorted dials and gauges dangled forlornly from its bowels along with various odd bits of wire, some of which still had some actual insulation on them. The whole thing had the air of having been so overwhelmed with shame at its parlous state that it had committed Hara Kiri and eviscerated itself. The hairline cracks in the water pipes sprayed a fine mist over the tangle of electrical wiring. We plugged in anyway – it was the only one within reach.

Everything went fine until the next day when Liz, while climbing the ladder, grabbed hold of the swim platform with one hand and the stern guard rail with the other. Luckily, the AC belt she got neither killed her nor threw her off the ladder. After farting around with a multimeter for some considerable time, we discovered that the problem was caused by an induced current and the fact that the shore supply's earth connection was neither an earth nor connected. I rectified matters by bonding the ship's AC earth to a large metal spike driven into the ground. Well, that's what I should have done. What I actually did was dangle a wire into a puddle on the ground. Seemed to do the trick.

The South Coast

Lagos to the River Guardiana

April 14th 2007 to April 24th 2007

The boat went back in the water on Liz's birthday so I enlisted the help of Tony and Joyce from Reeve as Liz decided to go and have a haircut, pedicure and general pampering instead of fulfilling her seawomanly duties. You just can't get the crew these days.

After five days of frantic preparation we shot dishevelled and gasping through the bridge at Lagos and turned left toward the Med. After four hours we were pretty sure no-one was still watching us so we pulled into Portimao and dropped anchor. Its tiring stuff this sailing business.

Portimao is only about half an hour by car from Lagos and we knew it very well, so we stayed just the one night. The next morning we motored into wind and swell for six hours toward Ria Formosa, a nature reserve near Faro. It's amazing that it's taken us a day and a half (well, ten hours sailing) to cover what you can do in 45 minutes on the motorway. The trip was a fine reminder of the less enjoyable aspects of sailing. The boat was pitching up and down, testing our hurried stowage to destruction and we survived on ginger biscuits. Am I selling the idea to anybody?

Conditions eased when, towards the end of the trip, we anchored in the salt marsh lagoons at Faro. Shallow creeks meandered between sandbanks, sheltered from the sea by an archipelago of low, sandy islands. The evening sun bathed the area in a soft rose hue and the yellow buildings and silhouetted palm trees reflected in the oily-calm water. It was idyllic. Sailing's like that, crap to sublime in what seems like nanoseconds (and the converse, of course).

Wanting to make good time, we were straight off the next morning to the River Guardiana, the border between Portugal and Spain. The skies cleared to another lovely day and we weighed anchor at about 09:50 and set off, keeping a wary eye on the depth sounder as we were leaving at low water springs. The lowest registered was 1.8 metres so Liz didn't have to do the bit where she stands on tip toe when it gets shallow as if this somehow reduces the draft of the boat.

What is it with fisherman, small boats and river/harbour entrances? There we are, trying to stick to the only bit of channel deep enough to let us through and we have to pick our way through hundreds of small dinghies with lines, nets and pots off them, whilst trying to dodge the behemoths of the fishing boat world steaming straight in at us at top speed. Still, we managed it.

What a change it was from the day before. Calm seas, sun shining and lots of (mainly juvenile) gannets. We even got a bit of a sail in on a beam reach (wind square on the side for non-yotties) before the weather gods decided we'd had enough fun for the day and the wind died.

A known hazard in these waters are the tuna nets, which can stretch for seven miles and are strong enough to bring a coastal freighter to a shuddering halt. We spotted them and avoided them easily enough, but so that we didn't get too bored the local fishermen had scattered the area liberally with pots. All along this area there are artificial reefs and other areas which are marked on the chart as fish havens, along with a big 'no fishing' symbol. Even without the chart the boundaries to these are easily found, as the borders are surrounded by lobster pots and fishermen with lines and nets, all packed cheek by jowl. One fin, tentacle or leg over the line and you're dead meat.

The river Guardiana forms the border between Spain and Portugal, meeting the sea between Vila Real de S. Antonio in Portugal and Ayamonte in Spain. It used to be a major crossing point with a little flat topped ferry carrying vehicles and pedestrians unsteadily between the two, but this has now been superseded by the large suspension bridge that carries the motorway across just up river. We decided to take a run the 25 miles up river to the twin villages of Alcoutim (Portuguese) and Sanlucar (Spanish).

The first intellectual challenge was to decide which courtesy flag to fly. Some officials can be very sensitive about this sort of thing. Theoretically the border runs down the middle of the river, but varying depths mean that you have to navigate between one side and the other as you avoid the many shoal areas. We didn't want to upset any nationalistic sensibilities and there are whole books devoted to the obscure rules governing flag etiquette. This is another area much beloved by men of a certain age in yacht clubs.

In essence, the courtesy flag should be second in status only to the boat's national ensign. No other flag should be flown in a superior position to the courtesy flag of the country in which the boat currently is. This means that it has to be flown on the starboard cross trees (don't ask why starboard is 'superior' to port – it just is, alright?). No other flag should be flown higher than the courtesy flag either. Therefore, we couldn't fly one above the other; neither could we fly one on the port side and the other on the starboard. So, in a solution that would have earned approval from Grauniad readers everywhere I whipped the two flags together with twine and hoisted them side by side on the starboard flag halyard so that, with the prevailing wind, it would show the Portuguese flag to the Portuguese shore and vice versa. Of course, to be really consistent I should have swapped them round when we went back down river or if the wind changed but I really couldn't be arsed. We flew the two side by side until we moored up back in Ayamonte, where we took the Portuguese flag down. Having been up since the previous August it was definitely looking a bit tired and frayed.

Travelling up a river is strikingly different to being at sea. We had been in a marine environment for so long that all of our senses had become accustomed to it. Once we had negotiated our way under the suspension bridge the whole aspect changed subtly but quickly. It affected everything – colours, sounds, smell, taste, even the feel of the wind was less harsh and sharp. The seascapes' restricted palette of pastel blues, greys and whites gave way to richer greens and browns, flecked with the reds and yellows of the profusion of spring flowers. The crash of waves and haunting cries of the terns and seagulls were replaced by the ripple of the river, accompanied by the lowing of cattle, the hollow, atonal ringing of the bells on sheep and goats, the constant zither of cicadas, the croaking of frogs and the choruses of swifts and kingfishers. The smell of agriculture, warm, organic, faintly foetid, took over from the sharp tang of sea air [14].

---

[14] This sea tang is not ozone as is popularly believed but, more prosaically, a mixture of sulphur compounds (chemically similar to those that give flatulence its characteristic fragrance) which are produced by rotting seaweed.

Further upriver the fragrant scent of orange blossom permeated the air. The whole experience was a vivid novelty. Even the feel of it was different. Such waves as there were in the river were very low and of too short a wavelength to have any effect on something of *Birvidik*'s size. The instinctive, subconscious counterbalancing that develops at sea, alternating the weight between one slightly bent leg and the other, was now superfluous.

Having successfully negotiated our twelve metre mast under the suspension bridge and (only just) avoided the shallows in the uncharted river, we anchored midway between the shores, just upstream of the two towns. The anchor bit first time and held against the force of the river and the engine. We sat back and relaxed. Just as we were congratulating ourselves on our immaculate pilotage in getting our 1.8 metre draft up the river a sodding great 200 foot cruise boat hammered round the corner, executed a nifty little 180 degree turn and moored up at Alcoutim. Show-offs.

The countryside was beautiful, and in a surreal twist there was even a beach at Alcoutim on a tributary of the river. It looked as if a section of the coastal tourist belt had been surgically excised and transplanted into the heart of the countryside. It had sand, a cafe, picnic tables, beach huts, even a blue flag. The only thing it didn't have were hordes of Northern European tourists with skin tones reminiscent of raspberry ripple ice cream. It was virtually empty, patronised only by a few local Portuguese and the odd Spanish visitor from across the river. Mind you, they must need it as it gets unbearably hot there in the middle of the summer.

We sat in the cockpit and savoured the smell of the orange blossom and the sounds of the river and countryside, which rose to a crescendo in the evening. This bucolic charm was penetrated by a puzzling sound, a single note 'peep' at regular intervals. At first we thought this was a bird call and thought 'how charming'. Then as time passed we realised how regular it was and decided it wasn't a bird call at all, just one of those electronic alarms that go off all the time. It instantly switched from the 'charming' category to 'bloody irritating'.

Then it stopped being regular and started moving around, so we decided it was a bird after all and it reverted to the 'how charming' psychological bracket. Mind you, if it keeps that up all bloody night... [15]

As night fell a slight niggling worry raised its head above the parapet. The river was still tidal, even this far up, and at the moment the tide was on the flood and so opposing and, in fact, overcoming the downstream flow of the river. When the tide turned (at about two in the morning) the tidal flow would augment the river flow and we would swing through 180 degrees. Would the anchor hold? Would it break out? If so, would it dig in again in the other direction? The worst case scenario gave the answers 'No', 'Yes' and 'No'. Under these circumstances the strong current would carry *Birvidik* careering downriver, bagatelling into all the other poor unfortunates downstream.

We activated the echo sounder alarm and the anchor drag alarm. Then we set the ordinary alarm for 1:30 a.m., just before the tide was due to turn. The echo sounder gave us depth and current flow, but gave us some peculiar (and worrying) readings which appeared to be written in a mixture of Cyrillic and Arabic script interspersed with Japanese pictograms. Things became clearer once we donned our reading glasses and peered, squinting, at the screen. Most of what had appeared to be data turned out to be small flies congregating on the screen, having been attracted by the illuminated display.

This highlighted another difference associated with being inland, namely the greater abundance of insect life, especially mosquitoes.

I have a deep and perfectly rational hatred of mosquitoes. They carry a litany of pathogens, including some

---

[15] This call was later identified as that of the Scops Owl, one of the smallest owls in Europe.

of the most unpleasant diseases known to man, among them malaria, dengue fever, encephalitis, heartworm and yellow fever. Mosquitoes are responsible for more human deaths and suffering than any other organism. Over one million people die each year from mosquito borne diseases.

Actually, on reflection, I may have to rethink that. About a million people worldwide die each year as a result of traffic accidents, around 8000 a year are murdered and, in 2010, roughly 3000 were judicially executed. The tobacco industry accounts for three million deaths a year worldwide and God knows how many died in the various wars and insurgencies around the globe. World War II killed around 60 million people in Europe alone, including 6 million Jews. It would take an awful lot of mosquitoes to match that. Altogether, we seem to make mosquitoes look almost benign by comparison.

No – what really gets me about mosquitoes is that I anthropomorphise them. I don't see them as organisms doing what evolution has cornered them into doing in order to survive and reproduce. I see them as nasty, vindictive little sadists who are personally trying to make me suffer. I wouldn't mind if they'd just bite me, slurp up enough blood to enable them to reproduce, leave a batch of assorted pathogens by way of payment and then bugger off.

But they don't. For a start, if all they wanted was to get their fix of blood and escape unscathed, it would make sense to wait until their victims were asleep, nip in silently, strike, and beat a rapid retreat. That's what a vampire bat manages to do and it's a damned sight more noticeable and less manoeuvrable than a mosquito. It even has a local anaesthetic and an anticoagulant in its saliva to make the whole process quicker and less likely to result in retaliation. Mosquitoes, no. They like a challenge. To them, rather than a biological necessity, it's more like the insect version of a bullfight.

First of all, she needs to wind me up. [16]

So, just to make it more fun, she lets me know she's coming. She waits until I'm snuggled cosily into bed, just dozing off and then makes her preparatory sortie. It starts with that irritating whine, perfectly pitched at around 500 hertz (around B natural) – high enough to be irritating but not at the two to five kilohertz, adrenaline producing level of the human scream.

After she's made a couple of circuits like this to make sure I'm awake she goes and hides. I then lay there, ears straining for about half an hour. Nothing. Eventually I begin to doze off again.

That's the cue to start phase two. This is the softening up process as usually performed by the picadors in a bullfight. A succession of low level passes over the head are enough to wake me up. At this point I usually decide to bury myself under the bedclothes and wait for the little bastard to die of hunger or boredom. Fat chance. She just perches on the headboard and waits. Soon enough the combined forces of suffocation and heatstroke bring me gasping into the air at which point the attack resumes. From here it can go one of two ways. Either all goes to plan and I'm debilitated enough to lay there and meekly accept my fate as the little sod homes in for the moment of truth or she cocks up big time and I leap out of bed in a fit of incoherent rage and head for the arsenal.

Liz has accumulated a comprehensive stockpile of anti-mosquito weaponry. These represent the entire range and history of military technology. A range of swats take on the rôle of the sword or mace. Chemical warfare is represented by cans of a Portuguese product called Dum Dum. How this stuff got past the Health and Safety regulators is beyond me. One squirt could knock out an elephant, reducing it to a twitching grey hulk with bodily

---

[16] It's always a she. Males don't bite. Sugars from plant sources are the main source of energy for all mosquitoes, but females need blood to enable them to develop fertile eggs.)

fluids oozing from trunk, eyes, ears and various other orifices. If Saddam Hussein had known about Dum Dum it would have altered the whole course of Middle Eastern history. The only life form impervious to it is the cockroach which, even if liberally coated with the stuff, will merely sneeze, give a peremptory twitch just to make you feel better, then lie down for 30 seconds and finally stand up, shake itself down and wander off whistling Dixie.

In addition we have a range of electrically powered chemical diffusers and the insect equivalent of the electric chair. A bright light attracts the mosquitoes (or so the literature assured us) and they then pass through a high voltage mesh which vaporises them with a satisfying crack. Fly paper took on the role of the pitfall trap and in desperation we had even resorted to the pseudoscientific charlatanism of ultrasonic deterrents. We deployed the entire arsenal.

None of it worked, of course. In fact I strongly suspect that the zapper light attracted them onto the boat without fulfilling its primary function of incinerating the bloodthirsty little shits. I emerged from the encounter looking as if I've just done five rounds with Tyson Fury. Luckily, Liz has the equivalent of an army field hospital stowed in the forward heads and we broke out the antihistamines to deal with the subsequent swelling and itching.

Walking around the area highlighted the dramatic difference between inland, agricultural Iberia and the tourism-blighted coastal strips. As little as 25 years previously car ownership was a rarity in these areas. Most transport, of goods and people, was done by donkey or horse. The small villages were little changed from how they were a quarter of a century ago, with the exception of the knock-on effects of car ownership. Most shopping is now carried by car from the larger towns and cities and the few remaining local shops struggle to survive. Mind you, given our experiences in the sole remaining store in Alcoutim, they don't seem to be doing themselves any favours.

We needed a few basic provisions; nothing drastic, a

few vegetables and some milk and bread – that sort of thing. We dinghied ashore to Alcoutim and went into the only shop. It was not, at first, immediately apparent that this was a shop at all. It looked just like all the other small cottages in the village. Peering through the open door, however, revealed a set of antique scales with two potatoes in the pan. We entered and waited for our eyes to adjust to the gloom. After a while the details of the interior began to emerge. Two women, one of whom we took to be the owner, were engaged in earnest conversation. They ignored us completely. The shelves and tables were almost completely empty. The entire stock consisted of half a dried cod, a carrot, three plastic bottles of 70 cent white wine, a bottle of bleach and the previously mentioned two potatoes.

We selected a few items from these sparse offerings and waited expectantly at the till. They showed no sign of having even seen us and continued their, by now quite animated, conversation. We attempted to engage them by the use of ineffectual hand signals and winding up our smiles to a manic rictus. They looked straight through us. I came to the conclusion that the only possible explanation was a warp in the laws of physics which had endowed us with a cloak of invisibility and transferred us to a parallel dimension. I subjected this theory to experiment by walking across and standing directly between them, holding the potatoes under the owner's nose and enquiring sweetly *Quant' sao estas?* She looked at me as if she had suddenly found the source of that unpleasant odour that had been assailing her nostrils all day.

I dug out the exorbitant amount demanded for the pathetic offerings and meekly handed it over to po-faced woman. She put it in her apron and instantly returned to her conversation without so much as an acknowledgement of our hypocritical thanks and good wishes for the prosperity of her business enterprise. We returned to the boat with our meagre provisions and decided to return to less rural surroundings. We weighed anchor and headed south, anchored a little further downriver for one night and then moored up in Ayamonte for a couple of days. Here we bumped into our friends Dick and Ginger from Alchemy.

Degrees of Separation is a concept associated with network theory and commonly applied to social networks. The idea was first put forward by the Hungarian Frigyes Karinthy [17] in 1929 and has subsequently been taken up by mathematicians, sociologists and internet dweebs. It refers to the number of person-to-person links that would need to be made to connect any two people. The popular figure for the smallest number of links that would, on average, be necessary to connect any two random people on the planet is held to be six, hence six degrees of separation.

Obviously, for members of a smaller and more linked group the number will be smaller. For twitter users (still a pretty large group) the figure was calculated as 3.43. For cruising yotties the average degree of separation appears to be about one point diddlysquat, which means that every time you meet other cruising yotties you either know them already or you have at least five acquaintances in common.

This should not, perhaps, be too surprising. There are likely to be considerably fewer cruising yotties than there are twitter users. It is difficult to be precise though. Due to their somewhat unconventional lifestyles, full time cruising yotties tend to fly under the official radar. Although this is generally a good thing, it makes it difficult to get reliable statistics on them. Nevertheless, in comparison with most other lifestyles, there aren't that many of us and those that do exist are spread out across the globe. Estimates I have seen range from around 15 000 boats to 50 000 boats. This still only accounts for about 100 000 people tops, which means you could get every cruising yottie on the planet into Wembley Arena and still have room for the entire population of the Falkland Islands. Although, to be fair, you could get the

---

[17]Karinthy (1887 – 1938) was a polymath, - a journalist, author, playwright, satirist, translator and poet. Among his many achievements was translating Winnie the Pooh into Hungarian, which resulted in it becoming a cult book in the country.

latter into the penalty boxes and still have room left over.

Although we are spread across the globe we are far from evenly distributed. There aren't a great many of us in the Barents Sea or Lake Titicaca for example. There aren't even that many in the lush, tropical paradises of the South Pacific. I'll let you into a little secret here. All in all, most of us aren't really that adventurous. We tend to stick to areas with relatively clement climates and reasonably easy access to the decadent benefits of civilisation. Marathon oceanic voyages are also contraindicated. This effectively puts about 97 percent of us in either the Mediterranean or the Caribbean.

Even within the confines of the Med, we still exhibit flocking behaviour [18], on both the large and the small scale. This is a result of geography, especially in the winter, and human psychology.

Most Mediterranean harbours and anchorages are usually open to the weather in at least one direction. If there is anything of a blow forecast (which is a lot of the time in most of the Med and almost invariably in the Aegean) then all of the boats in the immediate area home in on the relatively restricted number of protected spots like wasps on a picnic. In the winter, choices are even more limited as the chosen spot needs to be protected from all points of the compass. If you also take into account the other wintering hole requirements already mentioned under 'Lagos' then your choices are limited to a couple of hundred possibles, fifty or so preferables and around twenty favourites over the whole of the Med. Indeed the most desirable wintering holes are becoming so popular that more and more of them are refusing to allocate a place for the next winter unless you give them a hefty deposit before you even set off for the summer.

---

[18] Animals display a range of behaviours when threatened and they all begin with 'F' – Fight, Flee, Freeze and Flock. Humans can exhibit all four, but yotties tend to go for flocking.

There is also an even smaller scale flocking behaviour evident amongst yotties. Consider the occasional, but rare, occurrence that a boat arrives in an anchorage or harbour which has plenty of space and few boats in it. The etiquette, as will be discussed in detail further on, is that boats arriving later have to keep out of the way of those already ensconced.

The ideal position under these circumstances is to be the first to arrive in an empty anchorage. First of all you look at the chart and the weather forecast to judge which areas of the anchorage are likely to be best protected from the forthcoming weather. After that you take a mooch around the place, determining where there are suitable depths and good holding. Secondary factors, such as accessibility to shore and restaurants, distance from eyesores such as the local cement works and whether you are downwind from the overloaded sewage farm can then applied. Eventually you pick your spot and drop your hook.

Subsequent arrivals are progressively exiled to the less and less attractive options until eventually there are none left and the hapless latecomers either tie up to the sewage works or circle the anchorage forlornly looking for an available spot while territorially aggressive skippers glare at them from their foredecks. Any attempt to drop an anchor is met with wild gesticulations and sympathetic cries of *"Not there you bloody moron! That's right over my chain! I've got eight anchors out and they've all got 200 metres of chain on them. Bugger off!"* If the latecomer is British he will usually meekly go off and anchor off some horribly exposed headland and spend a miserable night rolling about and whinging about arrogant tossers hogging all the best anchorages. If he is German he will anchor wherever he wants and ignore the stream of invective coming from Mr and Mrs Yottie standing on their bow which is now about fifteen centimetres from his transom. If he is Italian he will do the same, except that once anchored he will produce a bottle of Chianti, a tray of glasses and proceed to charm the pants off Mrs (and preferably Miss) Yottie. Mrs. Yottie will then giggle girlishly, coyly lower her eyelashes and turn to her glowering husband saying "Oh Lionel, don't be such an old killjoy. I'm sure Signor Plentiflanelli's boat will be alright there for one night". Mrs. Yottie's point of view will prevail.

It does occasionally happen, however, that a new arrival will turn up in an anchorage to find a solitary boat at anchor. The interloper will frequently assume that the boat already in place has bagged the best spot. This is not necessarily so. It may be that there is no significantly best place in the anchorage and that more or less anywhere will do. It may be that the sitting tenant was a late arrival the day before and all those boats already anchored when he arrived have gone. He might be an idiot and not know where the best sites are likely to be. He might be a charter boat, which is similar to the previous example.

Whatever the case may be, the logical thing for the latest arrival to do is to go through the same procedures as would the first boat to arrive. Does he Hell. Rather than go through the strain of thinking he just assumes that the existing boat is in the best spot and proceeds to park as close to it as is humanly possible without triggering actual physical violence. The next boat to arrive assumes that, if there are two boats in that spot, it must be the best place and parks itself between the two of them. This continues throughout the day until you end up with thirty boats packed cheek by jowl in one small corner of the bay while the rest of a beautifully protected anchorage, big enough to take the entire US Pacific Fleet, lies empty.

Spain (Part 2 – The Costas)

The Costas are as different from Galicia as Blackpool is from the Isle of Skye and as different from each other as Torquay is from Skegness. They stretch from Ayamonte on the Portuguese border to Portbou near the French border, a distance of some 1500 kilometres and were the first parts of Spain to develop a tourist industry in the latter years of Franco's rule.

The package holiday industry started in Spain in the 1950s and took off in a big way. From around 700 000 tourists all told in 1950 it had risen to 34 million by 1973 and reached over 60 million by 2002. It dropped back a bit in the financial meltdown from 2008 onwards but has recently picked up again.

Like many people, I suspect, I read these sorts of figures in newspaper reports but I never really take them in or spend any effort trying to think about them. I'll read a headline such as "Spanish tourist figures hit all time high of 60 million" and think "Oooh – they're doing well, that's nice." Nice? It's like having the equivalent of the entire population of the U.K. popping in for a visit on a regular basis. That's bound to have a bit of an effect on the neighbourhood.

In the peak season around eight million tourists descend on the area in any one month. Assuming that they come for the traditional fortnight that gives four million extra people wandering round the place; all of them needing accommodation, food, drink and toilet facilities. This is a staggeringly difficult concept for me to try to get my head round. It's like transporting the joint populations of Birmingham, Leeds, Glasgow, Sheffield, Bradford, Edinburgh and half of Liverpool into the place overnight. Even if you spread them out evenly in a line along the whole 1500 kilometres from Ayamonte to Portbou you would still need to pack nearly three people into each metre of coastline.

In the wake of the tourists came the ex-pats, usually tourists who apparently liked the place so much they moved over permanently or semi-permanently. It's funny, isn't it, how someone from your town who moves abroad is an ex-pat whereas someone from abroad who moves to your town is an immigrant. Or bloody immigrant depending on your position on the Guardian – Daily Mail spectrum.

There are about one million British ex-pats living in Spain, mostly around the Costas, and around 50 000 in Portugal, mostly in the Algarve. From our experience they are generally drawn from a fairly limited demographic. The majority are retired or of independent means. Servicing this majority is a stratum of ex-pat entrepreneurs running businesses such as bars, restaurants, British food shops, estate agents, swimming pool installers and development companies. Servicing both strata are a rag-bag of assorted chancers scraping a living from their (usually imaginary) abilities as electricians, plumbers, hairdressers, satellite dish installers, fitness instructors or Feng Shui advisors. In general, the only ones that manage to show any real talent for their professed occupations are the time share touts, most of whom would make Arthur Daley look like Forest Gump.

It would be patently absurd to suggest that British ex-pats are a completely homogenous group. Absurd, but not that far from the truth. One could be tempted to draw up a kind of identikit character sketch of the archetypal ex-pat one meets in a typical ex-pat bar. I can resist anything but temptation:

Sex: Almost invariably male, even the women.

Chronological age: Rarely below 60

Emotional age: Pre school

Politics: Somewhat to the right of Genghis Khan.

Reading matter: The Daily Mail, or The Telegraph if he's feeling particularly liberal and mellow (this is unlikely if he has recently read the Daily Mail).

Hobbies: Xenophobia; writing letters to the editor bemoaning the state of almost everything; living in constant fear of being ripped off; bemoaning modern education and then writing internet posts containing 'seperate', 'priviledge' and 'their' for 'they're'.

Likes: Proper English food; whiskey; golf clubs (the institutions, not the equipment); gin & tonic; the saloon bars of waterside pubs; USING CAPITAL LETTERS ON INTERNET POSTS; the days when people knew their place; The Ladies, God Bless 'em (as long as they don't get ideas above their station); proper comedy (i.e. Bernard Manning).

Dislikes: Foreigners; taxes; unions; benefits scroungers; bogus asylum seekers (which is all of them); taxes again; political correctness gone mad; The EU; students; public sector workers; public sector workers' pensions; more foreigners; 'Elf n Safety; Dungaree-wearing bra-burning feminists; the BBC (except Strictly Come Dancing); Blacks; Asians; Gypsies; Eastern Europeans and most of the Irish. He's not sure about Jews.

George Orwell invented the term 'doublethink' to describe the ability to hold two contradictory beliefs in one's mind simultaneously and accept both of them. In psychological circles the opposite of doublethink is termed, 'cognitive dissonance', a condition where two incompatible beliefs cause conflict in the mind. The archetypal ex-pat displays all of the former and none of the latter. His mindset happily combines a deep seated belief that all things English epitomise the acme of human development and culture with the fact that he has chosen to leave England and live in a country appallingly mismanaged by a bunch of bloody foreigners who don't even have the decency to thank him for coming to their God-forsaken country and explaining to them how things really ought to be done.

Few that we have met, even those who had been ex-pats for twenty years or more, had made even the slightest attempt to learn the language, expecting instead that local tradespeople and shop assistants speak to them in English. There was one regular in the bar we used to run who maintained that he had made an effort to learn Portuguese and could communicate with the locals adequately. I was impressed until I heard him in action. His Portuguese consisted of putting 'o' on the end of most of the words in an English sentence: "You-o wanto a drinko on me-o?"

Another defining characteristic is that one of the main reasons given for leaving England (it's almost invariably 'England' rather than 'Britain' although many still use the anachronistic 'Blighty') is that it is over-run with bloody immigrants who "Come over to England, steal our jobs, go after our women, don't mix (uh?), carry on as if they were in their own country, eat their own food and don't learn the language". Doublethink is related to, but distinct from, hypocrisy.

The only disharmony apparent in this apotheosis of social cohesion is religious. A schism seems to have developed between those who advocate the deification of the Royal Family and the beatification of Margaret Thatcher and a breakaway sect who argue that it should be the other way round.

I realise that many will find this difficult to accept, but I generally try to hold my tongue in conversations such as these. Experience has taught me that no good will come of trying to widen the parameters of the discussion. Just occasionally, however, I can't resist asking, in a spirit of sympathetic concern, if they had actually made a wise lifestyle choice and suggesting that perhaps they might have a quieter, calmer and much less stressful time if they opted for a nice little bungalow in Surbiton.

The Costa de la Luz

Ayamonte to Gibraltar

April 27th 2007 to May 7th 2007

The next stop after Ayamonte was Mazagon for one

night at anchor; just outside the channel which carried bloody great freighters and carriers upriver to Huelva. We managed to avoid being run down in our sleep by judicious use of the riding light.

At sparrowfart the next morning we left for Rota, a journey of about 35 miles, which should have taken about seven hours. It was overcast with little wind so we set off under motor, rolling nauseatingly in the onshore swell. Twenty minutes into the trip a loud clunk reverberated through the boat and the engine stopped. In these circumstances the first thing to do is look over the stern to see if you've hit anything or caught something round the prop. Sure enough, we were trailing about a hundred metres of line behind us.

Birvidik has rope cutters fitted to the prop shaft. These are two sets of counter rotating, viciously sharp curved blades and are usually very effective. Indeed we have managed to completely shred our own moorings with them on several occasions. They were no match for this stuff though. It was a polypropylene mooring line, about ten centimetres in diameter, designed to hold 2000 tonne freighters in place.

I selected neutral and restarted the engine which, fortunately, seemed fine. I tried going astern to see if I could unwind the rope from the prop shaft. The engine just stalled again. A quick assessment of our situation didn't exactly engender a sensation of relaxed confidence. We were about half a mile off a rocky shore, towards which we were being carried by the current and what little wind there was. Sailing wasn't an option and we had no motive power. At the present rate of drift we would be on the rocks in about half an hour. It became apparent that someone (namely me) was going to have to go over the side to free it.

The one bright spot was that the echo sounder showed us in about eighty metres of water which appeared to be shallowing slowly. We carried an oversized Manson anchor on sixty metres of ten millimetre chain, all of which we deployed hoping to snag on something as we drifted into shallower water. While Liz kept an eye on transits to check our progress, I struggled into my wetsuit. I'd definitely put on weight over the winter.

The gnawing anxiety I was experiencing grew as the full implications of what I was planning to do sank in. My mouth dried up, my stomach started to knot and I began to feel slightly nauseous. By the time I was ready to go over the side the depth had shallowed to 40 metres and the transits indicated that we had stopped moving.

I deployed the stern platform and boarding ladder, attached myself to the boat with about five metres of safety line, donned mask, snorkel and fins, and jumped in. After much girly squealing my breathing eventually returned to mere hyperventilation. As soon as I hit the water I had no time to be worried or afraid. I found I was concentrating completely on the job in hand and that left no brain cells available for worrying.

The anchor had turned us bows on to the swell, causing the stern to pitch up and down violently. To avoid getting banged on the head by 16 tonnes of boat I had to grab hold of the lower rudder pintle as the stern rose and let it carry me down as it fell. Then I could hold on to the prop shaft to keep me going up and down in time with the boat. The dodgiest part was when I ran out of breath and had to surface as this necessitated balancing the opposing priorities of a screaming desire to breath and the need to wait for the right point in the boat's motion before swimming for the surface.

I dived down and took a look. It was not good. The line was polypropylene and polypropylene normally floats. We had hit the line near one end which was held under the water, just at prop depth, by a weighted monkey's fist on a throwing line. The rope had wound tightly round both the prop and shaft. The friction had fused the polypropylene into an amorphous mass of plastic, making unwinding it by hand impossible. I was by now desperate for air so I let go and swam up to get a knife.

It was at this point that the safety line attaching me to

the boat snagged round the prop and held me down. I immediately regretted my idiocy in not taking a knife with me in the first place. Fortunately I had had the foresight to attach the safety line with a snap shackle, making it easy to release. I surfaced and asked Liz for our fish filleting knife, which has a twenty centimetre razor sharp blade terminating in a wicked point. This, I hoped, would make short work of the knotted line. Its potential for making short work of me as well added the frisson of another thing to think about while pitching up and down underwater. Just to add to the challenge a swarm of jellyfish turned up to watch. There wasn't much of me exposed, but what there was - cheeks, ears, neck, hands, bald patch – was soon covered in stings. They were not particularly painful, more like nettle rash.

It took 45 minutes to clear the rope from the prop. By the time I came out, bruised and stung but triumphant, I was shivering uncontrollably despite the wetsuit. Before raising the anchor we started the engine and put it in ahead and astern to check if there had been any damage to the gearbox or prop shaft. A bent prop shaft soon starts letting in water and can wreak havoc with the gearbox and engine mounts.

All seemed well and so we upped the anchor and set off once again for Rota. I went below for a hot shower. We dumped the rope in Rota, but kept the weighted monkey's fist as a memento. It also doubles as a useful little shillelagh, going by the name of The Kadunka ; extremely handy for close quarters combat should we get boarded by undesirables.

We reached Rota without further incident, which was just as well – that was more than enough excitement for one day. We lingered there for some considerable time, the fine weather having given way to some seriously nasty storms.

Rota is a very characterful old town which manages to support a significant tourist industry without surrendering its soul to it. It also manages to live with an enormous American naval base without surrendering its soul to that either, which must take some doing.

While sitting out the bad weather we took the ferry

over to Cadiz for the day. It's a lovely city with a faded grandeur reminiscent of aging Aristos (© 'The Chickens meander in the general direction of Turkey'). If you ever want to be pretentious and irritate people (you know, like the continuity announcers do on radio three),use the Spanish pronunciation of Cadiz, which is like 'Cardiff', but ending in a 'th' sound rather than 'ff'.

We were now stuck in Rota, waiting to go to Barbate and then through the Straits to Gibraltar as soon as the weather cleared. We did try to use the time profitably and get lots done, but we failed to appreciate the significance of the date. It's one of the great ironies of life that May 1st is International Labour Day, and the Spanish drive this point home by ensuring that absolutely no labour is done whatsoever. In fact, I must report that, contrary to our expectations, Spain does not shut for International Labour Day on May 1st; it shuts for the entire week (with selected enterprises opening for short, sporadic and unadvertised intervals). Even some of the bars shut, one for the whole week. And don't get me started on Spanish post offices.

Oh, alright then, if you insist. Post offices fulfil many important roles in Spanish society. In fact you can do almost anything in a Spanish post office, from the obvious such as posting a letter, through the unexpected such as recharge your mobile phone, to the frankly bizarre such as gamble. Interestingly, the one thing you definitely can't do in a Spanish post office is buy a stamp. Those, you have to buy from a tobacconists.

Providing such a diverse range of services means that many people use post offices. Unfortunately, said people refuse to be responsible and come in at a constant and regular rate, but drift in and out as their personal circumstances dictate. This would result in expensive counter staff having to be paid to stand around cleaning their fingernails at one moment and then being rushed off their feet the next. It would also cause the management problems in trying to determine how many staff are needed.

They get round this in a cunning fashion, by only

opening for short and spectacularly inconvenient periods, thus forcing all the customers to abandon jobs, spouses and families to crowd into the post office at the same time. Unfortunately, this also ensures that everyone meets everyone in the post office at the same time. The resulting greetings, kisses, conversations and gossip mean that each transaction takes four times longer than it should and all the staff have to be paid exorbitant overtime as the place never shuts on time.

Spanish character five: officialdom nil.

We had wanted to leave Rota early on the 5th to catch favourable tides, but the notice on the marina office said that because of the ferias, it was only opening from 10 a.m. to 1 p.m. This was a pain as we needed to return the entry card for the pontoon in order to get the 12 euro deposit back. So, having delayed our departure, I went to the office at 9:45 to find that it had been open since 9. When I pointed out the notice the woman just shrugged as if to imply "No-one takes any notice of that".

The highlight of the trip to Barbate was the free dolphin show. Not just your ordinary riding the bow-wave type stuff, these were showing off personified, or dolphinified I suppose, the first in the queue if there was a cetacean version of 'Big Brother' or 'The X factor'. Each seemed to have its own special trick. One would jump vertically out of the water and splash down on its back. Another specialised in the barrel roll, jumping into the air and spinning round several times before hitting the water. The winner though, was the one who would rise up on the bow wave on his tail, facing the boat. He then rode the bow-wave, keeping himself vertically in the air by thrashing his tail, while surfing backwards, looking at us and flapping his fins together in a clapping motion. *Dix Points.*

We stayed one night in Barbate, sacrificed the 12 euro deposit on the card and left at 8 a.m. Getting the timing right in the Straits is complicated as there are the tides, the current (which is a constant flow into the Med to make up for evaporation) and numerous back eddies to try to keep track of. We struck lucky this time and were making speeds of up to 9.5 knots, and averaged 7.5 knots for the whole trip. We were in Gib by 12:30.

We moored in Marina Bay which would have been very convenient for the airport, had we been flying anywhere, situated as it was alongside the runway about 100 metres from the centre line. We didn't need to set any alarm clocks. Our early morning call was the 08:30 BA flight from London.

It's a strange place Gib. It has a surreal atmosphere, which gave me the feeling that I'd wandered inadvertently into a David Lynch movie. Everything is oddly familiar and yet at the same time slightly, disturbingly, different. The high street could have been transplanted from any reasonably sized English town. All the familiar shops are there. It bore a disconcerting resemblance to King Street in St. Helier. It had the same horrendous prices as St. Helier as well - we were getting spoilt by continental prices, but this brought it all back. Yet, whenever you look up, there is the overbearing presence of The Rock looming over you.

All the signs and advertisements are in English, and yet the most commonly heard language is Janito. This is the local dialect, a combination of Spanish and English with some Italian variants thrown in for good measure. It also has some Arabic elements, especially in the pronunciation which shows many of the guttural Arabic sounds. As a result, even aurally you experience the odd mix of the familiar and the unknown and exotic.

It is also appears to be a highly regulated society. The place is plastered with notices, all beginning with 'No' and threatening dire consequences for, among other things, parking, loitering, skateboarding, roller skating, washing cars in the street and conducting any sort of unlicensed vending. It also has the obligatory rash of building sites knocking up iconic, prestigious, luxury, fully appointed high rise apartment blocks. For God's sake don't let any Jersey politicians see it.

We had to stay until some spares arrived. We had ordered some replacement gauges by phone over two weeks before our arrival on the rash assumption that they'd be here ready for us when we arrived. Congratulating ourselves on our forethought and planning, we entered both smug mode and the chandler's, strode up to the counter and asked to pick up the gauges. No luck. We had failed to take into account the numerous public holidays that had occurred in the interval between our ordering the parts and our arrival in Gib.

The weather, however, was exceptionally good and so we used the time to do the tourist bit to the full. We donned our prat tourist hats, prat tourist shorts and prat tourist sandals and set off to brave the sneers of the locals and see what The Rock had to offer. As it turned out, there were no sneers; in fact no-one took a blind bit of notice of us, with the obvious exception of taxi drivers touting for custom.

What The Rock had to offer was a revelation. The first thing to do, of course, was to take the cable car up the 426 metres to the top and get an overview of the whole place. On disembarking at the top we encountered a rash of notices warning against interacting with the Barbary apes, which are, of course, not apes but macaque monkeys. The notices warned in about eight different languages that they can, and do, bite. Looking at their teeth, it would be a very nasty bite too. They also warned that the apes will grab plastic bags which they associate with food. Being good little Brits we obeyed the notices to the letter, packing everything away in our rucksacks and running away squealing if an ape came within 20 metres of us. Not so all the other nationalities, who gaily hand fed them. They then proceeded to pick them up and stick them on the shoulders of their infant children for that once in a lifetime photo opportunity.

We became blasé about apes after the 300th encounter. When we came across a rather appealing ape sitting on a wall on its own, Liz suggested to me that I might take a photo of her seated alongside said ape, at a cautious distance of course. Liz struck a pose with a smile in place - first photo. The ape suddenly decided it fancied a closer encounter. Liz allowed her smile to slip a bit - second photo. The next minute the ape had leapt up onto her shoulders, unzipped her rucksack, delved around inside and extracted the plastic bag with her new camcorder tapes in it. It then retired to a nearby tree to eat them. Liz still brings it up from time to time that throughout this traumatic episode, I did not make any attempt to come to her rescue, but just carried on taking photographs. Well, it was too good an opportunity to miss, but it is very difficult to hold a camera steady whilst attempting to suppress paroxysms of hysterical laughter.

We managed to rescue one tape. The other three the ape chewed, decided they weren't to its taste and so discarded them. It then expressed its disdain for these pathetic offerings by peeing all over them. We decided to leave them where they were.

The view from the top of The Rock is stunning. The vista along the Spanish coast and across the straits to Morocco clearly shows its strategic importance. Its current name is a corruption of the Arabic *Jabal Tariq*, or Tariq's mountain, being named after the Moorish general Tariq ibn-Ziyad who led the Moorish forces in the initial invasion of the Iberian Peninsula in 711. Prior to that it was known as Mons Calpe and was one of the Pillars of Hercules. Nothing can get in or out of the Mediterranean without passing under its watchful eye. As a result it has been fought over for centuries, falling under the rule of The Phoenicians, followed by a roll call of ancient and modern powers: The Carthaginians; The Romans; The Vandals; The Visigoths; The Moors; The Spanish; and finally (so far) the British.

This still rankles with the Spanish, who argue, probably with some justification, that The Treaty of Utrecht was a con, set up by the British and the Dutch. When we used to run the bar in Portugal we frequently had Spanish holidaymakers as customers. They would be friendliness personified unless the subject of Gibraltar came up, when they would transform, Doctor Jekyll fashion, into raving Anglophobes. "Gibraltar is Spanish!" they would shout, banging their fists on the bar, their eyes staring wildly and spittle spraying everywhere. "Always has been, always will be!"

I used to defuse this by agreeing with them. "Couldn't agree more, old chap. I mean, just look at the geography. It's actually attached to Spain. Britain is miles away. No question – it's Spanish. I think we should hand sovereignty over to Spain ASAP" This mollified, but confused them. Slightly perplexed smiles would appear on their faces and they would relax back in their seats. Bonhomie would return.

"And," I would then throw in lightly, "Just for the sake of consistency you know" (I know I shouldn't, but I couldn't resist it) "How about Spain handing Ceuta and Melilla back to the Moroccans. You've only had that for five hundred years. They had half of Spain, including Gibraltar, for over seven hundred."

That usually did the trick.

The Costa del Sol & the Costa Blanca

Gibraltar to Denia

May 18th 2007 to June 4th 2007

Diesel is one of the few things that are cheap in Gib so we took the opportunity to fill up and set off for The Med. It started off well - an attractive run, with high land in the background and numerous picturesque settlements along the coast. The snow-covered Sierra Nevada lay behind both. Further on the coast became very different. There were still the mountains in the background, but the lower slopes were all covered in plastic. Apparently any area suitable for hydroponics is covered and this part of Spain supplied the majority of Europe's vegetables.

As we approached Almerimar, we called the marina on the VHF, using our newly acquired Spanish (all 28 words of it). This gentle enquiry (*Buenas Tardes, Puerto de Almerimar. ¿Tiene un amarradero para nosotros? - el barco tiene doce metros.*) was met with a wall of rapid fire colloquial Spanish which meant absolutely nothing to either of us. We managed to latch on to the one word 'marinheiro' and blithely took this to mean that we would be met by one and shown where to berth.

It did too. Eventually.

It's strange, the effect that being confronted with a radio mike has on otherwise rational human beings. Perfectly competent, able, mature, articulate adults are reduced to gibbering bashfulness when asked to make a radio call. Put Noam Chomsky and A.C.Grayling on the VHF and their conversation would consist of a staccato of nervous Neanderthal grunts interspersed with stammering embarrassed pauses. Most people, Liz included, clam up completely when faced with a radio mike. When, in desperation, they do finally attempt to say something their voice jumps two octaves and turns into a strangled squeak. After about two minutes of this torture their eyes begin to dart frantically from side to side, seeking any avenue of escape as they try to work out whether it would be less painful and embarrassing just to stuff the radio down their trousers and throw themselves over the side. You would think they had been forced into a strait-jacket and ordered to give a lecture on the role of mimetic romanticism in pre-Raphaelite art to the second house on Friday at the Glasgow Empire.

The other extreme is represented by those whose loquacity on the airwaves is matched only by their ignorance of correct radio procedures. It is one of life's little ironies that, in Britain at least, anyone is free to buy a boat of almost any size and then rampage through crowded waterways and across oceans without any form of knowledge, ability, test or qualification whereas you need a licence to operate a radio.

Aldis lamps and semaphore having gone the way of the dodo, radio is the primary means of communication at sea and also, more importantly, the primary means of co-ordinating search and rescue operations. There are, though, a limited range of frequencies and unless some sort of order is imposed on the jabbering hordes it would degenerate into the equivalent of a Ukrainian parliamentary debate - everyone shouting at the same time combined with much shoving, punching and obscene gestures. There is also the problem that marine radio is used by ships and crew of all nationalities. Fortunately for Anglophones like us, the solution to this has been to adopt English as the official language of communication at sea. Except, that is, for search and rescue traffic, some of which is in French. A sop to French pride by the authorities I suspect.

One of the fundamental rules of VHF communication is that channel sixteen is the co-ordinating channel for search and rescue operations. Most ships and shore stations keep a listening watch on channel sixteen, although this has become less so since the introduction of DSC, the digital calling and alarm system. Nevertheless, channel sixteen is still the channel used for co-ordination once the alarm has been raised. The general rule is to listen on channel sixteen and to keep non-essential traffic to a minimum. If you want to speak to another boat, for example, you call them on sixteen, because they are likely to be listening to that. Once communication has been established you switch to another channel for your conversation. If the conversation sounds like it could be interesting, or even better salacious, every other station within range will also switch channels and eavesdrop.

The most important principle is to avoid interfering with safety traffic. If a Mayday call is in progress, any extraneous calls on sixteen result in the controlling station (usually the coastguard or equivalent) transmitting "Seelonce Mayday", which is officialese for "Shut the fuck up – I'm trying to work a distress call here".

As a general rule the anally retentive Brits tend to follow correct radio procedure fairly rigorously. Not so our more easy-going continental cousins. The most definitive example of this that I've ever heard was, inevitably, from an Italian. It was ten o'clock in the morning. We were anchored in the Ionian when a familiar refrain came over channel sixteen –

Volare, Oh!, Oh!,
Cantare, Oh!, Oh!, Oh!, Oh!
Nel blu, dipinto di blu,
Felice de stare lassù.

I assumed it was a temporary blip and would stop soon. Not so.

Ma tutti sogni nell'alba svaniscon perché
Quando la luna tramonta li porta con sé,
Ma io continuo a sognare
Negli occhi tuoi belli, che sono blu
Como un cielo trapunto di stelle.

Oh God! Please don't tell me she knows all the lyrics. Here comes the second refrain:

Volare, Oh!, Oh!,
Cantare, Oh!, Oh!, Oh!, Oh!

I looked out of the window. My jaw dropped and my face took on the sort of gormless expression usually only seen on an adolescent male who has just opened the fridge after his fourth spliff and found it unexpectedly full of chocolate ice cream. An absolutely stunning long-haired, olive-skinned, twenty-something brunette reclined languorously in an inflatable dinghy. She was dressed, if that's the word, in an exquisitely cut bikini that consisted of all of twenty centimetres squared of what was obviously a very expensive fabric, held together with small, tasteful gold clasps. In her right hand she held a long-stemmed flute of champagne and in her left a hand-held VHF, over which she was serenading a group of enthralled admirers, a category into which I fell headlong. All my self-righteous harrumphing about bloody foreigners playing fast and loose with radio procedures evaporated in a cloud of oxytocin. "Go on girl! Let's have verse two!" She obliged:

E continuo a volare, felice
Più in alto del sole ed ancora più in su.
Mentre il mondo pian' piano
Scompare negli occhi tuoi blu,

La tua voce e una musica dolce
Che suona per me.

We all joined in the final refrain, which culminated in her retiring gracefully to rapturous applause all round.

Volare, Oh!, Oh!,
Cantare, Oh!, Oh!, Oh!, Oh!
Nel blu degli occhi tuoi blu,
Felice de stare quaggiù.

It really isn't fair, is it, the disproportionate importance that humans give to physical attractiveness, especially as far as women are concerned? If exactly the same performance had been given by Mother Teresa herself in a voice that would have made Kiri te Kanawa sound like Lee Marvin in 'Paint your Wagon' she would still have been pelted with decomposing vegetable matter and told to sod off back to Calcutta and leave channel sixteen free.

The airwaves abound with examples of the varying national attitudes to radio procedure. I tend toward the extreme of even the British contingent in this. In contrast to our excitable Mediterranean cousins I affect the calm, measured understatement typified in British war movies from the forties and fifties. This is coupled with a liberal sprinkling of prowords such as 'Say again' , 'Affirmative', and 'Out'. These are used with punctilious attention to correct procedure. You won't hear an 'Over and Out' or a 'Roger Wilco' from us. [19]

---

[19] These common misuses are the shibboleths by which RT purists identify the plebian uninitiated masses. 'Over' and 'Out' are mutually exclusive. The former says 'I have completed my transmission and await a response from you', whilst the latter means 'Traffic has ended and no further response is required from you.'

'Roger' conveys 'I have received and understood your last message' whereas 'Wilco' includes the meaning of 'Roger' by conveying 'I have received and understood your last message and will comply' . Hence 'Roger Wilco' is a tautology and therefore beyond the pale. You're glad I told you that, aren't you.

This embodiment of British reserve can have its drawbacks, however. An example of this occurred in Corfu. It was early morning and we were manoeuvring out of a crowded marina in a strong crosswind when the engine decided to cut out, leaving us at the mercy of wind and current.

Birvidik started to drift relentlessly toward the expensive-looking boats on our starboard side. One of the marina staff had just passed us in a RIB and was heading out of the marina entrance. I tried to call him up on the radio, employing my best, calm, orderly radio procedure. He took no notice of it. With hindsight, it obviously didn't sound serious to him. He only heard the tone of the transmission and not the content. What I should have done was shouted in a high pitched hysterical screech and started screaming, sobbing and begging before building to a crescendo by banging the microphone repeatedly on the binnacle. Then he'd have thought it was serious. I tried again, persisting with my very British *sang-froid*, but to no avail.

At this point Liz lost patience with my starched-shirt efforts. She scrabbled around in the cove locker for our compressed air foghorn, pressed the button on the top and gave five loud blasts. Well, she would have done had she grabbed hold of the foghorn instead of the spray can of WD40. After I, the radio and most of the cockpit had been liberally doused in petroleum based corrosion inhibitor she found the foghorn and attracted the attention of the marinheiro. She also woke up the entire marina. Bleary-eyed yotties stuck their heads out of hatches, wondering what the hell was going on. Those on boats immediately downwind of Birvidik recognised their predicament and rushed on deck in various states of undress, ready to fend off. Not a sight for those of a sensitive disposition.

Luckily, fending wasn't necessary as the foghorn convinced the RIB operator of the severity of the situation and he came back and towed us to a quay just outside the marina where I set about trying to work out what had gone wrong.

In fact, once you get to the Med, not even the coastguards can be relied upon to follow correct radio procedure. On the way to Almerimar, channel 16 was suddenly taken over by either the Algerian or the Moroccan coastguard (they never made it exactly clear which). They appeared to be working a Mayday. In French. Picking our way through the heavily accented dialect, it transpired they were working a collision between an oil tanker and a coaster. I scrabbled down the original as best I could and laboriously translated it, noting the collision position co-ordinates. So did every other ship in a 200 mile radius.

I plotted the collision on the chart – it looked as if it would take us about three hours to get there. Standard procedure in these circumstances is to keep listening and keep quiet. Other faster, bigger and better equipped ships would get there sooner and do far more good than we would. We were more likely to just get in the way.

The airwaves got a bit busy. Several ships transmitted that they were in the vicinity of the position and asked for instruction from the coastguard. These transmissions were from ships of a variety of nations and were all in English. All replies from the coastguard remained, stubbornly, in French.

Soon after came transmissions from ships saying that they had arrived at the position given by the coastguard's co-ordinates and that there was no sign of a collision. Still the coastguard's transmissions continued in French. Eventually the frustration of the would-be rescuers boiled over. A German accented voice broke in: "Coastguard working Mayday at co-ordinates 35 decimal 985 degrees North, 02 decimal 958 degrees East, this is MV Compass Rose. SPEAK BLOODY ENGLISH!"

Which they did. "All stations, all stations, this is Coastguard. Please stand down. This has been an exercise. There is no collision. I say again, there is no collision."

International regulations specifically prohibit profane or obscene language in ship's radiotelephone transmissions, unbelievable as this might seem to a casual listener to the responses elicited by that last message.

Back in Almerimar, however, I demonstrated my mastery of both radio procedures and Spanish by calling up the Marinheiro and asking if it was OK to remain in our current berth. He replied immediately.

"Blimey" I said to Liz "This is a bloody clear signal".

"Of course it is, you idiot" she answered lovingly, "He's on the pontoon next to the boat. You can hear him without the radio."

We were stuck for five days in Almerimar, along with about 30 other boats, waiting for a weather window to round the dreaded Cabo de Gata and head up to Alicante and on to the Balearics. Five days was more than enough for Almerimar out of season. The marina was really cheap - only eight Euros a night, including water and electricity. The staff were wonderful – friendly, competent and helpful, but the whole place had the slightly desolate and depressing air of an out-of-season minor British holiday resort in the 1950s. A walk along the seafront involved hunching into the wind and rain, hands in pockets and neck sunk tortoise-like into the collar of the foul weather sailing jacket.

We left Almerimar on Thursday 24th May when the weather eased. Half the marina left the same day. Some were going to do an overnighter to Cartegena, but we decided to anchor halfway and do it in two days. The weather forecast gave light SW winds and little or no swell. This left us a choice of several anchorages which would all be well protected from South through West to North.

We ghosted round Cabo de Gata in the forecast winds and set off North North East, only to find a one metre swell from the North East. Where did that come from? Along with the unexpected swell was a two knot current against us, when all the books said there should be a one to three knot current with us. Hmmm.

Never mind, we had been looking forward to our first Mediterranean anchorage and we finally chose one, Horillo, which was sheltered from all directions except SSE. No problems there, with no wind or swell from that direction so in we went and dropped the hook in a nice sandy patch and stuck it well in with the engine. It was a very picturesque place as long as you didn't look south at the old quarry dicq.

As the sun set slowly over the smooth waters of the anchorage, we sipped our pre-prandials and relaxed in the calm of the evening. A starter of pear, parmesan and walnuts drizzled lovingly with extra virgin olive oil and freshly squeezed lemon juice and then lightly sprinkled with freshly ground black pepper was complemented perfectly with a chilled glass of white Rioja and all was well with the world. I went down to the saloon to serve the main course and was just passing it up to Liz in the cockpit when everything suddenly tipped sideways. Then the other sideways. Then back again to the first sideways.

The cockpit table, complete with glasses, cutlery, and bottle of wine slewed across to port and then back again, scattering its contents. Liz made an heroic save and rescued the wine and glasses. We don't know where this swell came from, but it seemed to have no intention of going away. The wind held us beam on to it and we rolled violently, the swell being exactly the same period as the natural roll frequency of the boat.

We came to the conclusion that it must be wash from a passing boat, and that if we waited it would go away and we could resume our civilised soirée. Far from it. It steadily increased. We abandoned dinner and I threw my drink over the side in a fit of pique. We now had to decide on a course of action. There were basically three options – head out to sea; lift anchor and try to re-anchor on the opposite side of the bay where there might be more shelter from the South South East, or grit our teeth and sit it out. It was, by now, dark. The rolling was putting no stress on the anchor as the boat wasn't pitching and the anchor was well set. We decided on sitting it out. We argued to ourselves that this was a considered and seamanlike response to the situation after analysing all the available data. In reality it was mainly driven by idleness and fear. Better the devil you know.

It didn't subside. It continued to throw us violently from side to side. All the contents of the shelves and cupboards were by now on the floor, which is where they stayed. Sleep was impossible as we had to make a conscious effort to remain in the bunk, despite the lee cloth. Every time the boat rolled to port I had to grab the mizzen mast compression post to prevent the pair of us from ending up a jumbled heap of limbs on top of the assorted books, clothes and other artefacts on the cabin floor. On the other roll Liz ended up wedged between the hull on the one side and me on the other with her face flattened and distorted against the window. This went on all night. Still awake at first light we thought "Sod this", weighed anchor and set off for Cartegena.

That wasn't much bloody better. Cartegena is a fascinating city and well worth a visit, but first a word of warning - don't let them moor you up on the North Mole. It's a lively little mooring in more ways than one. Firstly, you're about 20 metres from a range of bars and clubs that blast out competing music at 120 db until the early hours - quarter past six was the record. This is complemented by people throwing up, and climbing all over the boats (fortunately, while we were there, not simultaneously). Secondly, there's a nasty swell that finds its way into this part of the harbour and surges your boat up and down against the quay. The quay is designed for superyachts and so is built for much taller ships to rest against. Boats our size catch under the quay and then snatch up and land on top of it. We split our capping rail and broke one of the genoa travellers. A Dutch boat further down had its capping rail pulled right off.

Cartagena had a bloody part in the Spanish civil war, when Franco's Nationalists engineered a coup against the elected, left-leaning Republican government. Most of the Spanish navy remained under Republican control. There was a shortage of officers, though, as many either defected to the Nationalists or were shot by their crews for trying to. The Italian Government threw its support behind the Nationalists and harried the Spanish ships, driving almost all of them to spend the war holed up in Cartagena. It thus became a prime target. The city suffered almost continual bombardment from the Condor Legion, or Luftwaffe as it should perhaps more accurately be known. There is a hauntingly poignant museum housed in the air raid shelter tunnels hewn from the limestone upon which the city lies.

From Cartagena we sailed to Torrevieja and Altea before pulling in to Denia overnight prior to setting off for the Balearics. Here we charged the batteries and filled our tanks and every other container we could lay our hands on with water. This turned out to be just as well, as we weren't able to power and water up again for nearly three weeks.

Water and electricity are two of the main limiting factors in cruising. In fact, for us, water is usually the limiting factor. We carry 500 litres in our main tank and have a further 55 litres backup in cans. Electricity isn't too bad as long as we are careful as we have a 3.5 kw alternator on the engine, a 135 watt solar panel and a wind generator that wouldn't be out of place in an offshore windfarm.

In these matters, as in so many others, the cruising fraternity divides into two camps.

On the one side you have the Proper Hairy Sailors. These are men (and women) of rugged temperament. They relish the challenge of the elements and laugh scornfully in the face of anything the sea can throw at them. They will set sail into the teeth of a gale with a light heart and in joyful anticipation of spending 48 hours narrowly avoiding death or serious injury while leaning over at ridiculous angles, pounding up and down and getting bucketloads of freezing salt water thrown over them at regular intervals.

They are completely mad and impossible to reason with. It is futile to even try.

On the other hand you have the likes of us. We belong to the militant sybaritic wing of cruisers. We go by a number of sobriquets, prime among them being wusses, big girls' blouses, soft southern gits and great bunch of Jessies. We, however, prefer the term yotties.

Proper Hairy Sailors spend inordinate amounts of time at sea, day and night. On the few occasions they are not at sea they usually anchor and only go into a marina when it is completely unavoidable, for example if they are down to their last egg-cup of fresh water and on the point of expiring from dehydration, or if the boat has hit a whale and is taking in water faster than their bilge pumps can handle, or when struck by Hurricane Katrina. Yotties head straight for the nearest marina when they get down to their penultimate packet of jaffa cakes or if, through bad luck or (more likely) incompetence, a yottie actually experiences something mildly stressful.

Cruising is generally a fairly ecologically sound lifestyle. The cruiser's demands on the planet in terms of water, energy and pollution are near the bottom of the scale. This all changes when the yottie hits a marina, when conspicuous consumption becomes the order of the day.

First in line is electricity. In most marinas this is no problem as each berth has its own dedicated power outlet. In some other marinas, and most quays, however, power points are few and far between. Berthing then becomes a race to try to get tied up and plugged in before being pipped at the post, usually by a German. Consider the following scene, frequently played out at town quays:

Birvidik enters through the pierheads and I nervously scan the harbour through binoculars and try to identify the town quay. When I think I know where it is, we head toward it, with me still anxiously peering through the binoculars. The first thing I look for are spaces. Then, in descending order of priority are notices saying "Sod off - reserved for fishing boats/ferries etc.", then the presence of mooring rings/bollards (these are very useful), followed by electricity and water points. I choose my optimum spot and we head towards it. At this point I give a quick, nervous scan around and usually spot one or more predatory yachts (usually German, French or Italian) hacking into the harbour behind us. The game is on.

The other yachts are almost invariably more manoeuvrable than us so we employ our secret weapon, which is a 90 HP engine lurking below the cockpit sole. We whack on full throttle and steam in toward our chosen spot at about eight knots. This catches them on the hop, but we need to build up a big lead to compensate for our limitations at stage two, where we have to manoeuvre backwards into the space. We have frequently been outflanked in the past by some jumped up Tupperware container that can turn on a sixpence nipping in behind us while we are trying to line up to go in astern. It's a bit like a parking contest between a car transporter and a mini.

If things are looking too close for comfort we can try the marine equivalent of the handbrake turn. This involves heading straight towards the desired spot at six knots and dropping the bow anchor about 40 metres out from the quay. Let the chain run free for about 15 metres and then take the engine out of gear, snub the chain and hope the anchor bites. If it does, the chain will snap bar-taut with a satisfying twang and bring the bow to an immediate stop. The momentum of 16 tonnes of boat travelling at six knots then ensures that the stern impersonates a fairground ride and executes a rapid 180 degree turn, tipping the washing up on the floor and leaving the cat splayed on the saloon window like one of those stick-on Garfields.

Alternatively, the momentum of 16 tonnes of boat travelling at six knots could just rip the anchor out of the sea bed and the bow would then continue on its way unhindered and plough into the concrete quay with undesirable consequences.

Don't try this at home.

Having left our continental cousins staring in open mouthed frustration and admiration at our adroit seamanship and dexterity, we go slowly astern and I casually hop ashore and tie up the two stern lines. I then wink conspiratorially at the assembled onlookers, give them a jaunty wave and stroll confidently up and down the deck, adjusting lines and anchor chain until I'm happy that everything is ship-shape and Bristol fashion. Then I open the deck locker, dig out the power line, and turn to nip ashore to connect.

It is at this point that I realise that the German yacht is rapidly approaching the only other space, three boats down. What is worse, the skipper is poised on the bow with his electricity lead in his teeth. He jumps ashore, leaving the minor matter of tying up to his wife, and sprints to the sole remaining electricity point. I rush to the bow, but it is too late. He plugs in, turns, gives me a jaunty wave and strolls confidently back to help tie up his boat.

Bastard.

If we do manage to get plugged in, global temperature rises by a couple of degrees within hours. The inverter/charger goes on and starts to pour amps into the depleted batteries. Fans, kettles and water heaters stretch the local power distribution to its limits and the local sub-station starts to hum and give off a dull, red glow. The ice-caps shrink to a shadow of their former selves

Then we turn our attention to water. Water holds a special place in the cruising psychology. When we lived onshore we took it for granted. All that was involved was to set up a standing order to the water company and then turn on the tap. Not so on board. Our 500 litres of freshwater equates to about ten normal land-based showers or just about three baths. Average UK consumption is 150 litres per person per day, a miniscule proportion of which (about 3 litres) is actually drunk. Most of it goes on cleaning (selves, clothes, dishes etc.) and flushing toilets (20 litres per flush). If we stuck with our landlubber habits we'd have to refill every day and a half. We'd never get out of the marina.

In the absence of a watermaker, we have to make that 500 litres last. Unlike Thames Water, leaks are not tolerated. We have also replaced the shower head with a cunning water-conserving one and flush the toilet with salt water.

When cruising, we have three modes, careful, scrimp and scrooge. In careful mode we have one (brief) shower each per day. Washing up is aggregated and dishes wiped with paper towels to get most of the muck off before going in the sink. After swimming, salt is washed off with a pressurised garden sprayer. Under these circumstances we use about 25 litres a day each, which is about on a par with the sub-Saharan Africa average. This gives us ten days on a tank full.

Scrimp mode takes this further. We alternate days with a shower with days with just a strip wash. Washing up can be done in salt water and then lightly rinsed. Under this regime we knock consumption down to about 15 litres per person per day, which gives us around 2 ½ weeks.

Scrooge mode poses significant health risks and is seriously antisocial. Personal washing is done in the sea and rinsed off with the garden spray. Dishes are given a wipe and a spray. Water usage is pared to the bare minimum. Cooking is done in a 50 - 50 sea/fresh water mix.

This, of course, has knock-on effects. Tea towels take on the appearance of a Mark Rothko painting. Clothing begins to crinkle and supports a flourishing ecosystem of its own. When taken off it can be stood up and leant against the wall. An aerial view of us moving through a busy street would demonstrate an interesting phenomenon. The crowd mysteriously parts like the Red Sea as we approach and re-forms behind us, leaving us in the centre of an unconsciously group-selected exclusion zone. This is extremely useful in queues, which inexplicably melt away when we join them.

Under these circumstances we can cut consumption down to about 8 litres per person per day. That would give us 4 ½ weeks, which is enough to cross the Atlantic, although I suspect we might have trouble convincing the Health Authorities to let us in at the other end.

All of this is very ecologically sound, but when we finally get into a marina, well...

First of all we fill up the main and subsidiary tanks. Then we have long, long showers and wash our hair. Twice. Following that we load up every washing machine in a 500 metre radius with encrusted clothes, bedding, cushion covers and towels (especially tea towels). This only manages to remove the surface layer of bacterial and fungal culture, so we put everything through again, using the few machines that haven't succumbed to clogging up with salt, cat hair, pizza topping, bodily secretions, mouldy cat food and other crud too distasteful for even me to mention.

Then we hire a car and go shopping.

Looking back on this it has become apparent that my smug and arrogant assumptions of our minimal demands on the environment were completely unfounded. We probably place twice as much strain on the environment as the average American. It's just that we do it in concentrated bursts. If an analogy was made with alcohol we would be far from the near T-totallers my earlier boasts implied. Neither would we be the steady everyday drinkers typical of our age and class.

No – as far as water and electricity are concerned, we're the inner city binge drinkers - restrained for most of the week and then whacking down fifteen pints of lager and a bellyful of vodka and Red Bull on a Friday night.

The Balearics

Porto Roeg (Ibiza) to Mahon (Menorca)

June 3rd 2007 – June 29th 2007

The Balearics have become somewhat typecast in the popular imagination. Ibiza is all clubs, drugs and shagging; Mallorca is all Sangria, fish & chips and shagging; Menorca is all culture, middle class refinement and shagging, only there it's known as tantric lovemaking and is not carried out quite so frequently in public.

Porto Roeg, on the South coast of Ibiza, was our first anchorage. It was idyllic. Red cliffs almost completely enclosed the flat, clear waters of the bay. The sun dappled off the surface, with enough light penetrating to show the sandy bottom clearly. There were four other boats anchored, which left us plenty of room to pick a good spot and dig the anchor well in. We whiled away the afternoon swimming and snorkelling off the boat. At about four in the afternoon we settled down for a well earned snooze in the cockpit.

Just as we were drifting off a disturbingly familiar sound registered just above our hearing threshold and slowly swelled. As it did, the full horror of it became apparent. It was Boney M singing their bizarrely successful 1978 single 'Rasputin'.

RA RA RASPUTIN
Lover of the Russian queen
There was a cat that really was gone
RA RA RASPUTIN
Russia's greatest love machine
It was a shame how he carried on.

What a masterpiece that was. They don't write them like that any more. Cole Porter, Stephen Sondheim? Rank amateurs. As an example of lyrical perfection coupled with a stringent but accessible analysis of contemporary Russian history it is probably only bettered by Ross Bagdasarian's seminal 1958 work 'My friend the witchdoctor'. This reaches Joycean levels of linguistic complexity with its witty chorus, so resplendent in playful semantic ambiguity:

ooh eeh ooh ahah,
ting tang wallawallabingbang
ooh eeh ooh ahah,
ting tang wallawallabangbang
ooh eeh ooh ahah,
ting tang wallawallabingbang
ooh eeh ooh ahah,
ting tang wallawallabangbang

I was nine when that came out. I still have a full set of synapses devoted just to that chorus and can recall it at will. This is a total waste of my limited remaining storage capacity which could be far better employed remembering where I left my socks. As if that wasn't bad enough, I have another set of synapses, which also appear to have been file-locked, dedicated to the fact that Ross Bagdasarian was also known as David Seville and went on the same year to create The Chipmunks. I've tried to overwrite this information several times, but always to no avail.

Raising our heads above the cockpit coaming, our eyes

widened in disbelief as we saw a 50 foot charter boat hacking into the anchorage. It was full of German holiday-makers, all doing the shaky-head dance to the aforementioned cacophony and shouting "Party – here – four o'clock" in several languages. Oh, ineffable joy.

They were true to their word too. The only variants were the music, which alternated between Boney M and some drum & bass house/garage/garden shed crap, and the dances, which alternated between the Shaky Head Dance and the Hold Your Arms in the Air and Waggle your Backside Dance. At least that's what the women were doing. The men jigged around self-consciously from one foot to the other, occasionally twitching their fingers and forearms. They stared fixedly at the floor, all the time trying to avoid making it obvious that their attention was mainly focussed on the aforementioned waggling female bottoms. This attempted nonchalance failed miserably. All it achieved was to make them look even sleazier. Outright lechery would probably have been more dignified.

Outright lechery, in fact, was what was displayed by the Italian driver of a speedboat that came into the anchorage at about 20 knots and was instantly hypnotised by the array of undulating buttocks paraded at his head height. As he approached he flicked his hair back, adjusted his sunglasses, struck a pose and undid a couple of his shirt buttons. His gaze remained locked on the German boat as his speedboat carried on straight past it and on towards *Birvidik*. Luckily he wasn't completely testosterone loaded as he heard our frantic cries and turned his head just in time to execute a handbrake turn and slide past our stern, waving nonchalantly and acting as if he'd known exactly what was going on and had intended to do that all along.

The party went on for hours, beer, sangria and spliffs circulating freely. Luckily, by early evening they were pissed, stoned & knackered and careered off back to whichever unfortunate marina was going to have to suffer them for the night. Peace descended to be enjoyed for two nights.

From this haven we decided, for some unfathomable

reason, to go to San Antonio, the epicentre of the Ibizan Clubbing scene. Gluttons for punishment one might think. The front here is quite attractive - certainly plenty of 'young people' around, and huge adverts everywhere for various club nights featuring different DJs, including some that even we had heard of. All along the front were touts offering people free drinks to go to some club or other. Strangely enough, we were never approached in this fashion. We tried slowing down as we walked past the touts. We tried pausing and smiling at them expectantly. We even tried faux conversations such as "What do you think dear, shall we cash in the pensions and go out and give it large this evening?" but we might as well have been invisible. Don't they realise that we've probably got more disposable income than the spotty adolescents who were the focus of their attention. Admittedly, we're not going to spend it, but we've got it.

San Antonio is seriously weird. There's only one way I can describe it. You know those films in the late sixties, early seventies which purported to show the trendy London scene? Got that? Good. Now picture the bits where they try, with risible lack of success, to show the moment when the hallucinogenic drugs take effect. The colours turn garish and unnatural; people suddenly look strange with extreme make up and bizarre clothing; the sounds all become very loud, distorted and unintelligible, whilst strangers start lurching out towards you, talking gibberish into your face, and then receding. Well it's like that, but its 1:30 in the afternoon and you haven't taken so much as an aspirin.

We were tempted to go ashore that evening and sample the decadent delights of Manumission *et al.* On giving it further thought we decided that it would be expensive, not start until way past our bedtime and that I would have great difficulty trying to appear a disinterested academic observer of popular culture rather than the leering old perv I would, in reality, be. So we said our goodbyes to the Gomorrah of the Balearics and sailed twenty miles to the North coast.

It was stunning. High cliffs fell precipitously into the sea and flanked endless small calas, all tempting anchorages.

It bore a striking similarity to the North coast of Jersey. We settled on Cala Miguel, a beautiful anchorage with good holding and only two other boats in it. Limestone cliffs, riddled with caves, encircled the cala giving almost all round protection. Pine trees covered the cliffs and shore down to the water's edge. In the corner of the bay was a hotel, which offered the possibility of our getting internet access and therefore being able to get a weather forecast and check our email.

The next morning we dinghied ashore to check out the hotel. Actually, it was more of a hotel complex. In fact, it was really a fully fledged holiday resort complex. How can I describe it? Did anybody see the TV series 'Benidorm'?

We began to appreciate its full horror as we got closer. We heard it before we got to shore, a deep, bassy, PA system, distorted to the point of unintelligibility. Mesmerised, we followed the sound to its source. There was a stage. On the stage was a sweat-drenched, clinically obese man holding a microphone and wearing a T-shirt bearing the misleading legend "Entertainer". Next to the stage there was a pool. Around the pool were sun loungers and mattresses scattered chaotically, interspersed with small, low plastic tables. On the tables were the detritus of consumption: beer bottles, half empty glasses of warm Bacardi & Coke, greasy plates with the remnants of eggs, bacon and black pudding araldited to them. Chips proliferated in every nook and cranny.

On the sun loungers were the bodies; red, oiled, sweaty, blistered bodies; laid back with mouths open and eyes closed, some producing soft snuffling snores, some with strands of saliva stretched quivering between upper and lower incisors. Skin dried and wrinkled before our very eyes. Had it not been for the PA system you could have heard the incessant crackle of a million skins cells a second giving up the unequal struggle and bursting.

Slowly, the sound of the PA wriggled its way into our consciousness, competing with the Hieronymus Bosch visions assailing our eyeballs. It announced the start of The

Quiz. Just who amongst the assembled throng might be conscious enough to take part in such an enterprise was not immediately obvious, but the man with the microphone and misleading T-shirt was nothing if not an optimist and went ahead regardless.

The first twenty questions were all on the minutiae of recent editions of 'Eastenders'. Horizons widened somewhat in questions twenty one to forty which examined the events occurring in 'Neighbours'. We left before he completed the section on 'Big Brother'.

Oh - and did I mention the Karaoke night?

Probably best not.

I've only recently recovered enough to cut out the tablets.

OK - perhaps we were being a little unfair in rushing to judgment. It was high season and it was Ibiza. So we upped sticks and headed for Mallorca, to a (yes, you've guessed it) deserted little anchorage called Cala Santa Ponsa.

Santa Ponsa did not have The Resort. It did have beautiful surroundings and clear water. In addition it had a lot of Brit Gin Palace Powerboats, all with Gin Palace Wide-Boy types posing in them.

The British Gin Palace Wide Boys are a distinct subculture of the yottie tribe with their own, equally distinct, dress code. Whereas the standard yottie spends almost every waking hour in threadbare shorts and a t-shirt that could justifiably be mistaken for a mechanic's rag, the Wide Boys have developed their own style. As with your bog-standard yottie, temperatures dictate shorts and light shirts. This group, however, tends to favour Hugo Boss or Armani shorts set off by Fred Perry or Lacoste polo shirts.

These are accessorized with enough 24 carat bling to re-establish the gold standard. No Wide Boy worth his salt would allow himself to be seen without a medallion hung from his neck on a gold chain that puts the chain of office of the Lord Mayor of the City of London to shame. The medallion's tasteful and restrained appearance is further enhanced by two chunky 24 carat wrist chains and a single earring which looks like it was lifted from the props department of Pirates of the Caribbean. The combined weight puts him at serious risk of scoliosis, but on the plus side, obviates the need for a weight belt should he ever take up SCUBA diving. This is unlikely, given the fact that he is only ever seen in the water if he falls in from the dinghy after his eighth G&T. His chances of surviving such a mishap are slim as his total personal ballast usually ensures a swift and one-way trip to the bottom.

The crowning glory of the Wide Boy's appearance, though, is his Crowning Glory. All of them display the same hairstyle, which appears to have been modeled on Swiss Toni [20]. The copious grey has been artfully disguised, not by the obvious method of dying it darker, but by bleaching the whole bouffant artifice an almost platinum blond. Slightly darker streaks accentuate the curves brushed back over the ears into an artistic duck's arse and the whole flamboyant edifice is topped off with a gravity-defying quiff which is cantilevered precariously forwards so as to double as a sunshade. This intrinsically unstable structure is then held in place by liberal applications of enough lacquer to French polish a brace of Louis XVI armoires. The resulting impact-resistant carapace is impervious to water, UV radiation and most industrial solvents. The finishing touch is provided by a pair of Aviator or D&G sunglasses which remain firmly in place irrespective of the ambient light levels.

In addition to the gin palaces, Cala Santa Ponsa also had The Cat From Hell, fifty five feet of conspicuous consumption and in-your-face bling.

The Cat From Hell had one Hell of a music system on board. It must have needed a 4Kw generator to power that alone. It also had 'Lisa Darling', whose appallingly cheesy choice of music was made even more unbearable by the volume at which she chose to play it. When one of the others

---

[20] For the benefit of any non-Brits who may not understand this reference, I suggest you Google 'Swiss Toni' and 'The Fast Show' on youtube. The hair is a less moth-eaten version of Donald Trump's.

on her boat suggested tentatively that it might be a good idea to turn it down a teensy bit, she replied succinctly, in a 120 dB grating screech, that 'The next fucking fucker who tells me to fucking turn the fucking music down is in for a fucking good fucking slapping'. This tightly reasoned argument prevailed for an hour or so until Lisa Darling flounced below, collapsed in a G&T fuelled hissy fit and locked everyone else out of the cabin. We then had the audio drama of "Lisa, Darling please let us in" repeated at intervals, only to be answered by muffled abuse.

With deep and abiding regret, we left Cala Santa Ponsa the next morning and sailed on to Porto Colom. This was much better. Much more our cup of tea, don't y' know. Porto Colom had no Resort, no clubs, no party boats, no TCFH and no mooring fees (so far). It did have lots of smart looking restaurants lining the front. These all displayed gleaming cutlery and glasses, white tablecloths and pristine napkins, all under shading canopies. Liz looked rather longingly at them. I looked at the prices and walked quickly on.

One of the limitations of the cruising life is that there is a tendency to see just the coastal parts and miss out on the very different experiences of the inland areas. We counter this by hiring a car at intervals. We did so from Porto Colom and spent nearly a week seeing the sights of Mallorca, including taking the old tram and train from Soller on the North coast to Palma.

There were also some breathtaking caves, the Caves of Drach, which were well worth a visit. Unfortunately, they were also unbelievably busy. There were hundreds of people on each tour and, it being half term, hordes of screaming children. We hung back and let everybody pile on in front of us and then we dawdled along. After twenty minutes or so, we virtually had the place to ourselves. It was very large, impressive and effectively lit. The lights played on the many pools of crystal-clear water, reflecting the cave's formations.

Eventually, we came to a large cavern with a lake. Here there were seats forming an auditorium. The lights were dimmed and illuminated boats were rowed across the lake, with the musicians on them playing excerpts from the works of Mozart. The acoustics were exquisite, as was the music. Well, it would have been had the audience been able to keep their bloody traps shut for more than five nanoseconds and just listen. Can't they face the prospect of spending even the shortest period of their egocentric, idiot lives without subjecting all and sundry to the asinine, moronic drivel that appears to pass as their thought processes?

"Music with dinner is an insult both to the cook and to the violinist"

G.K. Chesterton.

"Inane prattle with Mozart is an insult to both the orchestra and the rest of the audience."

Me.

Italy (Part 1)

We had some reservations about Italy. After all, if they could re-elect Silvio Berlusconi with such tedious regularity they must be capable of almost anything. Add to that the rôle of the Cosa Nostra in the popular imagination and the fact that Bill and Laurel Cooper reckon that the state religion is theft and you can see why we were somewhat ambivalent about the place. We had visions of surly *mafiosi* relieving us of our boat at gunpoint while a bored *carabiniero* pocketed his *tangente* and looked the other way, cleaning his nails with a stiletto. [21]

On the other hand I love the food and the language.

Oh – and it's got a smidgeon of history and culture.

Like most countries, its history has had a marked effect on its culture, taking culture in its widest sense of the ideas, customs, and social behaviour of a particular people or society.

For most of history Italy was a rag-bag collection of principalities and city states such as Milan, Florence, Genoa, Venice, Pisa and Verona. Each of these states had its own traditions and dialect - language even in some cases[22]. They interacted in trade and warfare against the background of greater rivalries, notably between the Papacy and the Holy

---

[21] Sorry. Slipped into cheap travel writer mode there – using a load of italicized foreign words in an attempt to look sophisticated, impress the reader with my erudition and cover up the drab and mundane nature of the narrative. I'll try not to do it again. And anyway, why weren't Cosa Nostra and stiletto italicized? While we're at it, what about rôle? How far do you take this – should we italicise frankfurter, lager, cafeteria and coyote? What about garage and sabotage? Should we italicise Farage? There's a thought.

---

[22] This persisted into modern times. Until the advent of television and radio, few Italians spoke Italian as their first language.

Roman Empire and more latterly between combinations of virtually any European power that fancied its chances.

Italy existing as a nation state is a fairly recent construct. It wasn't finally established until 1861, under the stewardship of some toff called Camillo Benso and a raging revolutionary called Guiseppe Garibaldi.

Garibaldi was born in Nice which was then part of the Kingdom of Sardinia. He did well for himself, didn't he - creating an entire country and having a biscuit named after him? Not bad for someone who took part in a failed insurrection and was sentenced to death at the age of 27 before escaping to South America where he spent fourteen years demonstrating a keen interest in violence and mayhem by taking an active part in a variety of revolutionary wars before showing his face in Italy again.

As a result of this historical legacy, Italians don't feel the same identification with and loyalty to their nation state as do most other Europeans.

Take the notoriously unpatriotic Brits for example. Most may not consider themselves primarily British, but they will usually identify as English, Scots, or Welsh in the first instance.[23] After this an Englishman will describe himself as coming from, say, Kent and then from Maidstone.

The Italians do the exact opposite. They identify first with the town, or even district of the town. Then they feel a lesser obligation toward their province, then their region and finally, grudgingly, to Italy as a whole. This whole attitude is so deeply ingrained in Italian society that they even have a word for it, *campanilismo*, which doesn't translate directly into English. It derives from *campanile* (bell tower). This was traditionally the tallest and most prominent building in any town or village, and it has evolved, in the concept of campanilismo, into a symbol of devotion to, and love of, one's region, city, town, village or even *quartiere* (quarter, small district of a town).

---

[23] The Northern Irish are a special case in these matters and the position is far too complicated to even think about.

The innate parochialism this induces has led to another defining characteristic of the Italian psyche, *clientelismo*. This is the instinctive human tendency of tribalism taken to new heights. It is primarily based on looking after your friends and family and keeping strangers and outsiders out of the game. So, if you want to get on, or even get by, in Italy you need to get yourself into a tribe PDQ. The best way by far is to be born into it, preferably one with wealth, power and influence. Failing that, try to make friends with someone with wealth, power and influence. If this fails, try to make yourself useful to someone with wealth, power and influence. If you have no luck there, then I'm sorry but you're just going to have a shit life.

On reflection, not much different from Britain, then.

Sardinia - All the way round

(Clockwise)

July 1st 2007 – September 9th 2007

It is 200 nautical miles from Menorca to Sardinia, which necessitated another overnight passage, only our third of the entire trip so far. To get the timing right, and ensure that we arrived in Sardinia during daylight, I had calculated that we needed to leave Mahon at four o'clock in the morning. Liz greeted this news with weary annoyance, but no surprise.

Getting out of Mahon in the dark is an interesting exercise. The channel from the harbour to the open sea is three nautical miles long and contains a series of doglegs interspersed with islands and shallows. Such navigational lights as exist are virtually impossible to pick out against the background lights of the town. After three quarters of an hour of migraine-inducing concentration we emerged into clear sea just as the sun was coming up. If I had delayed our departure until dawn we could have made twice the speed and only have lost about twenty minutes on the journey time.

I had wanted to keep up at least 5 knots to get to

Sardinia when it was still light. As it turns out we must have picked up a current and were steaming along, getting up to nearly 8 knots. Ironically, having dug Liz out of bed at some ungodly hour of the morning I then had to announce that we would have to slow down or we'd arrive in Sardinia in the early hours of the morning, when it was still dark. But did she make sulky and sarcastic comments about this? Of course she did.

We had supper at sea and then Liz did the 22:00 to 01:00 watch and only saw one ship and no wildlife. I did the 01:00 to 04:00 and saw nothing. Liz then did the 04:00 to 07:00 and found herself on a dodgem track with swarms of enormous freighters and ferries. She had two radar alarms warning of potential collisions and things weren't helped by the fact that I had reduced the backlight levels on the radar/plotter (I tend to be rather obsessive about not compromising night vision). As a result, Liz could hardly see the screen. As ships loomed ever closer she was frantically scrabbling to put her glasses on and peer at the plotter, her nose nearly flattened on it. She managed to miss everything, but wasn't sure about the course she managed to get the boat back to so she had to wake me up anyway, just as the autopilot swung smugly back onto the correct course.

The wind rose steadily throughout the morning and we had her sailing well at six knots. The wind continued to rise and it was blowing a four to five and rising by the time we arrived at our planned anchorage, which didn't look tenable in the current conditions and so we set off five miles across the bay to Porto Scuso.

It was still blowing strongly in the marina and we were directed to an alongside berth with the wind blowing us strongly off. Luckily, on the second attempt we managed, with the assistance of four very helpful Italians, to get *Birvidik* moored up, to great sighs of relief all round. Ten minutes later the wind dropped completely.

But not for long.

We were stuck in Porto Scuso for a week, having had the unforgettable experience of sitting through a

Tramontana. This is where the French export their bad weather. If a nasty cold front has the temerity to enter La Belle France, it is directed down and to the right by the authorities and is therefore funnelled nicely between the Alps and the Pyrenees whence it shoots south-eastwards as Le Mistral. By the time Le Mistral gets to Sardinia it has managed to fan out, kick up a nice rough sea, and change its name (and sex) by deed poll to La Tramontana.

It appears out of nowhere like a large drinks bill, and can manage to go from calm to gale force in fifteen minutes. It also doesn't know when it's managed to outstay its welcome. This one blew for six days and it was another couple of days before we left, just to give the seas time to calm down.

The six days, however, had not been totally wasted. Five of them were taken up by an unequal wrestling match between me and the plumbing in the aft heads. (Note: those of a sensitive disposition should look away now)

On the way over from Menorca, I had decided to pump out the holding tank which, for the uninitiated, holds all those unpleasant bodily fluids and solids that one would rather not visit upon one's immediate neighbours whilst in harbour. During said manoeuvre, there was a 'Thunk' noise and the electric black water pump sounded as if it had developed an advanced case of constipation. I switched off the pump and tried the hand pump. It was blocked solid.

This was not totally unexpected as heads plumbing is subject to calcite build up, especially in limestone areas such as the Balearics. Various remedies are put forward by different authorities on the best approach in dealing with this problem. On the Liberal, Pacifist, Guardian-Reading Wing, opinion leans toward a dose of eco-friendly washing up liquid or, if feeling particularly annoyed, a gentle douche with lovingly hand-diluted organic cider vinegar. On the other side of the divide lie the far more numerous members of the Telegraph/Daily Mail axis who tend to favour a somewhat more bellicose response. I went with the latter and plumped for the 'Shock & Awe' tactic, deciding on deploying the most concentrated, aggressive mineral acid I could lay my hands on.

I got on my bike and pedalled into town in search of weapons of mass destruction. I was in luck. I found a nice little hardware shop tucked down a back street. Here you could freely buy the sort of lethal material that, in Britain, would have its sale restricted to Middle Eastern despots and Central African warlords. With the help of an Italian-English dictionary and ten minutes of unwholesomely graphic sign language I emerged ten minutes later the proud owner of five litres of forty percent hydrochloric acid.

It did the trick. I pumped it through the system and it produced grunts, bubbles, squeals, belches and a sound like a blue whale with amoebic dysentery. Further flushing spat large quantities of limescale and other, probably best left unidentified, substances out of the outlet. It got rid of all the limescale.

Unfortunately, it turned out that some of this limescale had, helpfully, been blocking a number of fairly large cracks in the pump casing, which just goes to show that nothing is completely without positive features. In the calcite's absence, pumping the system sprayed half the contents of the pump into the aft heads, where it drained down various pipes and surfaces and collected in attractive, if not particularly fragrant, little pools under the floor.

And so it began.

Step one was to identify the problem. This was easy – the pump was cream crackered. The second step was to list the possible solutions. These I narrowed down to:

a) Ignore problem.

b) Replace pump.

c) Bodge a repair on the pump.

The third step was to identify the best solution. Liz vetoed (a), and we carried a spare pump, so we went for (b).

Step four, however, turned out to be to discover a problem with the chosen solution. When I installed the holding tank I had selected special, expensive, odour-blocking piping. This had managed to weld itself onto the pump fittings and would now have to be cut off, thus necessitating new piping, which wasn't available locally.

So step five was to move on to solution (c). This now involved using special epoxy sealing materials, bandages, ingenuity and a previously unknown talent as a contortionist to seal the cracks in the pump. I left it to cure for twelve hours and pressure tested it – it stubbornly persisted in spraying noxious pebbledash everywhere. I repeated step four several times. It still leaked. More drastic solutions were required.

In desperation I removed all evidence of the previous three days work, and went back into town to buy large quantities of fibreglass mat, polyester resin and hardener. The man in the hardware store was by now becoming my close friend, confidante, technical advisor and therapist.

This brought us on to step five, in which I usefully discovered a hitherto unknown even greater talent as contortionist. Squeezing myself into a space smaller than that legally required to house a battery hen, I coated the pump outlet and casing with polyester resin. Also, but inadvertently, I managed to coat the inspection hatch, floor, wall panels, toilet bowl, carpet, various items of clothing, hands, arms, knees, hair and glasses.

After another day leaving it to cure I reran the pressure test. Against all expectations it leaked not a drop. All I had left to do then was to spend a further three hours putting the aft heads back together.

It's a full life this cruising.

One of the joys of cruising is meeting other people, both yotties and locals. Another is having visitors from our previous life and so being able to give old friends a taste of the cruising life. The problem associated with this is that you have to make arrangements to be in a specific place at a specific time. This is not always easy on a cruising boat where the many variables result in there being a large degree of uncertainty as to where you'll be and when you'll be there; or even whether you'll be there.

We had arranged to meet our friend Karen and her

son Jamie in Cagliari in the middle of August. As it turned out, we had made much better time than we had anticipated and so now had seven weeks to travel the 65 miles from Porto Scuso to Cagliari. That's under ten miles a week. Even we could manage that. So we decided to spend the time really getting to know Sardinia. We would go right round the Island, clockwise.

And on the seventh day, *Birvidik* set off up the West coast in a dead calm, and motored up to Capo St. Marco in the Bay of Oristano. We had originally planned to go into a marina here (Torres Grande) but found more of the 'Save the Seaweed' mooring buoys on the West side of the bay, just off the Ruins of Tharros, a Phoenician/Roman city.

I dived on the mooring and found it was a solid piece of kit - a concrete block two metres square by three quarters of a metre high, with four metres of fourteen millimetre chain attached. On top of that were two thick rubber snubbers, about forty millimetres in diameter, braced together with stainless steel bridles and then twenty millimetre nylon line attached to a ruddy great buoy with a fourteen millimetre stainless steel eye on top. It would have held a battleship in a full gale.

This was just as well really, as the weather forecast indicated yet another Tramontana blowing through. Impressed by the solidity of the moorings we decided to sit it out there. We were joined in this enterprise by another couple of Brit boats, *Marlin*, and *Taminori*. This would normally have resulted in much socialising and consumption of alcohol, but we were all faced with the same problem - no booze. (Well, little booze).

Capo San Marco is a lovely spot, and Tharros is fascinating, but it suffers from one, quite serious drawback - no shops. A couple of bars and cafes, a gentleman selling printed African clothes, another gentleman selling leather masks for what could well be Satanic rituals and that was it. No shops. Anywhere. No bread, milk, vegetables, fish, condiments, toilet paper, other sundries, and most pertinently, no booze. Enquiries (entreaties?) elicited the information that the nearest shops were in the town of Cabras, 12 miles away, with no public transport, which leads us to tonight's bedtime story as told by Liz (Jackanory) Newbury:

Once upon a time there was a man who had two beautiful folding bikes. They were sleek and shiny, and designed with exquisite engineering to travel the open road in freedom, with the wind whistling through their spokes.

But the nasty man kept them locked away in a big, dark locker on his boat, and that was where he made them stay, with only the occasional spray of WD40 to ease their lonely unhappiness. Until one day, the nasty man looked in the fridge and cried out in alarm "No Beer!!!"

In the twinkling of an eye the bikes were pulled blinking out of the locker and stowed in the dinghy along with four panniers, bike tools, socket set, footpump and a map of the local countryside. They were then taken the mile and a half to shore, assembled in nanoseconds and pedalled furiously in the direction of Cabras, where the nasty man bought lots and lots of beer. The nasty man strapped the heavy, heavy load onto the poor bikes and made them carry it all the way back to the boat. Mile after mile the poor bikes struggled back to the boat. "Perhaps now the nasty man will see what useful bikes we are and will treat us better" hoped the bikes. "Perhaps we will more often travel the open road in freedom, with the wind whistling through our spokes, only this time without having our poor frames distorted by carrying 50 kg of beer over rutted, potholed roads" they thought.

Sure enough, when they got back to the boat the nasty man turned to the bikes and said "Bikes – I have been cruel to you and treated you badly. And yet – in my hour of need you saved me from the horror of no beer and carried out your appointed task without complaint. I promise to treat you better in the future. More often will you travel the open road in freedom, with the wind whistling through your spokes. I will even pump up your tyres and grease your chains and cables regularly".

The bikes sighed contentedly as they were lovingly folded and taken back to the boat. The no longer nasty man gave them a friendly squirt with WD 40, gently wrapped them in their covers and put them cosily to bed in the locker. Then he drank his beer and forgot about them.

The end.

Our last night in Capo St. Marco was one of those hauntingly peaceful and beautiful experiences that stay in the memory for ever. We spent a gloriously warm and still evening sitting in the cockpit. After dinner we relaxed with a drink, while watching a pilot whale making its leisurely way around the anchorage as the sun set behind the ruins of Tharros. Such moments are absolutely sublime. Time seemed to stretch to a standstill. We lived purely in the present, savouring the experience through all our senses. Hardly a word was said; speech was superfluous as we sat in companionable silence, luxuriating in the colours of the sunset, the gentle lapping sounds as the whale made its rounds, the smell of the maquis and the caress of the odd zephyr of wind on our faces. Episodes like this are rare, even in the cruising life, but once experienced they are never forgotten.

The next day we set off for Bosa Marina further north. Don't be fooled by the word 'Marina'. In Italy this just signifies something vaguely to do with the sea, much like the suffixes 'on sea' or 'super mare' as applied to English place names. It definitely does not imply the existence of anything as sophisticated as fresh water, electricity, toilets, showers, pontoons, or even shelter. In this case it meant the coastal suburb of the town of Bosa which was two miles inland upriver. Bosa Marina sported an anchorage and precious little else.

Getting anchoring right is important, especially if you want a good night's sleep and you don't want your home to disintegrate and spread all your possessions over a wide area. As a result our technique undergoes continuous modification. By this stage we had evolved system 27(b). Before reaching the anchorage, in fact frequently before leaving the previous one, we would consult the weather forecast, the pilot book, the charts and the I-Ching to determine where was likely to afford the best shelter. On approaching the anchorage we would scan the area and see to what degree the reality matched our expectations from the charts. Next we look at the other boats and try to work out where they have dropped their anchors. This is not as easy as it sounds. If there is no strong wind blowing it is quite possible that a boat can be sitting right above its anchor with 50 metres of chain snaking in a rough circle on the sea bed.

The next stage is to choose a likely spot to drop our own anchor. This should preferably be somewhere with a depth of between five and ten metres that provides good shelter and allows for the swinging room needed should the wind come up from any direction. To do this you need first of all to make an informed guess as to how much scope each of the other boats has put out on its anchor. This will depend on whether they are lying to a rope and chain mix or to all chain. Scope is typically around five times the charted depth of water but can vary considerably according to conditions and the particular foibles of the skipper. As you can probably tell, the area of uncertainty is increasing exponentially.

Following that, mentally picture every boat, including your own, swinging in a full circle of the estimated radius around the estimated position of its anchor. While trying to hold all this in your head, you then choose a spot to drop anchor where, whatever happens to the wind, you will neither crash into any of the other boats, nor end up on any of the shallow patches, rocks, fish farms, wrecks, military exclusion zones or sewage outfalls that almost inevitably clutter up any decent anchorage.

The next stage is to go over the selected spot, confirm the depth and, if possible, check if the substrate is such that the anchor has even the slightest chance of digging in to it. Sand is good. Thick, heavy mud is better but it makes a terrible mess of the deck when you haul the anchor up. Wrecks are good holding. As a rule you are unlikely to go far if your anchor is tangled in the superstructure of an 8000 tonne coastal freighter. It is, however, generally impossible to get your anchor back when you leave unless you have diving gear and a full set of professional salvage lift bags; so we generally try to avoid wrecks.

Having committed ourselves we preset the GPS anchor alarm and head upwind to the selected spot. Liz steers and keeps an eye on the depth sounder while I release the anchor and leave it hanging ready. I then stand on the bow, one foot on the anchor and a hand shading my eyes, striking a noble and seamanlike pose. Using our sophisticated and finely tuned hand signals [24] I guide Liz to bring *Birvidik* to a dead stop right over the mark. She then yells out the depth and I let go the anchor. Liz sets the GPS alarm.

We then allow the wind, if present, to drift us back. This puts tension on the chain and thus pulls more of it out of the chain locker and also begins to dig the anchor in. When the planned length of chain is out I lock off the windlass and let the wind pull the chain tight and (we hope) dig the anchor in.

Then it's testing time. I look for a couple of transits (thingies in line with other thingies) and signal Liz to put the engine gently astern. The boat moves backwards until the chain is bar-tight and then, if we're lucky, stops. Heart in mouth I signal to increase revs and Liz slowly brings the engine up to 1000, then 1200 rpm. This frequently pulls the anchor out and we have to lift it up and go through the whole palaver again. Our record is eight times. If it holds, we cut our losses and shut the engine off. It would need a force 9 or 10 wind to equal the force of a 90 H.P. engine at cruising revs. No sense in pushing our luck.

We sigh with relief, but it's not over yet. Leaving the windlass taking the strain of the anchor is not a good idea. It's designed to lift it up, not take snatch loads. Any serious force on it could rip it out of the foredeck. This would be somewhat inconvenient, so I then attach a snubber line to

---

[24] In reality, this is more like Marcel Marceau being attacked by a swarm of African Killer Bees.

the chain and tie that off to a cleat. This transfers the load to something much more substantial. Being highly elastic it also absorbs snatch loads, which both protects the cleat and reduces the likelihood of pulling the anchor out. $F=mV/t$ and all that.[25]

Despite all this I am usually still a nervous wreck and so, visibility permitting, I snorkel over and dive down to check that the anchor has set. The best case scenario is that it has dug in so deeply that you can't see any of it, just a chain appearing from the sand.

The penultimate job is to hoist the anchor ball and riding light. These tell other vessels that you are at anchor and are therefore highly unlikely to get out of their way, no matter what the colregs might otherwise indicate. Many boats don't display these, but if they are then hit by another boat they are deemed at fault and have to pay for all the subsequent repairs. Finally we hang the cat ladders over the side. (Don't ask)

After being given the once over by the Carabinieri, we took the dinghy upriver to Bosa, which is an atmospheric, cluttered picturesque town, with wandering narrow streets, cafes, supermarkets and waterfront, all supervised from the hilltop by a cathedral and a castle. These two were sited at the end of another of our long climbs in the heat of the day. The castle claimed to offer fantastic views of the river, anchorage and surrounding countryside. Indeed, it would have done, had it been open.

We went all the way back down, and then came all the way back up when it opened at 4 o'clock.

On the 15th July we left Bosa for Alghero. The idea was to sail up on a beam reach with the forecast Westerly. As it was, the wind did its usual trick of heading us each time we turned a cape and so we ended up motoring all the way.

---

[25] That should have made the publisher break out in a cold sweat. Apparently the conventional wisdom has it that for every equation you put in a book you halve the sales figures. Except for e=mc2 which inexplicably doubles them.

There are several options for mooring in Alghero, among them the town quay, which was central and Ser-Mar marina, which was further out, but promised a RIB to assist in mooring, so we called up Ser Mar on the radio in our best, halting Italian, and booked a place, albeit in the name of "Moby Dick", which they insisted on calling us.

Sure enough, as we approached the entrance to the harbour, a RIB came out, asked us if we were Moby Dick, and instructed us to follow them.

I'm not sure if we were boatnapped or offloaded, but we were taken to the town quay and helped to moor up. Never mind - it was where we wanted to go anyway.

We spent 3 days in Alghero doing essential jobs such as washing, sorting out Italian mobiles, stocking up on provisions, going out for a pizza and going to the funfair. We did, however, completely fail to find a laundry or launderette. Thankfully we were living in shorts and T-shirts, of which we have a plethora. The dirty washing locker, though, was threatening to erupt.

There followed a series of swift hops up the West coast and round the corner onto the North coast. From Alghero we took a short run to Porto Conte, which the pilot said was now a part of a marine reserve and anchoring was prohibited. Others we had met said this was absolute cobblers and it turns out they were right – there were boats anchored all over the place. There was still plenty of room though and we anchored in crystal clear water.

The next day took us up the rest of the West coast and through the Passaggio Fornelli, an interesting exercise in pilotage which winds its way between Isola Asinara and mainland Sardinia. The passage is as little as 25 metres wide and 3 metres deep in places and requires keeping transits accurately in line.

The stop for that night was Isola Rossa, which takes its name from the pink granite of which it is composed. This anchorage was crowded when we arrived, but most of them were just out for the day and left by early evening. It's always worrying when that happens and you're left as the only boat overnighting - Do they know something we don't?

The next day's trip was a short hop to Liscia, in the approaches to the Straits of Bonifacio. This was a stunning anchorage with a sand bar at the end of the bay and a salt water lagoon behind it. The problem was that it was very deep and steep to, and (unusually) the water was not very clear. With me on the bow and Liz on the helm we scouted round the bay looking for shallower water. We both found it at the same time, Liz on the forward looking echo-sounder and I by seeing rocks appear suddenly under the bow. At this I turned round, waved my arms franticly and shouted "Hard Over, Hard Over". For the non-boaties amongst our readership, this is the nautical equivalent of "For Christ's sake turn left".

At this we decided to anchor in deeper water (15 metres) and let out all 60 metres of chain. It wasn't a completely relaxed night as a combination of depth and poor water clarity meant that I was unable to dive on the anchor to ensure that it had set properly.

The next day it was the Dreaded Straits of Bonifaccio, the narrow gap between French Corsica and Italian Sardinia. Once through these we would be in the land of the Agha Khan.

Proper Sailing! We went through the Straits of Bonifaccio on a beam reach – seven knots and steaming along. We turned right into the channel between the Maddelena Archipelago and mainland Sardinia and wondered what had hit us. There were boats everywhere. Bloody great sixty-plus foot yachts under sail and hundreds of power boats, mostly around sixty foot, some smaller, some like mini-liners, but all hacking around at high speed in all directions, but mostly towards us.

Up until now, our use of the colregs had mainly been along the lines of 'Give way to pot buoys and tuna nets'; we had seen so few close quarters situations. Here we were confronted with boats swarming like bees with us being the honeypot. To cap it all, we were on a dead run, which isn't the most manoeuvrable point of sailing. I decided to put blind faith in the colregs and gybed onto a starboard tack. This should mean that we need only give way to vessels aground, vessels restricted in their ability to manoeuvre (such as dredgers) or the Marie Celeste.

So, teeth and knuckles clenched, and manically shouting the mantra "Boat under sail - starboard tack - get out of the way!" we ploughed through the pack, praying we didn't meet another boat on starboard tack to leeward of us, to whom we would have to give way.

We did, of course.

Liz felt that these were not the circumstances under which the crew would want to hear the skipper comment in a bemused tone "There seems to be something wrong with the steering". There wasn't. Like an idiot I had forgotten to disengage the autopilot before trying a crash gybe to avoid the inconsiderate flash git bearing down on us at 8 knots in his damned great status symbol. Luckily, those clever people at Raymarine had anticipated such incompetence and had built in a failsafe whereby a manic skipper wrenching the wheel over when on auto causes the autopilot to gracefully retire and switch itself onto standby. We emerged, miraculously unscathed, at the other end.

This area is known as the Costa Smeralda and it has been exquisitely developed, with the architecture blending perfectly into the stunning scenery. It is also the playground of the rich and famous, who flock here in their thousands. As they flock, they bring their toys. We had wondered why the French and Italian traffic control radio stations kept calling up "Motor Yacht This" and "Motor Yacht That" to clear them through the traffic lanes. This is normally only done for large merchant ships. Leisure vessels are usually left to their own devices and expected to get out of the way.

You understand when you see them. They may be 'Motor Yachts', but they're like mini passenger liners and bigger than many merchant ships. They come equipped with their own fleet of RIBs, jet-skis and other irritating accoutrements - one just over from us at that moment had a bloody helicopter on the back. Not to be outdone, the one further down had a sailing yacht, bigger than *Birvidik*, suspended in davits.

They're also, almost invariably, British registered. At first we thought there must be a lot of rich Brits around here, but in most cases the owners and crew are not British but Italian, so we suspected that it must be some sort of tax dodge. Subsequent investigation revealed that it was. Well, shortly before then the IMO had, apparently, classified Britain as a tax haven. Perhaps the Red Ensign will soon command as much international respect as Panamanian registration.

We anchored in Golfo de Cugnana, in order to ride out yet another Tramontana. I'm sure the French were breeding the things up there. The anchorage was just off Marina de Portisco. This was classified in the pilot book as charge band five, which meant it cost the equivalent of the GNP of Paraguay for one night. OK, that is a slight exaggeration, but only slight. Out of a sense of mischievous curiosity I enquired how much it would cost for us and was quoted 250 euros for one night. We stayed at anchor, surrounded by superyachts as previously described (all British Registered).

As I looked at them I could feel the old, long suppressed, atavistic class hatred welling up. They press all the right buttons for me. Much muttering of "Rich, arrogant bastards", "Flash Gits", "Conspicuous consumption", "Exploiting the masses", "Bloody crooks" and "First up against the wall when the revolution comes" rumbled around the boat.

My only saving joy was that international maritime law means that the aforementioned rich bastards have to put up with the likes of us parking in their anchorages and lowering the tone. This fills me with a deep and abiding delight (not to mention unbearable smugness) especially when some unscrupulous rich tosser enters the anchorage in his shiny white mechanical equivalent of a sock down the front of the trousers and finds there's no room for him because *Birvidik* and some scruffy French and German boats have taken up the only space.

Lowering the tone? - I love it.

My underlying conviction that these boats were all owned by a load of amoral crooks was confirmed when another helicopter-equipped penis gourd arrived and anchored too close to us. The owner spent most of his time in the picture-windowed aft deck cabin, posing about in a purple and white silk dressing gown with a pair of Dolce & Gabbana designer sunglasses (I told you they anchored too close) pushed back on his slicked back, jet black, (probably dyed) hair.

Early that evening, a launch was despatched from the boat and driven off to the landing stage. It returned soon afterwards. The two original crewmen, resplendent in their starched white uniforms, had been joined by a gaunt, bird-like man in a suit. As he was being escorted up the boarding ladder we could see that he was carrying a briefcase chained to his wrist. At the top of the ladder he was patted down before being sandwiched between a couple of goons and marched in to meet The Man. As they approached the cabin door The Man slid his sunglasses onto his eyes, sat at the table and picked up a book, feigning disinterest.

At this point Liz decided she wanted a better look and got out the binoculars. I nearly had a coronary and snatched them from her, visions flashing before my eyes of an eagle-eyed *Capo di Tutti Capi* spotting a flash of light reflected off the binoculars and sending a couple of henchmen over to remove our livers with a couple of deft flicks of a stiletto.

We slunk down in the cockpit, aping Mr. Big by feigning interest in a book while surreptitiously staring wide-eyed over the top toward the developing scene. Mr. Sparrow unlocked the case from his wrist, laid it on the table, flicked it open and turned it so that Mr. Big could see the contents. Mr Big looked impassively at the contents and just nodded to Goon number one who took an envelope from his pocket and handed it to Mr. Sparrow who was then escorted back to the launch and ferried ashore.

It was all a bit of an anticlimax really; no kiss of death, no falling to the knees and begging for mercy, no blade slid effortlessly between the ribs, no phut of a silenced 9 millimetre parabellum. All for the best really. If there had been any of that they'd have had a really good look around and could hardly have missed a couple of gormless yotties staring at them open mouthed. I suspect our life expectancies could then have been measured in minutes.

The tramontana arrived right on cue and continued to blow for days, especially at night. This reached its climax one night when I was woken at about 3:30 in the morning by a series of thuds and scrapes down the port side of the boat. A Greek boat had dragged its anchor and drifted down on us, banging its way down the side. I woke, rushed on deck in my pants (not a pretty sight) and helped fend off until it had dragged well past us into deeper water and was able to re-anchor. My smugness now knew no bounds as Liz managed to sleep through the whole episode. She will no longer be able to recount her party-piece story of my sleeping through a grounding with quite her usual brio. We had a look the next morning and there didn't seem to be any significant damage. I can cause more during an average mooring procedure.

Fed up with the wind, which after four days eased slightly, we decided to poke our noses out of Cugnana with a view to heading on down the East coast. When we got out of the anchorage, however, the wind dropped almost completely and it was a beautiful day with smooth seas. It appeared that we'd been sitting out a purely localised weather phenomenon, probably caused by the immediate topography, and we could have left days before.

The wind picked up, unusually from just the right direction, and we had an exhilarating sail down to Isola Tavola, hoping to pick up one of the AMP mooring buoys that the pilot book assured us were there. They weren't. What we did find there were a load of little day-tripper motor boats anchored in all the prime sites. We had one go at anchoring, but ended up too close to other boats and gave up. I don't know, scruffy cheap little things stopping proper big boats like us from anchoring - shouldn't be allowed.

The pilot also mentioned another two places that should have had AMP mooring buoys, but the buoys were conspicuous by their absence in both places. As the charts showed these to be part of a marine reserve, with free anchoring prohibited, we gave up and headed on to La Caletta on a cracking sail, averaging about six knots. We arrived about five p.m., having made several unsuccessful attempts to rouse the harbour authorities on the radio.

We went into the harbour and milled around, hoping that someone would notice us and take pity upon us, but we continued to be ignored. Seeing an English boat at the end of a rather dilapidated pontoon, we edged close enough to have a conversation. It would seem that it was pointless trying to call up the marina as they never answer and anyway are probably still at lunch. The English boat was on a freebie, an old pontoon with no charges, but equally no facilities.

There was another pier that was also free without facilities. The drawback was that you had to moor med style, with an anchor holding you off. We weren't set up for this yet, and didn't feel like trying it now but, lacking any response from the marina, the pier seemed our only option. There was a large space on it, so we went alongside; thinking that such a blatant disregard for the rules would draw the authorities out of their hidey holes. It didn't, so we stayed there.

La Calletta is a delightfully ramshackle sort of place, with the air of somewhere that's going places but hasn't quite got round to doing much about it yet. It also appears to be a hotbed of Sardinian Independence Fervour. All along the breakwater were slogans and symbols, and the phrase 'I am not Italian' written in a multitude of different languages except, rather pointedly we felt, Italian.

I suppose they could have a point.

There was a large catamaran next to us, British registered, but definitely Italian. It was crewed by a Grandfather and Granddaughter who seemed to have a very vocal and volatile relationship. She spoke some English and always came out to help any boat moor up. Grandfather, by contrast, just stood there running down their boat handling techniques and shouting out obvious and unnecessary advice in loud, voluble Italian, something like: *"Non volete farlo in questo modo, si vuole fare in questo modo si carica incompetente di stranieri"*. We're now pretty sure that's the Italian for 'Oooh, you don't want to do it like that, you want to do it like this you incompetent load of foreigners'.

The next day the couple from the English boat dropped by, Maurice (French) and Barbara (English). We got on really well and were having a lovely time when the Harbour Master appeared blinking out of whichever hole he'd been hiding in and told us in no uncertain terms and Italian that we couldn't moor alongside, we had to moor stern to with an anchor off. Oh dear.

Maurice and Barbara offered to help, an offer that was rapidly and gratefully accepted. We tied lots of really long ropes together and ran them over the quarters (back corners) to Maurice and Barbara and then motored off the quay while they hung grimly into the lines, keeping our stern in. On the second attempt we successfully dropped the bow anchor and our assistants hauled us back into position. Barbara said she particularly appreciated Grandfather's advice as she struggled to heave sixteen tons of boat back in, and no, he didn't offer to help.

We were up early the next day and no problem getting out of the berth as the wind had dropped completely. We set off and motored towards Arbatax. You can see Arbatax from a long way off as someone appears to have left an oil rig lying on its side there. Despite this, it is a beautiful place. The marina is in a spectacular setting, surrounded by hills and mountains. The offices and a small bar/restaurant are built of clapboard and painted in beautiful shades of blue and white. Bushes of oleander and bougainvillea add to the colourful picture, offset against the ever-blue sky and sea. It was an absolutely perfect spot.

The day after we arrived was the hottest day of the year so far. It was 40 degrees in the shade and there wasn't a breath of wind. So how did we spend it? Well, I'll tell you since you ask. We spent it doing laundry and servicing the engine.

That's one of the unfortunate truths of the cruising lifestyle. You may be in paradise but everyday life continues frustratingly unabated. Bedding has to be washed. Plugholes need unblocking. Fridges have to be defrosted, tap washers replaced, teeth cleaned and rubbish disposed of.

And engine maintenance needs to be done.

Every 200 hours.

Birvidik's engine is a Mermaid Melody, a 90 horsepower marinised Ford tractor engine. It is a basic, unsophisticated donk, designed as a reliable workhorse on farms. Nevertheless, it needs a good sort out every 200 hours.

Every 200 hours? That's nothing! Modern cars have service intervals in the region of 30000 miles, which is around 600 hours driving at 50 miles an hour. How come a tractor engine needs servicing over three times as often?

However, squawk I may, but pay I must. If you break down on the road you can always pull in to the side and walk. Try doing that in a strong wind on a lee shore. I keep a record of engine hours and service it as soon as it gets within spitting distance of 200 hours. I also like to keep a full set of spares and so try to replace any parts or consumables as I use them.

This is a simple enough exercise for the landlubber. Just pop in the car, drive down to your local hardware store, garage, supermarket or motor factors, select what you want from the extensive display on offer and drive back. Sorted.

Not so for Mr Yottie, who has to overcome several impediments to the process. Firstly, he has no idea where the relevant retailers are. The only thing he can usually assume with any degree of confidence is that they're nowhere near the boat. The most likely location will be in an industrial zone about five miles out of town, down a potholed, desolate, dusty road with no pavement.

Having overcome the first hurdle of finding where to buy his requisites he then faces the logistical challenge of getting there and, more importantly, getting back with his bulky and weighty spoils. Hiring a car is an option but the cost is usually prohibitive and the hire car office is almost certainly in the industrial zone, probably next to the motor factors. The usual solution is to walk there and back pushing a trolley. Not the trusty shopping trolley mentioned previously, which would be unable to cope with the weight. What is needed here is the special heavy duty metal trolley which has to be dug out from the bowels of the boat. This usually involves first digging out the mountain of assorted clutter that has been piled on top of it over the three months since it was last used.

The final obstacle is posed by the fact that the descriptions and instructions of all the products on display are never written in English or, for that matter, in any of the other two European languages that our hero stands even the faintest chance of understanding. If he's lucky there might be some information in Italian, usually in 4 point font on a shiny, mottled surface. All other instructions are in an eclectic selection of the most obscure tongues ever to assail the human ear – Bulgarian, Turkish, Basque and Hebrew seem to be among the favourites.

"Here, this looks like it might be motor oil

Източване по-чист(BG)."

No, that turned out to be drain cleaner.

"Ah! How about hamamböcegi sökücü (TR)?"

Don't think so – that's cockroach eradicator.

"What about margotzeko meheagoa (EU)?"

Paint Thinners, as it happens.[26]

---

[26] I gave up trying to insert Hebrew into the text as it ends up all over the place. I suspect that this is because it is written (and read, of course) from right to left. This stubborn individualism is bettered only by Arabic, in which text is written right to left, but numbers are written left to right. So an Arabic speaker writing something containing both text and numbers, such as a scientific paper, has to think in two directions simultaneously.

Once these little local difficulties have been successfully overcome, and the booty lugged laboriously back to the boat, all that needs to be done is to carry out the actual engine service. This first requires running the engine for a while to warm it up and make the oil less viscous. This enables the old oil to be pumped out more easily. On the downside, it knocks up the ambient temperature in the engine bay from an already sweltering 40 degrees C to a heatstroke-inducing 60 degrees plus.

The next step is to dismantle half the boat and crawl into a cramped engine bay which is liberally festooned with obstructions, narrow access points, sharp edges and blistering hot metal. Then you spend half an hour pumping scalding hot oil into a series of plastic containers, using a hand pump that struggles to produce a thimbleful every three strokes. Over the years, I have evolved a cunning system of plastic pipes that enables me to pump out the old oil with only a couple of second degree burns and usually less than a foot of old oil sloshing around in the bottom of the engine bay.

Stage two is the removal and replacement of all the filters, namely oil, fuel and air. This usually doubles the amount of oil in the bottom of the engine compartment and dilutes it with a gallon or so of diesel. After that, top up the antifreeze, refill with fresh oil *et voilà* – Job done.

All that you need to do now is steam clean the engine bay, throw away your clothes and give yourself a long soak in industrial degreaser.

After putting 600 quid's worth of diesel into the tanks we set of for Cala Pira, which, looking at the chart and pilot, promised to be a beautiful anchorage, well sheltered from the forecast North West winds and open only to the South East.

The setting was, as promised, lovely. The wind (and swell) however were not as promised and came straight out of the South East. Until the evening, that is. Then the wind backed to the North East, which put us beam on to the swell. Both of us felt a little sea sick for the first time in months.

Giving up on Cala Pira we set off the next morning for the short trip to as more promising anchorage at Capo Carbonara. Just as we were leaving the autopilot went into a sulk, said "drivestop" and refused to play any more. We'd forgotten quite what a pain it was having to hand steer all the time.

It was a beautiful anchorage, a white sandy strip of beach backed by what looks like vines and hills covered in maquis and prickly pear. The sea once again was that gin-clear turquoise blue. No relaxation for me, though. I contorted myself into the cockpit locker in a vain attempt to fix the autopilot. The cockpit lockers, although large, are not a place of comfort for someone of my size. On top of that, the residual heat from the engine, combined with the 38 degree ambient temperature just about finished me off. I phoned Raymarine, but even with their help I couldn't resolve the problem, so I got the phone number of the main Italian Raymarine distributors. As a result we had to leave the idyllic spot and head in to a hot marina in Cagliari to try and get the autopilot fixed.

I phoned ahead and booked the marina berth for two days. We reckoned that as it was August and the whole of Europe was on holiday, our chances of getting it fixed quickly were minimal. We also feared that we'd need a new drive unit at a cost of about £900 as I had narrowed the source of the problem down to the drive unit clutch.

I went to the marina office, sorted out the formalities and payment, and explained the problem with the autopilot. The woman in the office was a gem. She phoned the main Raymarine distributors in Milan and got the details of the two agents in Cagliari. She then called them and explained the problem.

One of the agents sent a mechanic over within fifteen minutes. He was about a foot taller than me but still managed to squeeze himself into the locker. Feeling guilty, as it was again about 38 degrees, I set up two fans and blasted as much air into the locker as possible.

Two hours later, he emerged, drenched in sweat but

triumphant. The problem was a linkage inside the unit. A grub screw had worked loose and disconnected the drive motor from the electromagnetic clutch. What we had feared would take three weeks and cost nearly a thousand quid ended up taking a total of three hours and costing us £75. I don't know where the Italians get their totally undeserved reputation for disorganisation. All through our time in Sardinia they were invariably, helpful, friendly and hospitable (with the exception of Granddad).

From Cagliari we headed for Pula, an anchorage just to the West, which promised Roman ruins above and below water. What it didn't promise, but delivered, was a nice sloppy swell which rolled the boat from side to side, making most activities difficult. Liz even had to resort to strapping herself, bikini-clad, to the cooker. I have photographic proof of this, but have been forbidden from publishing it. This is probably just as well really as we wouldn't want our male readers getting too excited and losing their catheters.

The ruined Punic/Roman city of Nora (honest – it *is* called Nora) was worth a visit, but as usual we managed to choose the hottest part of the hottest day to visit. We tagged onto the end of a guided tour that was being given in English, led by a woman holding a big orange sign with the number six on it in the air. No-one seemed to notice us, or query our advent, which was surprising really as we stood out by being the only ones unadorned by a bright orange number six sticker.

Giving up on the swell we weighed anchor and set off for Malfatano, another anchorage about 20 miles further West. Malfatano offers three bays in which one can anchor. We were put off the larger, Western, bay by Hytrapia's log which told of their grounding there twice in rapid succession due to extremely variable depths. We pottered around to the centre bay which had the added protection of two small islands.

After we had dropped the hook, I dived to check it and found that the seabed was a mass of intersecting rock and shingle outcrops rising steeply off the bottom, weed patches and the occasional patch of sand. Depths varied by three to four metres in a matter of less than a metre - prime running aground territory. Good job we had the forward-looking sonar. We had managed to drop the hook in some weed and then pulled it through until it had hooked into one of the rock ridges. We weren't going anywhere unless we had a 180 degree wind change. Even then we thought we might have difficulty weighing the anchor.

Malfatano was an idyllic anchorage. We sat in the cockpit on the first night, sipping our sundowners and watching a pair of Golden Eagles (well, that's what I told Liz they were, having taken a surreptitious squint at our well-thumbed copy of 'Wot dat birdie').

The shore on the mainland part of the bay was crowded with Italian holidaymakers. Rich Italian holidaymakers as it turned out. Prices ashore were about three times the average in the rest of Sardinia. When Karen and Jamie were over we returned here and thought it might be nice if we hired a pedalo with a slide on it for an hour or so, so that Jamie could indulge his aquatic yearnings. Not at those prices we didn't. You couldn't hire for an hour, it had to be by the half day, and a half day was 130 Euros. A Hundred Quid?!

The next morning we picked up a met which predicted winds of force seven gusting nine. It was difficult to determine whether this would actually apply to us as we were at the junction of three forecast areas. Nevertheless, it looked as if there was going to be a fair blow and so, given the uncertain holding we were in, we gathered up our skirts and headed off for the nearest marina, Teulada.

Remember your geography lessons at school, where you'd look at the siting of industrial areas, cities and ports and it would all be clear as to why they were sited where they were - transport links, ease of defence, sources of raw materials and, especially in the case of ports, shelter from the weather. It all made sense didn't it.

Historically, the development of the leisure boating industry has followed this sort of pattern, with marinas and yachting centres springing up in or around existing ports. In fact, developers looked at coastal sites as being a town in need of a marina. Not any more. Modern civil engineering techniques enable shelter to be constructed where there was none before by the quarrying, transporting and dumping of thousands of tons of rock.

Teulada is one of this new breed. Far from being a town in search of a marina it's a marina in search of a town. The marina is called Teulada, but the town of Teulada is about twenty kilometres away and can be reached only by car or the thrice daily bus.

Don't get me wrong - it's a lovely marina, well constructed, good shelter, excellent ablution facilities, but there's something missing. Well, in fact there are several things missing; atmosphere, activities, chandlers, workshops, boatyards, supermarkets, bars and people. There is a big sign which lists the aforementioned among a list of the delights to come, all nestling in the tasteful development (artist's impression) lovingly drawn on the hoarding. Nothing beside remains...

Actually, I lie. There is a campsite with a primitive general store. This is situated about two kilometres away along yet another dusty, potholed track. Such an arrangement is, of course, ideal for shopping trolleys.

Which leads us to our trip into Teulada Town. The day's plan seemed simple enough and started off OK. We got to the bus at stop at 10:15 and caught the bus into Teulada. Excellent - it had a tourism office, which we were staggered to find in a small town. We bought a map of the town and got the office staff to mark an internet point and two supermarkets on it.

We went for the internet first. It was in a bar, and there was only one computer terminal. Never mind, we ordered coffees and fizzy water and asked if it was OK for us to use the internet. Very sorry, came the reply, It's broken - might be fixed later today. Ah well - no internet. We drank our drinks and did a tour of the two supermarkets. One was a virtual waste of time but the other was OK and even had bread.

We planned to shop just before the supermarket closed at one p.m. before catching the bus back. We had a short walk, bought a paper and then shopped. Loaded with shopping we found some shade in a small park and read for half an hour before returning to the bus stop. We waited and waited - no bus. Liz checked the times again. Whoops. She had misread them and the bus left at 13:35, not 13:50. I was very good and didn't say very much. I just looked very pained and rolled my eyes a bit.

The next bus wasn't until 19:05, just over 5 hours time. Believe me, there was nothing to do in Teulada and anyway we were hampered by bags of shopping, included in which were several temperature-sensitive items such as milk and butter. A taxi seemed to be the answer, if only we could find one. We returned to the tourist office which, of course, was closed and didn't re-open until 19:00 but there was a list of telephone numbers on the door, including one which, along with the promise of car hire also offered taxis.

I summoned up my best Italian and rang. I hit some confusion over time, having trouble getting over the fact that we wanted the taxi now. We huddled in what shade we could and waited and waited - no taxi. Perhaps he had misunderstood and instead of bringing the taxi at two o'clock he thought we wanted it in two hours' time, at four o'clock.

A return to the bar seemed to be the best option, for some refreshment and maybe see if the internet had been fixed. It was shut - didn't open again until six p.m. I tried ringing the taxi again but it defaulted to a messaging service. All we could do was return to the Tourism office and see if he turned up at four p.m. We found a bench in a patch of shade and read the paper as the shade slowly shrank.

The best bench, in the deep shade, was occupied by the local branch of the Old Boys' Club, a constantly changing melee of old men, amongst whom the conversation ebbed and flowed but never died right out. This phenomenon seemed to have a self-sustaining quality. Members came and left frequently. Over the course of a few hours the membership probably changed completely. There was probably no single individual present when we left who also been there at the beginning. Nevertheless the organisation remained essentially the same. Comparable to the way in which a human being is reputed to change its component cells completely over a period of some seven years but still remain recognisably the same person.

Four o'clock came and went, along with the realisation that our only remaining way out was now the seven o'clock bus, over three hours away. So, back to the park we trudged, butter dripping in our wake. We've never read a paper so thoroughly, even the sports and business sections. At six o'clock we headed hopefully back to the bar. We'd had nothing to eat since toast that morning and Liz hadn't dared drink any of the water we had left as her bladder was full and there was absolutely nowhere to have a wee. Dehydration and mummification seemed the only civilised course of action.

Liz waited on a corner in the shade with the shopping while I checked the bar at six o'clock, six oh five, six ten and six fifteen - still shut. Then a middle aged Italian in vest, trousers and slippers appeared out of nowhere with a bottle of beer and an opener. He'd been watching us out of his third floor window and guessed we must be thirsty and had come down with a beer for us - what a nice bloke. Everywhere in Sardinia we have been overwhelmed by the friendliness, hospitality and helpfulness of the Italian people and this was yet another example.

At long last we headed for the bus stop and waited once again. The bus pulled up. At first I thought it wasn't the right bus as it had 'Guia' on the front. Luckily, I asked the driver and it was the right bus, just travelling incognito.

"Two tickets to Teulada Port, please" says I (only in Italian, obviously).

"No can do mate" says the driver (also in Italian) "You have to buy them from the tobacconist's down the road".

"Aaaagh" says I (in Esperanto).

Luckily he seemed prepared to wait while I ran all the way back to the tobacconists, stood in the queue, bought the tickets and ran back. Can't imagine that from a Jersey or UK bus driver, but perhaps the workforce of Italian bus companies don't labour under quite the same rapacious shareholder and management pressures as do their Anglo-Saxon counterparts.

And so ended the longest shopping trip ever experienced in all our years on board. We arrived back in the marina at seven thirty in the evening and we still needed water, wine and beer.

From Teulada we sailed to Zaffarano. This is a closed area for most of the year as it serves as an artillery firing range for the Italian armed forces. In July and August, however they all seem to go on holiday and leave the Italian peninsula vulnerable to attack and invasion. During these months boats, local and foreign, can anchor here without being used for target practice. As a result of its almost year round isolation it is unspoilt (apart from the considerable amount of spent ordnance lying around).

On arrival we took the dinghy ashore and went for a wander, where we gaily tripped over old munition casings, bits of impeller primed shells and other rather worrying debris. In July and August all and sundry are free to clamber around and blow themselves to pieces. We worked on the assumption that the target practice took place with unprimed shells, reckoning that even the somewhat laid-back Italians would draw the line at letting Joe Public blunder about amongst the remnants of live, unexploded ammunition.

The area is (not surprisingly) totally uninhabited and therefore unspoilt. Its only drawback is the very isolation that makes it so attractive. There are no facilities or provisioning opportunities. Once you've run out of food, drink and water you have to slink regretfully back to civilisation.

Back in Cagliari I decided to give the toilet pipes a quick once over with acid again before we left for Sicily. In went the hydrochloric acid, gurgle, gurgle fizz. I left it for a while. To and fro went the pump to pump it out, clank, clank, boing, snap, crunch, break. Ah - hydrochloric acid was now laying in system with no way of pumping it through.

A little knowledge is a dangerous thing, true enough. I'm a physicist really, not a chemist. The seeds of doubt started nagging away in the back of my mind: bronze seacock, hmm. Bronze is copper and tin. Copper isn't affected by hydrochloric acid, is tin? It's fairly low down the series. Look it up. Oh Bugger:

$$Sn + 2\ HCl = SnCl_2 + H_2\ [27]$$

I dismantled half the aft heads and looked at the outlet seacock. There was a small amount of wet stuff seeping through.

Panic.

Take deep breath.

Calm down.

Visualising a corroded seacock disintegrating halfway between Sardinia and Sicily and letting large quantities of Mediterranean into boat, I began to hyperventilate. I considered the probability that this seepage may be normal due to the seacock bedding down but remained unconvinced. Soddit. I went and paid a man an inordinate amount of money to lift the boat out with a bloody great crane.

When the boat was out we dismantled the seacock – it was not corroded at all. I ground it smooth, regreased and rebedded it. While I had the opportunity I also cleaned the hull, prop, bowthrusters and anodes. The boat went back in water six hours later and we were £300 poorer. All this meant that we missed the weather window for Sicily and so had to spend an extra week in Cagliari waiting for the next one.

---

[27] That's the book sales quartered, then. If physics equations halve the sales, chemistry equations must send them into free-fall.

We used the time to do a bit of maintenance.

"When was the last time we tested the engine driven bilge pump?" asked Liz, innocently.

"Lost in the mists of prehistory" I replied.

"Don't you think we (= you) ought to do it then?" asked Liz with what appeared to be a question but was, in fact, an imperative.

Once again being driven to good practice by Liz, I poured a few bucketsful of water into the deep bilge, started the engine, turned on the pump and looked over the side and waited for the Niagara-like flow spurting out the side of the boat like a firefighting barge. Nothing. Well, there were a few gurgling noises but no water. Not so much as a trickle.

I entered analysis mode. Perhaps the impeller was damaged. Remove casing - impeller fine. Perhaps it was too high a lift from the bottom of the bilge and the pump couldn't prime. I split the inlet hose at a join, filled it with water and asked Liz to switch on the pump, confidently expecting water to pour out of side of boat. To my surprise, this failed to happen. On the contrary the entire contents of the hose and pump were ejected with considerable force straight in my face and chest with a similar effect to that of water cannon on rioting students.

This was unexpected and confusing, not to mention dispiriting. The pump was pumping the wrong way. The interesting implication was that if we had got into trouble and tried to use it, all we would have succeeded in doing was pump water into the boat even more effectively than the leak would have been doing.

After double checking the hose connections, I spent some considerable time impugning the parentage of whoever installed the pump - "*What kind of incompetent, half-witted, shit-for-brains would install a powerful bilge pump and then fit the inlet and outlet hoses the wrong way round?*"

Then, after spending a couple of hours cutting, re-routing and joining hoses, the awful and embarrassing truth hit me.

Impeller pumps will work equally well in both directions.

The pump is driven by a belt from the main engine.

We had a new engine fitted a few years ago.

When the engine was fitted we had to have a new propeller fitted.

Because the new engine rotated in the opposite direction to the old engine...

Sicily

The South Coast

Sciacca to Pozzalo

September 10th 2007 – September 15th 2007

We left Cagliari in the pitch black at 04:45 as is usually the case when we have a long passage in the offing. It started a bit blowy but eased and the sun came out so we had a very pleasant trip during the daylight hours. We reefed the sails as darkness fell at about 19:30. Liz took the first watch from 22:00 to 01:00 and I sloped off to bed.

By the time Liz's watch finished at one in the morning the poor love was quite drained. It's pretty busy between Sardinia and Sicily; ferries, freighters and tankers zipping about all over the place. She had to call me up a couple of times when something big and nasty looked like it was getting a bit too close. One was frighteningly close - it looked like a brightly-lit apartment block going past at speed almost within touching distance. Liz's nerves took a good hour for to settle after that. At one o'clock she roused me for my watch and crawled, relieved, into bed.

My watch from 01:00 to 04:00 was quieter on the traffic front, but the wind piped up and I had to waken Liz to help reef the sails even further. She took over again from 04:00 to 07:00. I hit the sack and sank immediately into a deep and dreamless sleep, only to be roused not long afterwards by the sound of fast flowing water gurgling and splashing. I leapt from the bunk and rushed into the cockpit, convinced that a seacock had failed and that water was pouring into the boat. Water was, indeed, pouring into the boat, but not from the sea. A squall line had hit us and the rain was so heavy that water was flowing in torrents off the wheelhouse roof and into the cockpit. Luckily it then poured back into the sea via the cockpit drains. It was this gurgling noise that had woken me.

The rain became so heavy that it reduced the visibility to almost zero, to the point where we couldn't see the front of the boat. 'Not to worry', we thought, 'We have chartplotter and radar'. Just as that comforting piece of data zapped across our synapses there was a brilliant flash, followed almost immediately by a bloody great bang. Then another. And another.

As I mentioned earlier, a really good, top grade, humdinger of a lightning strike is the Gotterdammerung of the yottie world. It will fry all your electronics for a kick off. So no GPS, no chartplotter, no wind or speed instruments, nothing. It can also blow the alternator and fry the batteries so you can't start your engine (if it's a diesel and it's running at the time of the strike it will probably keep going. Just don't, whatever you do, switch it off).[28]

Your compass will be re-magnetised and will spin wildly before settling down to point in any direction except north.

If you're really unlucky it will blow the rigging wires and your mast will come down and then pound against the side of the hull. In the worst case a couple of thousand amps will discharge through your metal seacocks and blow them out sinking the boat in minutes. Oh – and you can't call for help because the radio resembles a badly overcooked kebab. Not that I'm trying to do a maritime Daily Mail and stir up

---

[28] This is what we thought at the time, but subsequent events proved us wrong.

totally unreasonable fear and prejudice against thunderstorms. Well, actually I am. They scare the bejeezus out of me. As usual, the military think the whole idea is an absolute wheeze and are investigating the development of an EMP 'gun' which could take out enemy communications, including GPS satellites.

As the lightning was right on top of us, and seemed to be following us around, I started having niggling little thoughts about the abovementioned effects of electromagnetic pulses on delicate electronic equipment (such as radars, chartplotters, GPS, depthsounders, radios, computers and the like). I disconnected and demounted them all, cobbled together a series of impromptu faraday cages out of the cooker, garden twine, sticky-back plastic and several rolls of aluminium foil, and stowed them all safely away from the nasty electrical fields. OK, I made up the bit about the sticky-back plastic.

Whilst safeguarding our beloved electronics, this did leave us in the somewhat awkward position of being effectively blind, with no information as to position, speed, depth or the whereabouts of other large, fast, hard things that might be out there, all of this while just about to make a landfall on an as yet unvisited coast.

So it was back to trad-nav. Despite all the promises I had made to myself after the fiasco in Audierne, I had failed to keep in practice and had to try to remember how to use a pencil, pencil sharpener, eraser, Breton Plotter and dividers, and then use the information so gleaned to point us away from anything nasty, like land.

After about two hours of this the storm got bored and wandered off so we turned back toward the coast and put all the toys back up which, to our surprise, indicated we were where we thought we might have been.

We tidied up the rather soggy mess that was the boat, a process which included picking up three dead flying fish which had managed to land on the boat and knock themselves out. One even managed to make it into the aft cabin. At 13:30 we called up the marina at Siacca, and arranged a berth. With considerable relief, we tied up, tidied up, ate, drank and then slept for fourteen hours.

From here it was only a few short hops to Pozzalo, the jumping off point for the fifty mile leg to Malta, our next wintering hole.

Malta

September 16th 2007 to May 4th 2008

The second winter

Msida marina was the best situated, best protected and cheapest marina in Malta. As a result, it was very popular, and they didn't take bookings. There's a knack to getting a berth there. It only took us five days to work it out.

The 60 mile crossing from Pozzalo to Valetta took about ten hours. It was calm with just enough wind to fill the sails and steady us and we didn't see any wildlife except for an inflatable green crocodile halfway across. Following protocol, we called Valletta Port Control when we were six miles off and they gave us clearance to approach, telling us to call again when we were two miles off, which we did. After that they seemed to lose interest in us.

Arriving at Valletta by sea, especially in the late afternoon, was an almost spiritual experience. The low afternoon sun reflected off the golden yellow sandstone of the buildings and bathed the whole scene in a warm, ethereal glow. An air of timelessness permeated the scene, which seemed to ooze history from every inch of weathered stone. At the angle from which we viewed the city, there were few signs of modernity and we gained the sense that what we were experiencing was little different from that experienced by sailors ghosting in under sail in the late 1500s, when the Islands were still run by the Knights of St. John.

The spell was broken by the need to find somewhere to moor up. We edged our way into Msida and, following the instructions in the pilot book, tried to find a space on the customs quay. It was full. So we tried the recommended alternative and looked for a space on the guest pontoon. Also full. We tried calling up the marina on the VHF – no answer. So we tried calling Valletta Port Control. They told us to call the marina, which we did. Still no answer. This is one of the downsides of cruising – arriving somewhere tired and hungry and not being able to find a mooring.

We shuffled around disconsolately for a while and eventually saw a notice for Manoel Island yacht marina, which also listed a VHF channel. This one answered our call and directed us to moor up alongside the quay in front of the disused plague quarantine hospital. We gratefully followed his instructions.

We did, at first, entertain the idea of staying where we were for the winter; it certainly seemed well protected from all directions; a good, solid mooring against a stone quay. Water and electricity were available and it didn't look far to the shops, bars and restaurants. Seemed good to us.

Then Mister Doomsayer came along on his bike. He stopped, dismounted and looked down at the boat.

"Hello Boyo", he said in a strong Valleys accent. "Just arrived?"

"Yup" I replied, "Seems a good spot. We're thinking of staying here for the winter."

This was met with a sharp intake of breath sucked through the teeth, followed by a world-weary shaking of the head in resigned despair at the endless follies of mankind. "You don't want to do that, Boyo. First *Gregale* you get will pound you to pieces against this quay."

I had heard of the *Gregale*, a strong north-easterly wind that occurs when a low pressure system moves south of Malta. We appeared to be well protected from that direction by a bloody great island and its attendant stone quay and three-storey plague hospital. The sea here should be in the lee of the island and so should be flat. In addition, any wind that did manage to get to us should be blowing us off the quay, which is the ideal situation. I proffered this alternative interpretation of the local topography to our local Cassandra.

"Oh no Boyo" he replied. "The waves hit those walls and breakwaters behind you and bounce back here. Like a bloody washing machine it is." Looking at it from that point of view, his explanation looked all too horribly possible. This was somewhat disconcerting as there was a Gregale forecast in just under a week's time.

"What you want to do, Boyo" he continued, "Is to get yourselves into Msida PDQ". With that he mounted his bike and cycled off before I had a chance to ask him how, exactly, we were supposed to achieve this objective, given that both the visitor pontoons were crammed to bursting and the office appeared to have imposed radio silence.

After a few fruitless attempts to contact Msida on the VHF, I decided to walk round to the office and see if a personal approach might meet with more success. It didn't. The office was locked and in darkness. On the door was a hand-written note sellotaped over the opening hours, bearing the terse message 'Gone for a swim'. In all fairness, it was a particularly hot day.

Luckily, there were a number of visiting yotties working on their boats, and I engaged them in conversation. It transpired that Msida had a somewhat lackadaisical berth allocation system. To be more precise, it didn't have a berth allocation system at all. As soon as a boat left, there was a free for all and the first boat to barge its way into the vacated spot won. Then, once in, you daren't leave for fear of losing your spot to some marauding new arrival.

I asked around further – no one was admitting to leaving in the immediate future. I arranged with Ian, one of the overwintering skippers, that he would call me on the VHF as soon as he became aware that someone was on the point of leaving. I would then cast off and hotfoot it round to the pontoon. I got a call the next morning and we hurriedly cast off and charged across to Msida on full throttle only to be pipped at the post by a yacht that had been squatting on one of the residents' pontoons. Crestfallen, we skulked back to Manoel Island.

The next day Ian called again. A boat was in the

process of leaving and there appeared to be no other boats waiting. While we were casting off, a visiting Italian boat came into the harbour, went straight to Msida and nobbled our spot.

Bastards.

The weather forecast was not encouraging. The Gregale continued to draw closer. We needed to set up a backup plan in case we couldn't get into Msida. We certainly couldn't stay where we were. In a last ditch attempt I went to Msida office, which I found unaccountably open. I threw myself on the harbourmaster's mercy, explaining that I had a wife on the edge of a nervous breakdown and that I wasn't far behind.

He took pity on me. "Bring the boat round now" he said, "We'll find somewhere for her until a better spot arises." I rushed back to *Birvidik*, cast off and shot round to Msida before he changed his mind. He tied us on to the outside boat on the quay. It wasn't at all protected and we would be very vulnerable when the Gregale hit. We were, however, in pole position should anyone move from the pontoon, which someone did the next morning. Over the next couple of days we gradually shuffled our way inwards as further boats left, until we were in a nice, secure, protected berth, and there we stayed. We were snugged in for our second winter and I wasn't going anywhere and risk losing our berth.

Since leaving Jersey we had passed through France, Spain, Portugal and Italy. All of these were nominally Catholic. In reality they were secular countries with a strong Catholic heritage and tradition. Their citizens in general, with a few pious exceptions, seemed to take the dogma and teachings of The Church with a large pinch of salt, as can be seen from their attitudes to contraception. Italy, the home of The Vatican, has a birth rate of 1.32 children per couple, one of the lowest in the developed world. So either they're using a lot of contraceptives or the Government was lacing the water supply with bromide. I could see Berlusconi doing it – stacking the odds in his favour.

The Maltese, though, really are Catholic. They make

Pope Pius XII look like Richard Dawkins by comparison. Everywhere you turn there are religious icons and signs: in shops, market stalls, houses, cars and busses; especially busses. In fact, the Maltese usually cross themselves when they get onto a bus. It makes you wonder what they consider their chances are of getting off alive.

Maltese busses are cheap, frequent and they cover the island. They are also charming and idiosyncratic, counting amongst their number many old (1950s and 60s) Leyland, Dodge and other marques. They're quite a tourist attraction in their own right.

They are also personalised with pictures of the driver's extended family and lavishly adorned with religious decorations and slogans. One of the favourites is "Take Jesus into your heart and enjoy eternal life". I don't care what the odds are, that's one hell of a top prize. Beats the National lottery hands down.

On the down side, however, any suspension that may have originally been fitted has long since expired. Don't sit over the rear axle. The grating, grinding and thunking sounds are disconcerting and a twenty minute ride gives the physiological equivalent of riding a rodeo bull. They'd be bad enough on decent roads and Malta's roads are a collection of potholes interspersed with the occasional patch of uneven tarmac.

In addition, you're not spared the effects of the buses if you cycle. There are so many of them that you'll inevitably end up behind one. Ten minutes on a bike behind the average Maltese bus has the same effect as smoking forty fags a day for twenty years.

These engines didn't meet emission standards when they were built. After nearly half a century of limited, if any, maintenance they dish out enough smoke, particulates and aromatic hydrocarbons to camouflage the arrival of an invasion fleet. If they'd had them in the 1940s it would have changed the course of the war. The German bombers would have had no chance of finding their targets and the Maltese wouldn't have had to go to all the trouble and expense of rebuilding Valletta.[29]

The story of Malta's resistance during WWII stands as a prime example of courage and fortitude against overwhelming odds and extended suffering. Throughout my schooldays it had been held up to me by teachers and newspapers as an example up to which I should strive to live. That, of course, was before Dom Mintoff decided that they didn't really like the Brits all that much and kicked us all out. The British press were incandescent. What ingratitude – we allow Malta to get bombed back into the stone age for us while defending itself with a trio of WWI biplanes, a couple of pop-guns and a large catapult, then we give it virtually no assistance to rebuild after the war, including no share of the Marshall Aid and they have the bloody nerve to boot our military bases out. This was at the height of the cold war and they twisted Mintoff's non-aligned stance so as to make him appear nothing more than a Soviet puppet.[30]

Interestingly, when talks on the possible granting of independence took place in London, the Catholic Church in Malta interdicted Mintoff and the rest of the Malta Labour Party leaders and supporters, threatening to deny them burial in consecrated ground. It then declared voting Labour in the 1962 general elections a mortal sin. More than forty thousand mortal sins were committed in one go on polling

---

[29] This used to be the case, but this narrative has been overtaken by events. The service was privatised to Arriva in 2011. They lasted until 2014 when the whole shebang was re-nationalised before being re-privatised later the same year. So everything is more comfortable and less polluting, but it has lost something in the process. I think it's called *soul*.

[30] In fairness, it should be pointed out that Mintoff was originally quite pro British and supported the idea of integration with Britain. This concord fell through when the British Admiralty decided to scale down its expenditure on the island and dismissed 40 dockyard workers. Dockyard employees formed a substantial part of Mintoff's electoral power base.

day. There are limits to even their piety.

They did rebuild Valletta, and a magnificent job they made of it. I had expected to see a modern city rising from the ashes of the old. What they did was to rebuild it almost exactly, although to be fair the worst bombing didn't take place in Valletta itself but in nearby Three Cities area – Vittoriosa, Senglea and Cospicua. Maltese architecture is a prime example of the dichotomies of modern Malta, of which there are many. Valletta and a few other sites such as Mdina, Naxxar and Mosta are oases of organic architectural evolution. Outside of these the island has been blighted with the worst of post war brutalist design: hideous tower blocks for high density housing and equally soulless holiday apartments blighting the seafronts. Mind you, there are nearly half a million or so people crammed into these small islands - they all have to live somewhere.

As a result of the population pressure Malta is very built up, with little green space and almost nowhere where you can escape the buildings and traffic. Gozo is very different with a much smaller population density and much more open space and greenery.

The people present a similar contradiction. They are open, friendly, genuinely hospitable, helpful and they all speak English. On the other hand they have little regard for their environment and dump rubbish (including bodily secretions) in any available public place; the street, parks and, especially, in the sea. We were walking along the seafront at Ta' Xbiex, following a Maltese carrying a large black bin bag full of rubbish. He walked straight past two wheelie bins and threw it in the harbour. No-one batted an eyelid.

Italy (Part 2)

After the usual last-minute panics we left Malta at 06:00 and motor sailed back to Porto Palo, where we anchored for the night. The next day we went thirty miles north to Syracuse and anchored in the northwest of the bay, just as the wind started to blow up.

According to the pilot, this anchorage can be a bit choppy (true), has very good holding (true) and is a short dinghy ride to the big supermarkets (sort of true - it's a short ride to the shore, but once at the shore there appears to be nowhere to leave the dinghy and get ashore). So we ended up dinghying the 500 metres to the town quay, walking the 1 ½ kilometres back the way to the supermarkets and then reversing the route.

Back at the boat, I went to do the engine checks and found the engine bay awash with salt water. Having drained it out, we found that the muffler (a large box which collects the mix of raw cooling water and exhaust fumes and then squirts it overboard) had developed a crack and was squirting the mix of water and exhaust gases into the engine bay. Two days of contortions, epoxy, glass fibre and polyester resin later the leak was fixed. With a peculiar sense of déjá vu, I gradually shed my newly acquired carapace of epoxy, glass fibre and polyester resin over the next day or so.

Syracusa comprises the new town and the original town of Ortigia, which is on an island connected to the mainland by two bridges. Ortigia is a stunning place, winding streets with balconies overhead and courtyards off to the sides, magnificent squares and a genuine ancient Greek temple stuck in the middle of the town. The quay area leads on to the southern part of the island, where there is a freshwater spring welling up in a shaded garden and arboretum. It is altogether a sublime place.

We did a bit of exploring with the dinghy, going up the Ciane River and then dinghied back into town. Here we learnt from other yotties that, despite the friendliness and helpfulness of the Syracusans, Bill Cooper was right and the state religion in the area does appear to be theft – in particular dingy and outboard motor theft. Apparently outboards here cost over twice as much as they would in the UK and they disappear from tethered dinghies like confidence from a banking system. The arms race runs something like this:

* Yotties leave dinghy tied to quay and go into town. On return outboard gone from dinghy.

Syracuse 15 Yotties love

* Next yotties padlock screw handles on outboard together so it can't be removed.

15 all

* Syracusans either remove dinghy and outboard intact, or smash off cast screw handles with lumphammer.

Syracuse 30 Yotties 15

* Yotties run chain through eye on transom and outboard to strongpoint on quay.

30 all

* Syracusans smash eye off transom with lumphammer.

Syracuse 40 Yotties 30

* Syracusans get large set of bolt croppers out of car just in case.

Game, set and match Syracuse.

Tiring of constantly devising cunning new plans to

keep our dinghy and outboard intact, we decided to leave the anchorage and take *Birvidik* to the town quay where we could leave the dinghy and outboard safely (?) locked up in the davits. A stroll into town from this quay led us to our next little learning experience – crossing the road in Sicily.

This is nothing like Inspector Montalbano. He never has any trouble parking or crossing the road. Despite the Don Corleone reputations the Sicilians are a gregarious, hospitable and friendly lot. Until they get behind the wheel of a car that is. Then they undergo an Incredible Hulk type transformation. White knuckles grip the steering wheel, the eyes bulge, veins in the neck and temple swell and begin to throb rhythmically and the right foot slams to the floor and stays there. Crossing the road therefore poses a unique challenge. There do appear to be strange markings of alternate black and white stripes going across the road with flashing lights at either side, but these seem to indicate either 'Please park your large truck here' or 'Suitable space for erecting a stall selling obscure knick-knacks or cholesterol laden snacks'. The technique we developed goes something like this:

Stand at the edge of the road and choose The Opportune Moment. This involves looking for a gap of at least four picoseconds between successive vehicles and ensuring that the driver of the vehicle next in line to flatten you can see you. They will give no indication of seeing you, but the following are no-nos:

- Turning round to have an impassioned conversation with the rear seat passenger.

- Reading a message on their mobile phone.

- No sign of driver (bending down to tune radio, pick up dropped mobile, polish shoes etc)

Having ascertained The Opportune Moment, take a deep breath (it may be worth a quick prayer to whatever supernatural entity seems appropriate, St. Jude springs to mind) and stride straight across the road at a steady pace. Like Moses at the parting of the waters, you will find that all the traffic miraculously swerves and jigs around you and you arrive unscathed at the other side. You may now grasp the nearest lamppost just as your knees give out and you start sobbing uncontrollably.

It is most important that you walk straight across. Do not deviate, speed up, slow down or (worst case) bottle out completely, turn round and run for your life. They will not know how to react to this and will plough into each other and you. The police at the subsequent investigation will almost certainly hold you responsible.

Syracuse was the first place where we had to moor bows to the quay and hold ourselves off with a stern anchor. This an interesting manoeuvre on several points:

1. If you drop the anchor too near the quay it doesn't bite and the boat surges forwards and rams the quay.

2. If the anchor does bite, but you drop it too far off the quay, you run out of rope and you're left dangling too far from the quay to get a line ashore. The wind then takes charge and you cut a swathe of destruction through the other boats on the quay as you swing around on your stern anchor.

3.If you get (1) and (2) right, whoever's on the helm has to try to keep the boat in position when one end refuses to move because it's connected to the seabed by a sodding great lump of metal and 10 metres of 10 mm chain.

4. Even if you get (3) right, then whoever's not on the helm has to adjust the stern anchor line, tie it off and then hot foot to the bow of the boat and, if he's lucky, throw the bowlines to helpful souls waiting on the quay. If he's unlucky there are no helpful souls waiting on the quay, merely the usual collection of ghouls and sadists waiting for disaster to strike. He is then expected to provide them with a frisson of entertainment to brighten their sad and inadequate lives.

In this case, our intrepid crew member has to gather the two bowlines in gritted teeth, balance on the bow anchor and leap gallantly to shore to attach the lines before the wind catches the boat and carried it off (swathes of destruction etc). The key to this manoeuvre is to ensure that you have sufficient slack in the rope to allow you to complete the leap to shore before it tightens, brings you up short in mid air and drops you, limbs flailing, into the uninviting waters below.

It was decided that we'd try this with Liz on the helm and me doing the heaving, grunting and running around. It was here that Liz had reservations, having worked out that the male problem solving technique went something along the lines of:

1) Identify problem and devise plausible (preferably simple) method of solving it.

2) Apply method. If no success:

3) Apply more force.

4) If no success, repeat steps (2) & (3) until either:

a) Problem solved or (more likely)

b) Something breaks.

Nevertheless, she decided to give it a try.

As it happened, there were helpful souls on the quay and it went like a dream. Safely moored up, we set up the passarelle so as to get ashore and went ashore. The first stop was the archaeological park, which contains a Greek theatre, a Roman amphitheatre, and an assortment of caves and grottos, including a relatively small one where Dionysius the Tyrant (do you think he chose that name himself? Doesn't quite have the ring of 'Vlad the Impaler', does it) kept 7000 Athenian prisoners. Not for long, though, he very decently slaughtered the lot of them a few days later.

Also well worth visiting are the catacombs of S. Giacomo and the new, modern cathedral. This is a very restrained, understated and interesting piece of architecture that doesn't suffer from the 'sacred bling overload' of most RC cathedrals.

It is very noticeable that Syracuse and its environs are a Mecca of Italian school trips. Everywhere you go there are crowds of school kids trooping in all directions. School uniform is not a characteristic of Italian society and so they identify their charges by giving them all baseball caps of identical colour. How, we wondered, do they ensure that two groups with the same coloured caps don't meet and cause chaos and confusion as the harassed teachers collate their charges for the return trip? Think of the turmoil that would ensure if Gucci-adorned Angelo and Guiseppina ended up in a slum in Naples whilst street-urchins Paulo and Maria found themselves sitting bewildered in front of silver service at a plush dining room in one of the swishier areas of Milan? Is there a central registry of school trips where forms are filled in, itineraries are logged and compared and baseball caps allocated and sent by DHL to ensure such disasters never occur?

We were stuck in Syracuse for over a week as the weather changed a couple of days before we intended to leave. The prevailing north-westerly wind decided it fancied a change and cleared off to Germany whilst a strong south-easterly offered to fill in for it whilst it was away. As a result we had five metre waves pounding the shore on our intended route and cloud, rain, wind and swell in the harbour. Apparently it was 24 degrees and wonderful weather in the UK.

Bastards.

During this time we found ourselves casting nervous glances at the stern anchor line. We have faith in the anchor itself, it's a ruddy great Danforth, but the line holding us onto it is a device called an ankarolina, a reel of 25mm polyester / nylon braid. It looks like we've moored up sixteen tons of boat by a strip of typewriter ribbon, but the man at the boatshow said it had a breaking strain of two and a half tonnes. I believed him at the time but when you see it in use it looks a bit frail for the job. Still, it's held so far in some trying conditions.

Of course, if there's a first time going in bows-to with a stern anchor then there's also a fist time coming out. Luckily this went without a hitch. The new system of Liz doing all the cerebral steering and stuff whilst I do the grunt-heave-hernia stuff seemed to be the answer.

The Toe & Heel

Naxos to Santa Maria di Leuca

May 22nd 2008 – May 28th 2008

The trip to Catania was uneventful, although we had to motor-sail the whole way, but at least the swell had eased. Catania has four marinas - two expensive and two cheaper. We took the cheaper one. The staff were very friendly and helpful, but then again they ought to be at 43 euros a night. I dread to think how much the expensive marinas were. I suppose you're paying for the fact that you can see Etna erupting from the comfort of your own cockpit.

Having moored up and sorted stuff out by lunchtime we set off to find a tourist information office and organise going up Etna as well as the usual necessities (supermarket, internet, town map etc). Catania is a large town/small city that has been cunningly designed to improve the mental abilities of visitors by presenting them with a constant stream of intellectual challenges and initiative tests.

This started right at the harbour (a large industrial job, not a picturesque little fishing haven). The first challenge was to get out of the harbour area, which was all walled in. Not to worry, we came upon a sign saying 'uscita' (exit) and trustingly followed it into a blind alley which led solely to the end of the breakwater. It didn't specify that this exit was for amphibious vehicles and disgraced Secretaries of State for Posts and Telecommunications.

Having retraced our steps we eventually found the main (only) exit and, to our delight, a tourist information office - unfortunately closed. Undeterred, we negotiated the homicidal intentions of the Sicilian traffic and followed a sign to the railway station where we were told there was a tourist information office. We then followed the signs to the tourist information office through a long circuitous route which took us over an hour. The place is designed for cars you see – we walked all the way round the one-way system. It only took us twenty minutes to walk the direct route back as shown by the map.

There were two other boats with us - John and Carole on *Aquatint* and Walter and Margaret on *Lady de Vie*. Between us we managed to work out that to get to Etna we needed to take a bus from the main bus station at some time between eight and eight fifteen the next morning.

Arriving at the bus station the next morning we found the Etna bus surrounded by people clutching tickets. These, we discovered, had to be bought from a bar/café over the other side of the square, and I was sent off to do it. The bus actually left at eight thirty and took an hour and a half to get up to the cable car station at the base of Etna (including a twenty minute coffee and fag break for the two (yes, two) drivers.

Having arrived at the cable car we walked into the empty ticket office and looked around for some indication of what sort of options there were. Failing in this, we went to the ticket booth and asked them. We could walk up to the crater, cable car up and walk the rest, or cable car up and four wheel drive the rest, after which we would be guided around the crater. Or, for a further fee, we could go over to the hut opposite and book a guided tour including a visit to the site of the current eruption and its associated lava flow. 'Ooh - that sounds fun' we thought and headed off to the hut opposite.

When we got there we found lots of lithe, fit young things milling around and equipping themselves with climbing boots, picks and Nordic sticks. Still - no sign of karabiners or crampons, so that's alright then. Then we saw the signs (in six languages): 'People suffering from the following are not permitted to undertake this activity. Listed were a range of debilitating medical conditions, including asthma (Margaret kept quiet) and heart conditions (I whistled nonchalantly and looked insouciantly out of the window).

The guy behind the desk looked at the four of us standing in the middle of a sea of the young and the fit and asked pointedly "Do you know what this trip involves?"

"More or less" we answered confidently. He proceeded to tell us anyway. What it involved was a five hour hike all over the mountain at heights of around 3000 metres. "We usually get back before the bus back to Catania leaves" he said meaningfully, giving us the opportunity to back out with honour intact; an opportunity we gratefully accepted. I mean, we were puffing a bit climbing the steps to the cable car office and that was only at 2 000 metres.

So, we returned to the cable car to buy tickets. Shouldn't take long, we thought. Unfortunately, while we were making fools of ourselves in the hut, about five coach loads of German tourists had arrived and set about filling up the ticket office.

The ticket office staff were helpfully explaining all the options (there being no other source of such information) and issuing tickets to them all on an individual basis. There were two queues, and so we split ourselves between them with the understanding that whoever got to the front first would buy all the tickets and the others would regroup.

Walter got to the front first and we were just about to exit our queue and go down the side corridor to the cable cars when another coachload of German tourists decided to start their own queue there and effectively blocked all routes in or out.

When we got up there though, it was all worth it. The landscapes were surreal, almost lunar, with black frozen lava flows pocked with craters. Here and there were the roofs of buildings poking out of a frozen sea of solid rock and plants were starting to colonise some of the older flows. My photographs don't do it justice, firstly because it's difficult to capture on still photography and secondly because my Canon packed up. Bloody technology.

Our guide, Giambattista, was excellent - knowledgeable and enthusiastic. He made an already brilliant day even better. If you ever get the opportunity to go up Etna, don't pass it up.

After a couple of days in Catania we set off up the coast to Naxos. This is the village and bay that lies beneath

Taormina. It's a stunning setting; Mount Etna in the background, lava flows visible at night, castles and pretty towns perched vertiginously on cliffs and the long arc of a sandy bay.

We stayed there for a couple of days so that Liz could indulge in her usual hobby of finding the highest point in a five mile radius and dragging me up it. This involved a three mile climb to Taormina, followed by a further mountain goat impersonation up to the village of Castelmolo.

The next stage involved four long slogs across the toe and heel of Italy to get to Ionian Greece. First stop was Rocella Ionica, which had the disadvantage of having no electricity, but the distinct advantage of being free. On the way there, we were sailing along the Southern coast of Italy, doing about six knots on a beam reach, and all was hunky dory. Then the wind started to build, probably a topographic effect, funnelled down between the mountains. The waves built and spray and foam streaked downwind across the sea. By the time we were doing eight and a half knots and leaning over at 45 degrees with the leeward gunwales in the water we thought it might be just a smidgeon past the time at which we ought to have reefed.

Having reefed and got things vaguely under control, we then approached Rocella Ionica. The pilot issues dire warnings about the approach to this place: sand banks, breaking waves, boats rolled over and dismasted; doom, defeat, disaster; fire, famine flood and traffic jams. Luckily we avoided these, but mooring in a strong wind was made more difficult by picking up something round the propeller which managed to impede the steering. After an interesting and unusual mooring technique, which kept the assembled onlookers amused, we set off to explore, which involved a four kilometre walk into town.

We met up with *Aquatint* and *Lady de Vie*, and went for a pizza at the pizzeria at the marina. They sell pizza by the metre. A quarter of a metre satisfies even my appetite.

Two long runs from Rocella to Crotone and then on to Santa Maria di Leuca brought us to our leaving of Italy and it was then a trip across to Corfu.

Greece

We originally planned to set off for the Greek Islands on *Minivet* in 1981, but didn't make it past the pier heads. Twenty seven years later we arrived in Ionian Greece. We may be slow, but we get there in the end.

In the summer it's easy to get misled by the bustle, but in the winter it soon becomes apparent that Greece is really more of a Levantine county than a western European one. It may be in the EU, the currency may be the Euro (at least, it was at the time of writing), but don't make rash assumptions. The society is qualitatively different from that to which we're accustomed.

The Greek tradition of Χενοφιλια (Xenophilia) , or hospitality, makes them very loth to disappoint anyone, even when they have no intention or ability to fulfil a request. In the interests of Anglo-Hellenic friendship we offer the following translation service:

Spoken:

"Of course, Sir. No Problem. We'll have it by tomorrow"

translation:

"Hmm - dunno mate. Might be able to get you something almost completely unlike it by Tuesday fortnight."

Spoken:

"We weren't aware there was a fault with your internet connection. We'll have it fixed by tomorrow."

translation:

"We've known about this for weeks but either we don't know how to fix it, or we really can't be arsed to try. We might think about doing something about it before Easter, but don't hold your breath. And no - you don't get your money back."

Spoken:

"Almost certainly Sir. I'll have a word with my brother in law and we'll probably have something by tomorrow."

translation:

"No."

The people are friendly, hospitable and honest. You can leave your car or boat unlocked with a light heart. Drop a fifty euro note on the floor in a shop and the owner will run after you down the street to return it (leaving his shop unsupervised).

Should, however, you be brave or foolish enough to enter into a business transaction with a Greek then it's as well to be aware that he (or she) is honour bound to get the most exorbitant amount of money out of you as possible. Morality or ethics don't even get a look in. Being British, we seem genetically incapable of producing the correct response to being quoted an astronomical and totally unreasonable price for some piffling product or service such as, oh I don't know, £30 for a couple of postage stamp sized passport photographs , to pick an example purely at random.

The correct response to this, as evidenced by any Greek, is to clutch ones heart and screech "HOW MUCH??!!!" at the top of your voice. This should be followed by imploring looks at all the other customers in the shop. Then you should launch into a sobbing description of the total unreasonableness of the demand and a heartbreaking description of the effect paying this amount would have on the already precarious wellbeing of your wife, seven children and God knows how many poor distraught grandchildren, all of whom are even now living in conditions of Dickensian squalor.

The important point here is never to impugn the character or motives of the vendor. Instead you need to give him a get-out clause whereby he can reduce his Shylockian demands to the merely scandalous in the guise of showing sympathy for a fellow human being. He also takes advantage of this to proclaim to all within earshot just how much he and his extended family will now have to suffer should he reduce his price to this poor, unfortunate customer.

This process continues to and fro like a table tennis final until you both converge on the reasonable price that should have been asked in the first place. You then pay that amount and leave, with everyone; buyer, vendor and audience, being happy. The fact that in the time taken up buying this couple of photographs, Michelangelo could have painted the Sistine Chapel and still had time to dash off a gross of dirty postcards is totally immaterial.

We, of course, will have none of this. Being British we meekly hand over the thirty quid, then leave the shop muttering under our breath and spend the next five days bitching to everyone and anyone about how we got ripped off by swarthy, thieving Johnny Foreigner.

The Ionian

Corfu to Cephalonia

(And back again)

(Several times)

May 28th – September 28th 2008

We had intended to stop off at one of the small Islands NW of Corfu, but unseasonal SE winds persuaded us to anchor in Ormos Vroulias on the N coast of Corfu itself.

It was as we approached Northern Corfu that we came across our first flotilla. Charter boats in general, and flotillas in particular, are the *bêtes noirs* of the cruising world. For many cruising yotties they take on the same scapegoat/outgroup/hate figure role that gypsies and immigrants do for shaven-headed Neanderthal thugs across Europe and for all the cynical, amoral, opportunistic, rabble-rousing, lick-spittle politicians that pander to them.[31]

Cruising yotties, well, most of them anyway, are not quite as ruthlessly vindictive toward charterers as the Nazis were to gypsies (and quite a number of European governments and police forces still are). Organised mass extermination is not generally practiced on flotilla crews and Molotov cocktail attacks are rare. Forced sterilisation is frequently considered but rarely carried out in significant numbers. Cruising yotties have yet to be seen relaxing happily on a beach, blithely ignoring the bodies of two flotilla children, as happened when two Roma girls drowned near Naples in 2008 and were left where they lay for over an hour while those around them carried on sunbathing. I wouldn't put it past some of them though.

Current scientific thinking has it that tribalistic tendencies have been hard-wired into the brain by evolution, with social cohesion and co-operation within the ingroup maximising survival rates and reproductive capacity. Primatologists had long established that primates, man included, operated in social groups of varying sizes. This was investigated by Robin Dunbar, an anthropologist at Oxford University. He noticed a correlation between the size of social groups in primates and the size of the neocortex, the most recently evolved part of the brain and the part that is involved in the higher mental functions including spatial reasoning, conscious thought, and language.

Dunbar argued that the social group was cemented by grooming, a process controlled by the neocortex and made much more efficient by the evolution of language. For a human social group to function effectively, each member needs not only to recognise every other member, but also to

---

[31] I know it's a lot more complicated than this, and that there are problems associated with clashes of culture, but I've got a book to finish. Anyway, if politicians and the tabloid press can use simplistic, unsubstantiated and irrational appeals to baser instincts in a cynical attempt to game the system and boost their chances, then so can I.

grasp all the individual relationships within the group. Essentially, the larger your forebrain, the larger the social group you can get your head round.

The maximum size of a workable, groomable social group, calculated from the size of the neocortex, is known as the Dunbar Number. For humans this is about 150. Interestingly, this figure is around the estimated size of hunter gatherer communities, early farming villages and army companies. This size of basic military unit has been unchanged since Roman times.

According to this argument the establishment of an outgroup further promotes cohesion and identity within the ingroup. All this, though, evolved over millions of years of a hunter-gathering lifestyle in small bands. Physical evolution, in Homo Sapiens at least, is a tediously slow process. Psychologically we are still wired up for functioning in bands of up to about 150 individuals, not nation states of several millions. Our circumstances have changed so relatively quickly that our poor old brains just haven't been able to keep up. The wiring and thought patterns are still there though.

Canny demagogues exploit this. That's why every tin-pot dictator who feels he has finally pushed his luck just that bit too far with his own populace conveniently manufactures an external enemy to serve as a focus for all the discontent. If he is really sneaky he manufactures and exaggerates an internal enemy as well; Jews, Communists, Capitalists, Fifth Columnists, Bogus Asylum Seekers, Millwall Supporters, Traffic Wardens etc. just to sow discord and enhance paranoia. Of course, if he's too idle to do that himself he can always let suitable elements of the press do it for him and then plead that he is just responding to the legitimate concerns of his people.

Cruising yotties have a little bit of a problem satisfying these atavistic desires. Defining the outgroup is difficult. The traditional fall back of the nation state isn't really available. The cruising community, especially in the Med, is made up of lots of relatively small groups of many different nationalities. Language is no help – virtually everyone speaks to everyone else in English. Skin colour is useless as, to all intents and purposes, there are no blacks, browns or yellows – we're all pinks almost without exception. Non-whites are so rare that they can only be viewed as a novelty rather than a threat.

There is no dominant religious affiliation to latch on to unless you count "*I don't believe in God as such, but I do consider myself a religious person*". That's not a religion, that's Church of England. Or New Age Bollocks I suppose. You know - the sort of crap that you see in bookshops that have tapes of whale-song playing over the speakers while *fragrance eau de smug* (as endorsed by mumsnet.com) is subtly pumped into the atmosphere by aerosols hidden behind the posters of soulful-looking willowy blondes riding a unicorn through a sylvan setting.

What really drives me incandescent is that they usually file this exploitative dross under a section called 'Popular Science'. 'Popular' maybe, but 'Science'? Not by any stretch of semantic relativism. It should have its own section.

"*Excuse me, have you got 'Tachyon emitting crystals and Tibetan singing bowls – How to empower your life and heal your spirit' by Chakra T. Gimlet and L. Ron Cobblers?*"

"*Oh yes Madam – it's over there in the 'Bollocks' section, right next to 'Tarot-guided homeopathy. The synergistic ancient healing art that the Medical Establishment doesn't want you to know about' by Gideon McStruth M.D.(struck off)*".

Ingeniously, yotties achieve the seemingly impossible task of creating an outgroup by demonising charter boat and flotilla crews. This takes a fair bit of mental and moral gymnastics, especially considering most of us have been on flotillas before, but we manage it.

The criteria for successfully defining an outgroup are three fold: They have to be easily identifiable; there has to be a plausible reason why they are inferior to the ingroup, thus enabling the heart-warming sensation of self-satisfied superiority; and finally there has to be a believable, if tenuous, explanation as to why and how they are a serious threat to the well-being of the ingroup.

The first one is easy as the charter companies do it for us, which is very considerate of them. All charter boats fly an enormous flag advertising the company. Just in case we miss this they invariably paint the company URL on the boom – something like www.greekislandcarnage.com or, possibly, www.hereIcomewatchthefuckout.gr . If all else fails look at the number of people onboard compared with the size of the boat. Modern boat manufacturers love to advertise the berth capacity of their boats. They maximise this by squeezing what they laughingly describe as 'double berths' into inaccessible spaces the size of a cutlery drawer and also by enabling the saloon table to be converted into another so-called double berth by an ingenious system of slots and levers which can be executed by any three dimensional chess grandmaster in just under three hours. When non-yotties strike up a conversation with a cruiser, the first question they ask is usually "How many does she sleep?" The answer is "It depends on how friendly you are." Adlard Coles put his finger on it when he described his boat as accommodating 'One in comfort, two in tolerance, three in tenseness and four in bitter enmity'.

Most cruising yachts use about a quarter to a third of their theoretical berths. *Birvidik* is listed as sleeping seven. It's just about right for the two of us. Charter boats, however, shoehorn them in. If it says it sleeps six, then six there will be; unless they can get away with eight by sleeping a couple on deck. Fortunately these are usually the most visually attractive members of the crew, although it does make you wonder what's lurking below in some cases.

Having identified the boat as belonging to our despised outgroup, we now move on to stage two: how do we find a plausible reason for their inferiority and therefore, more importantly, our superiority. Well, it stands to reason doesn't it? I love that phrase. It imposes and reinforces prejudices without the inconvenience of having to resort to thought or reasoned argument. Whenever I hear someone declaim that something 'stands to reason' I can be damned sure that the one test it has never been put to is that of reason.

It stands to reason doesn't it? We've been doing this boaty stuff 365 days a year for years and they're doing it for a fortnight. Therefore we are seasoned and skilled sailors and they're a bunch of bloody amateurs who shouldn't be let loose on a boating lake with so much as an inflatable plastic goitre unless they're under the direct supervision of someone clever – such as us, for example.

This leads us on to the last criterion, the one that really cranks up the hate hormones. It is their very incompetence and lack of experience that makes them a clear and present danger to us and everything we hold dear. ***They*** don't know the colregs. ***They*** can't handle the boat. ***They*** crash into us while mooring and wreak havoc with our topsides. ***They*** anchor incompetently and too close. ***They*** drag their anchor and ours with it, condemning us all to an unwanted encounter with the rocks. ***They*** should be strung up from the main halyard. By their testicles. It's the only language those bastards understand.

Unfortunately, there is just an eensy teensy weensy little bit of truth in this last point. Charter companies are a business. They need punters to survive. If they were too stringent about the required competence of their customers they would be out of business before the end of their first season. Inevitably, therefore, they tend to be fairly relaxed about checking on clients' sailing abilities. This is akin to finding someone who once rode a bicycle in rural Shropshire, giving him the keys to an articulated low loader and letting him loose in central London during a snowy December rush hour. In the immortal words of one lead boat skipper at the beginning of a flotilla: "Go out there and enjoy yourselves. Don't worry – it's not your boat, and it's insured".

What we conveniently forget here is that all of us started off with a total sailing experience of zero and a great many of us gained much of our cruising experience by going on flotillas. On top of which, many charterers are very highly qualified sailors with years of experience in far more challenging sailing grounds than an Ionian summer.

But we won't let that stop us.

Having heard of Greek bureaucracy we decided to go straight to a port of entry (Gouvia marina) and get all that sorted out. They were very friendly and helpful. After visiting a couple of offices, filling in about five forms and handing over a not insubstantial number of euros along with crew list, ship's stamp, inside leg measurement and other vital pieces of data, we were given a DEKPA, or transit log. This is a large document (some obscure Greek standard which never quite fits into any standard document wallet) with space for sixty official looking stamps.

Greek maritime bureaucracy is designed for huge merchant shipping fleets, not the little piss-in-the-wind yachts that merely get in proper ships' way and send in claims for damages when the wash from a 20 000 tonner going at fifteen knots smashes them to kindling against a concrete quay. As such, the DEKPA sternly instructs 'The master of the vessel' to check in and have the DEKPA stamped immediately upon arrival and to further have it exit stamped 'not more than two hours before departure'. It is pertinent, though, that the English word 'pragmatic' has Greek roots.

"How do I do this in deserted anchorages and small harbours where there are no port police?" I asked, plaintively.

"You don't" came the off-hand reply from the port policeman.

"What about these stern instructions on the front of the DEKPA?"

"Ignore them. Get it stamped if they come round and ask you, or go and find them if it's more than about 30 days since your last stamp."

"Oh good - can I have that in writing?"

"No."

We took the bus into Corfu wearing our 'Look at the pratty English tourist' hats and set about sightseeing, getting

Greek SIM cards for the phones and trying to get the Canon repaired. We met with success on (1) & (2), and abject failure on the third. No camera shops anywhere. I googled 'Canon' and discovered that Greece is about the only European country without any agents. It was exceedingly galling to finally get to the Ionian and not be able to take good quality pictures.

It was also on this expedition that I did one of those little things that seem trivial at the time, but which subsequently turn out to have an effect out of all proportion to their expected importance. I bought a rucksack.

I put little thought into this. In fact I only bought it as an afterthought, my existing rucksack being on the verge of collapse. I chose it on the grounds of fit and capacity, assigning no import to its colour or general appearance. This could have been deduced from the fact that it was a garish combination of red and white, with a decal on the back showing the profile of a Greek god and the word Ολυμβιακοσ in large print and Συδεσμος φιλαθλων πειραιως in smaller print around it.

Well, how was I to know that Olymbiakos was a football club? I'm not a proper bloke – as far as I'm concerned, a car is merely a device for getting from A to B without getting wet and football is a riddle wrapped in a mystery inside an enigma, surrounded by crowds of sweaty men chanting indecipherable rallying cries. I later discovered that Olymbiakos is not just a football club, but **the** football club – The Greek equivalent of Manchester United, apparently. It even has the same colours, I am told.

I have never had any interest in football, or any other spectator sport for that matter. I was vaguely aware on an abstract, conceptual level, that it was a crucial part of many people's lives and fulfilled a range of social and psychological needs but it had never impacted upon me personally. I suspect that this was in part due to my hatred of sports and P.E. at school, mainly as a result of my then being seriously overweight and appallingly unfit. Mind you, the same handicap doesn't seem to have managed to discourage many of the armchair football experts I have been unfortunate enough to witness. They sit for hours in the pub, drifts of fag ash building up on their beer bellies, while they proclaim to everyone in earshot that various professional football managers would achieve far better results if they just bowed to our pundits' superior grasp of the subtleties of managerial tactics.

Football, I now realise, is not about sport. It is about belonging. It is about male bonding and group cohesion. It is a means of classifying unknown males as potential threats, potential allies or potential prey. It is inter-tribal diplomacy and warfare, stylised and regulated. The least important thing about it is that it happens to be a sport.

My ignorance of all this knew no bounds. I shouldered my new rucksack and strode jauntily along the main road toward Corfu town. Up until then I had been more or less invisible to the locals, just another tourist in daft shorts, geeky sandals and stupid hat; of interest only to proprietors of tourist-tat shops or touts trying to drum up custom for overpriced bars or cod-traditional folklore extravaganzas. Everyone else looked right through me.

Not now. Subsequent research, observation and thought has shown me that there is a strict protocol regarding discussions and interactions regarding football, and that the protocols differ according to whether the participants are in civvies or are wearing The Colours.

In civvies, a delicate *pas de deux* takes place, in order to subtly establish the mutual positions. Most importantly, loyalties are not disclosed, or if they are, this is done slowly and step by step. The opening goes something like this (with the subtext added in italics):

A: See the match last night? (*Are you willing to be engaged in conversation?*)

B: Yeah – lucky goal in the 2nd half (*OK – as long as you're not a homosexual coming on to me.*)

A: Wenger shouldn't have fielded Ramsey. (*No way mate! Straight as a die me – never worn Hush Puppies in me life*)

B: Nah – and they'd have been thrashed if Mourinho had played Costa. (*OK then, but just watch it, that's all*).

Once a rapport has been established they can move on to motors (opening gambit 'What are you driving these days?) and discuss torque converters, the relative merits of cars that neither of them will ever be able to afford and the best way of getting from Brent Park to Heathrow while avoiding the Hanger Lane Gyratory System. [32]

In contrast, once bedecked in The Colours a very different set of rules come into play. Members of the same tribe will roar encouragement to each other and crank up the testosterone with particularly crude disparaging remarks about the gross inadequacy of the opposition's genitalia and courage, coupled with highly defamatory and completely unsubstantiated assertions regarding the sexual proclivities and availability of their close female relatives. These are frequently accompanied by a range of obscene and threatening gestures.

By donning my rucksack I had come out of civvies and had now hoisted my colours. In military terms this is a declaration of the opening of hostilities. In Footballing terms it has much the same meaning. My rucksack was a badge – no, the word 'badge' doesn't do it justice. It was a flashing neon sign rallying and reinforcing the faithful. To infidels, however, it read 'Come on then, if you think you're hard enough'. Fortunately, Olymbiakos was the most popular and supported club in the country and so my new found tribe was usually present in greater numbers.

It took me a while to work this out. For the first few days I thought I had inadvertently featured in the Greek version of Top Gear or whatever programme Jeremy Clarkson's fronting at the moment. Young men whom I had never met in my life smiled at me, cheered and gave me the thumbs up. Cars full of a similar demographic slowed down, beeped, smiled and waved. Just as I was getting comfortable

---

[32] Apparently the problem wouldn't arise if they widened the road by knocking down that hospital just off the A406.

with my new found status as a local celebrity, the illusion was shattered by jeers, catcalls, monkey noises and cries of Ολιμβιακος Μαλακα ('Olymbiakos malaka') [33] emanating from a car that had slowed down to a crawl as it passed me. I was nonplussed by this, a fact that, fortunately, was not lost on my aggressors. Once I had explained that I was English, and that I had no idea who or what Olymbiakos was or were, they downgraded my threat level from flashing red to a zero-rated 'idiot foreigner'. Then they gave me a condescending smile and shot off at speed.

You might think that after such an unsettling experience I would consign the rucksack to the bin. Not me. I am made of, if not sterner, then more Machiavellian stuff. I can get the best of both worlds. There are many more Olymbiakos fans out there than there are rivals, so the rucksack tends to open more doors than it closes. On top of that, if I do happen to come across any rival supporters I just play the 'idiot foreigner' card and all is forgiven.

Come on You Reds!

It was on a trip into Corfu town that Liz managed to fulfill a lifetime's ambition and got me on a little tourist train. These first started to appear in tourist resorts in the 1980s and have spread like an allergic rash until they threaten to reach critical mass and explode, burying the whole of western Europe under a suffocating layer of charred kitsch.

Don't get me wrong – I'm not against guided tours per se. They're a good way of getting an overview of a place and building up a basic background knowledge of its history and situation. My problem with little tourist trains is that I'm an appalling intellectual snob. This is a bit rich given that I'm

---

[33] 'Malaka' is probably one of the most commonly heard words in Greece. Its exact translation is 'wanker', but it has some similarities to the Australian 'Bastard' as it can be used as an insult or a term of endearment depending on context. It also has parallels with the epithet 'nigga' as used by black Americans to engender a sense of friendship or brotherhood. If used as an insult it is serious indeed and has even been known to lead to court cases and violence.

middle class, middle brow and ended my working days as middle management. I've managed to elevate blandness to an art form.

No, what gets my goat is their presentation. It's a matter of taste, Dahling. Why does the tour have to take place on hard bench seats behind an old tractor that has been tarted up with plastic and aluminium sheeting so as to look as if it has just been lifted out of the pages of the 1953 Noddy Christmas Annual?

Like all the best snobs, my major objection was not aesthetic, moral or ideological. It was image and status. I was horrified at the prospect of being seen on it. What would people think of me if they saw me on such an undignified, plebian excursion? It was immaterial that the likelihood of anyone I actually knew seeing me was infinitesimal. It was, of course, equally unlikely that I would later become acquainted with anyone who happened, by chance, to have spotted me on the train and memorized my face for future reference.

"Hermione, shall we invite the Newburys round for cocktails on Friday? They seem an awfully good sort."

"Oh no, Jolyon, darling, we couldn't possibly. I distinctly saw him on a little train in Corfu last August!"

"Oh, how ghastly! I'll scrub them out of the address book right away."

I put on my sunglasses, pulled my tasteful straw Stetson down over my face á la Clint Eastwood and climbed on the train wishing I had a copy of Stendhal's autobiography in the original French so that I could stick my nose into it ostentatiously whilst feigning indifference to my surroundings.

In fact, it was fascinating. The history of Corfu, like that of most places of strategic importance, was a litany of strife, conflict, invasion, insurrection, alliance and betrayal. Over the years it was occupied or attacked by the Spartans, the Romans, the Byzantines, the Vandals, the Ostrogoths, the Normans, and the Venetians.

That only takes us up as far as 1259 when the whole

bloody island; every field, every farm, every town, animal, house, hovel and peasant was given to King Manfred of Sicily as part (part?) of the dowry when he got married. I wonder what it felt like to wake up one morning to find out that you, along with your wife, all your kids and tiddles the cat had suddenly become a wedding present. Did they all have to wrap themselves up in tinsel and stand on the table at the reception?

This gave the Corfiots about a hundred years of stability. Life was still shit but at least it was stable shit.

Then the Venetians came back closely followed by the Ottoman Turks. Close on the Turks' heels came Napoleon (he did bring quite a few other Frenchmen with him). This lasted two years before the Turks came back, this time in cahoots with the Russians. Then the Russians gave it back to Napoleon without so much as a by-your-leave to the Turks. The locals must have been getting thoroughly confused by this time.

Napoleon fell in 1814 and the Brits got in on the act, running the Island as a British colony under a series of autocratic Lord High Commissioners.

The position of Lord High Commissioner was in the gift of The Crown, advised by the Government. They seemed to use it as a way of getting rid of genetic throwbacks whose eccentricities were such that they even managed to embarrass the notoriously self-assured British aristocracy. Possibly the most extreme example was Sir Thomas Maitland. He was loathed by the local population for his arrogance and rudeness toward local petitioners and was known by the Corfiots as 'the abortion'. In modern times he would probably be defined as clinically insane. He refused to wash and insisted on receiving visitors whilst dressed in mock Roman attire. He also, according to scurrilous local rumour, had a penchant for dressing up in womens' clothing and frequenting the less savoury parts of town. Such an activity was unlikely to have been unknown among others of his class, but they probably indulged their passions with a tad more circumspection. For the irredeemably macho local

Greeks, being bossed about by someone with such proclivities must have been a difficult cross to bear.

This sorry state of affairs lasted for 50 years until 1864, when the Ionian Islands became part of Greece and everyone lived happily ever after.

Just kidding.

The Italians turned up briefly in 1923 and repeated the trick in World War II until September 1943 when the Germans took over. They hung on for just over a year until the British liberated the island in October 1944. Then everyone lived happily ever after except for the Junta taking over from 1967 - 1974 and the economy going down the pan from 2008 to the time of writing.

Other than that, everything has been just hunky-dory.

From Gouvia we sailed (yes - actually sailed) to a little bay in the North Corfu channel called Ay Stefanos. This is an idyllic spot just a mile over the water from the Albanian mountains. It has clear water, perfect for swims every morning and evening, and excellent tavernas in which to idle away the warm evenings. It also had a bloody great superyacht called the Queen K moored off it. We watched it with keen interest, wondering if we might get a repetition of the Cugnana mafioso incident in Sardinia.

It was not to be, although what we didn't realise at the time was that there was probably even more sinister skulduggery going on there than there had been in Sardinia. We found out later that we were anchored off the villa of Nathaniel Rothschild and that the Queen K was owned by Oleg Deripaska, who was at that moment acting as host to the abovementioned banking scion plus Peter Mandelson and George Osborne. So near to centres of power, privilege and intrigue and yet so far.

We then began to work our way down the mainland coast, Pagania, Igoumenitsa creek, Platarias and Mourtos before crossing over to Paxos. Then the plan was to explore the gulf of Amvraikia before heading to Levkas to check out the marina there for overwintering.

The trip from Ay Stefanos to Pagania was marked by

the complete absence of wind and the complete blockage of the aft heads when we tried to pump the holding tank out. I pronounced this a 'wait for a marina with full protective clothing' job. Luckily we have two heads. Many will have noticed that this is a recurrent theme in the cruising almanac - trouble at t' heads.

We anchored in Pagania, which was a deserted, fully enclosed bay, with the only signs of civilisation being a gigantic fish farm blocking the entrance and a tiny little smallholding in the corner. We dropped anchor after a day's motoring without any wind, at which point the wind decided siesta time was over and started to rise. And rise. And rise. By the evening it was blowing thirty knots and the anchor chain was bar tight. We had looked forward to a quiet evening relaxing over dinner to the trilling of birdsong drifting across from the wooded hills. Fat chance. We had to shout to be heard across the cockpit over the screaming of the wind and the howling of the rigging.

By morning the wind had dropped and we went on to Valthou creek, just North of Igoumenitsa. (If you think these names are difficult you should see them written in the Greek alphabet.) After a lovely couple of days here we got a met over the radio predicting strong winds and thunderstorms. In fact we got this met repeatedly over the next few days but all we got was flat calm and general muggy weather, so we ignored it and motored down to Platarias where we moored to a stern anchor again and I set about the aft heads piping with hacksaws, hammer, wire coat hangers, levers, hydrochloric acid and vigour, if not enthusiasm, all washed down with concentrated bleach solution.

Platarias was a welcome change from Gouvia. Instead of fifty Euros a day we paid three euros a night, plus three euros if we wanted water and electricity. Bargain.

The met had given up predicting thunderstorms and strong winds. We suspect it was having a sulk as no-one was taking any notice of it. It now predicted light southerly winds and clear skies. Off we went under motor and anchored in Mourtos roads. These are a collection of little anchorages, set in small bays between the mainland and a number of small islands. There were quite a few other boats there, but we managed to find a space to swing, dropped the hook and I dived on it and proclaimed myself satisfied.

As we were settling down to prepare dinner, several other boats came in and the anchorage became pretty crowded - fine as long as we all swung in unison (This is a technical nautical term and not a euphemism for orgiastic activities carried out whilst simultaneously performing choral evensong) and no-one dragged (this refers to anchors - transvestites are free to do whatever they wish in the confines of their own boats).

Among the late arrivals was a ruddy great charter catamaran crewed by eight very large German gentlemen swilling beer and smoking cigars. We watched their anchoring technique with interest and a growing sense of the requisite smug superiority. Said technique involved motoring vaguely in the direction of a space fractionally bigger than their boat, throwing the anchor and a pile of chain over the side, switching of the engine, slapping their thighs a couple of times and then going below for more beer.

'Look at them' we commented to each other. 'That'll just be an anchor lying on its side with a pile of chain on top. Didn't set it in, lay out the chain or dive to check it. They're lucky there's no wind forecast for tonight otherwise they'd drag through this crowded anchorage and cause mayhem.'

Not long after, I looked across to the North and saw some large, dark purple clouds building up which didn't make me feel at all comfortable. The bright flashes and dark rumbling noises didn't help either. The flashes got brighter and more frequent, the thunder got louder and more frequent and the clouds grew as darkness fell.

Then it hit. The light southerly wind against which we had anchored swung through 180 degrees and blasted out of the North at about 35 knots. Boats lurched and pivoted all over the place and one by one started to drag their anchors. Several made a number of attempts to re-anchor, failed and headed up to Monastery Bay where there was a little more shelter from the North.

Strangely enough, the German cat was not one of those that dragged. Its pile of chain had pulled out straight and so it had moved back about two boatlengths, but it was still in position. As, fortunately, were we.

The wind continued to build, with *Birvidik* snatching at her anchor and leaning over in the gusts. Then it started raining so heavily that it was like trying to look through a waterfall. More boats dragged and either reset their anchors or motored off north in disgust. Still *Birvidik* held firm.

So did the bloody German cat.

In the end, my nerve cracked first. Hoping to leave more space in the anchorage we had anchored fairly close to the (originally windward) southerly rocks and the boat had swung away from them as planned. The 180 shift had now swung us directly toward them, and straightened the chain rigid to bring us even closer. This meant that if the anchor did drag, we'd have no time to react before we hit them. Just to add to things, some kindly local fishermen had left floating ropes and moorings just off the aforementioned rocks in a prime position to foul our prop should we drift back any further.

I put a waterproof on over my shorts and T shirt, Liz took the helm and we raised the anchor and set off to reset it in some of the space made available by the recently departed yachts.

Still the bloody German cat held firm.

It took four attempts to get the anchor to reset. By this time the storm was directly overhead. The rain was falling in sheets, the lightning and the thunder simultaneous. Several strikes were so close we could hear the hissing crackle as the air ionised and one was so close it made my hair stand up and I could feel the charge tingling on my skin. Soaked, scared and pissed off, I looked across the bay. There was the German cat, still in place, lights glowing cheerfully through the fug of cigar smoke and beer fumes in the cabin.

By two in the morning the storm decided it had had enough fun in this area and slowly wandered off to cause mayhem further south. When the sun rose it revealed calm seas, crystal clear water, *Birvidik*, one Canadian boat, and the bloody German cat.

'Hubris' is also a word of Greek origin. Suitably chastened we slunk out of the anchorage before the crew of the cat woke and started on the beer and cigars again. Lakka on Paxos beckoned. It was good holding and fully protected from every direction. Sounded good to us.

Overnight, summer hit. Every day was sunny, with light winds except for the afternoon sea breeze (which can get quite strong). The temperature in the cockpit rose to the low to mid thirties every afternoon.

The summer was one long bout of blundering round the Ionian Islands playing a (usually unsuccessful) game of 'Dodge the Flotilla'. It's was very relaxing (most of the time) – a welcome change from the passage making of the previous two years. There were no long trips and the weather patterns were generally predictable. The only real downside was that the whole area is so popular that all the anchorages and harbours get full to bursting with hordes of Italians, and masses of Germans, Austrians and Brits, enhanced by the multitude of flotillas.

To get round this we cunningly set our passage plans so as to arrive in harbours around midday when they've all gone out sailing. They have to leave sometime. As they get ready to leave, *Birvidik* and a few other likeminded cruisers cruise gently round the harbour like circling sharks. As soon as a boat leaves, a berthing frenzy ensues as predatory cruisers fight for the available space. This tactic has been spectacularly successful, but has two main drawbacks:

1 - If any distance has to be travelled, then it involves getting up at some ungodly hour in the morning.

2 - The winds are, as mentioned, predictable. Calm in the morning, sea breeze builds in the afternoon to about a force four and then it dies off again in the evening. As a result, getting into the available berths means you miss out on the best sailing weather and tend to motor everywhere.

In the really busy places, though, even these tactics fail. A prime example of this is Fiskardo, on Cephalonia. Many cruisers pooh-pooh Fiskardo, and I can understand that, but we quite like it.

OK, it's very touristy and expensive, but the pontoon is free and you can get water and electricity.[34]It's chi-chi almost to the point of twee and although some would describe it as sophisticated, others consider it vain, shallow and pretentious. One restaurant owner told us "We cater mainly for upper middle class English". And My Word but he was right. You can tell that from listening to the ambient RP - all stockbroker belt vowels and carefully enunciated consonants. No dropped aitches, flat 'a's or glottal stops sully the ears. The vocabulary is all lavatories, sofas, napkins and puddings, not a toilet, settee, serviette or dessert to be heard. Other than from me, of course.

By rights I should loathe it with a passion, but we both love it and were looking forward to it like a couple of excited kids in the run-up to Christmas (i.e., around September if you're an English retailer).

We are not the only ones who like Fiskardo. It's one of the most popular ports in the Ionian and is almost always packed to the gunwales in the summer. This is prime country for the tactics outlines above. In August, though, even this tactic is doomed to failure as the harbour is full of Italians who, once they get a slot, stay there for the duration. Most of the circling yachts are also Italian and they drive boats like they drive cars, so you've got no chance of getting in. Even if you've dropped your anchor and have started backing in they'll screech in behind you, execute a handbrake turn and slot into your space, barging the other moored boats out of the way if necessary.

By September, though, things are a little quieter as all

---

[34] Events have overtaken this account. The pontoon fell victim to a series of winter storms in 2013/4 and the harbour is now even more crowded, with water and electricity in short supply. These currently have to be blagged off a quayside tavern.

the Italians clear off back home en masse on the last weekend in August. As we approached we could see that the pontoon was still full, but this time the boats were mainly Dutch.

Yotties, especially Brits, are as prone to national stereotyping as anyone and usually denounce the Dutch as terse to the point of brusqueness and generally a bunch of crabby old misanthropes with the social skills of a congenital sociopath; sort of Germans-lite really.

We disagree. We've met many Dutch cruisers and, without exception, they've been open, friendly and helpful as well as excellent conversationalists, especially as most of them speak better English than did most of the kids I used to teach. So - Fiskardo and lots of Dutch. Oooh we were looking forward to it. So we circled and waited.

Sure enough, a couple of boats pulled out, leaving one reasonably wide space. We went for it, dropped the anchor and started backing in to the space, letting the anchor run as we went. There was, though, one slight little problem, namely a cross wind blowing us sideways.

Liz does a sterling job of manoeuvring *Birvidik* in tight situations, but this was really awkward. Nevertheless, we would have done it first go had it not been for the bloody obnoxious Dutch congenital sociopaths on the downwind boat. We dropped the hook in the clear spot between the two anchors and started to reverse in. He didn't see us until we'd drifted off a bit downwind and immediately started shouting abuse. "Fuck off!" he screamed, "You're over my fucking anchor, you fucking prick!"

I told you they spoke good English.

I pointed out that we weren't over his anchor and that we could pull straight when the stern was in, but he just threw his arms in the air, gave me the finger and went below. We continued in, which brought him and his wife back on deck with alacrity. We got the stern in and I asked if they could take our stern lines ashore, which would pull us into position neatly between them. We could then pull in on the anchor and square up. The wife, upon whom I suspect the character of Rosa Klebb was based, pointedly ignored my proffered rope. Instead, she threw me a venomous look that could have curdled milk at twenty paces and hissed "Why did you come in here - go away!" I pointed out that it was the only space available and that if I had had any choice at all in the matter I certainly wouldn't have chosen the Chuckle Brothers here as neighbours. The wind was starting to cause havoc by this time, but we still had a chance to get in if only they would take our lines.

Unfortunately, they did the opposite. They ignored the lines and both pushed our stern forwards out of the gap, causing us to slew sideways across their bow and catch the keel on their anchor chain. "Now look what you've done you bloody fool" screeched Rosa in a decent enough impression of a cat being put through a mangle. We now had no choice but to extricate ourselves, pull off and try again. We lifted the anchor and I pointed out that it was not over his. He ignored this helpful demonstration.

We tried again, but the wind had increased to the point where it became obvious that we weren't going to able to get in, so we aborted. He took this opportunity to shout out "Why don't you go back to school and learn how to fucking sail!"

So I gave in to temptation and gave him the finger.

Luckily, another gap had opened up and we decided to abandon trying to go in stern to, and instead head in bows to and lie to the stern anchor. This is a piece of cake, but has the disadvantage that it's not as secure and it's a bugger to get out in a hurry if things go pear-shaped.

Once tied up, we had a cup of tea and indulged in some therapeutic chocolate. After about an hour and a half we had managed to suppress the urge to go out and punch every Dutchman we came across.

Funny, isn't it, how a lifetime of positive experience counts for so little against one obnoxious exception.

After a couple of days a sense of perspective slowly returned. *Menheer & Vrouw Klootzak* were now seen as the exception that proves the rule and the Dutch were reinstated as Most Favoured Nation. We continued on our Ionian perambulation.

This was the first time we had experienced an entire season of 'potter mode'. We categorise cruising into three modes: 'Hell-for-Leather', 'Passage Making' and 'Pottering'.

We've never really done Hell-for-leather, unless you count crossing Biscay. This mode has the objective of covering as much distance as possible in the shortest time possible. Meeting this objective requires stocking up with enough provisions to relieve the Siege of Mafeking then setting off at some God-awful hour in the morning. After that you just keep going, day and night, for weeks on end until you reach your destination. This often involves arcane tricks of seamanship, such as setting an obscure dog-leg course which goes miles offshore and doubles the distance travelled but saves you time because it takes advantage of wind and current. It's tiring all the time and alternates between boredom and abject terror. Aficionados consider it the high point of cruising, the acme of the sailing experience.

No thanks.

Having eschewed Hell-for-Leather mode, we had spent almost the whole of our three years in Passage Making mode, which is just the sort of wishy-washy compromise that appeals to a pair of indecisive wooly liberals such as us.

It gets you where you want to go. OK, it takes forever but that's a price you pay for travelling at an average speed of around one statute mile per hour. [35]

It takes forever because we have a couple of provisos built in to our passage making protocol.

Firstly, there shall be no night passages unless they are absolutely unavoidable. This means that each day's leg should be no more than sixty nautical miles, so that it can be

---

[35] Difficult as it may be for proper hairy sailors to believe, this is a reasonably accurate estimation of our average speed when passage making. It is based on sailing one fifty to sixty nautical mile leg every three days or so.

completed in daylight. Secondly, there must be at least two days break between legs, so as to give the poor old dears time to recover from the rigours of the voyage. This also provides time for exploration and experiencing the place. That, after all, is the purpose of the whole exercise.

Despite these precautionary measures, passage making mode is not without its drawbacks. You never completely relax as you're aware that you have to squeeze all your exploring, provisioning and passage planning into your two day furlough. Any bad weather, maintenance or other unexpected tasks also throw the whole schedule into disarray, necessitating longer stopovers and thus reducing your average speed to that of an out of condition slug. This, of course, sets up a tension between stopover times and the requirement to get to your overwintering spot before the horrors of the Mediterranean winter set in.

Then you have the navigational and pilotage aspects. When passage making you never go into the same place twice. Every harbour, anchorage and town quay is new. While this is intellectually stimulating and helps stave off dementia, it is also stressful. Charts and pilot books are all very well, but they are no match for the confidence imbued by having been there before and knowing just what to expect.

Pottering mode is probably the nearest the cruising yottie comes to the popular image of cruising – anchored in an idyllic bay, lolling in a hammock strung between the masts while sipping at an ice-cold G&T, stress levels bumping along the bottom of the graph.

Pottering mode is characterised by short hops, frequent revisiting of previous anchorages and harbours, well-known pre-determined routes and the relaxed confidence that comes from knowing you can easily get to a safe haven in almost any eventuality. Not only that, but you'll know the easiest approach, the best spots to drop anchor, where provisions can be obtained, how to get hold of water and electricity and where, what and who is best avoided.

We criss-crossed the Ionian from Corfu in the north to Zakinthos in the south and from Cephalonia in the west to

Astokos in the east, visiting most of the islands and much of the mainland coast. Our track resembled the webs that were produced in the 1995 NASA experiments where the spiders were force fed about eight spliffs' worth of dope. [36]

However, as the oracle at Delphi advises, μηδέν αγαάν - nothing in excess. One season was enough. By September we had had enough of pottering mode and made our way back to Gouvia for the winter, with the intention of resuming passage making mode and heading for Turkey the next year.

Via Delphi, as it happens.

Gouvia, Corfu

The third winter

(mainly wet)

September 30th 2008 – May 4th 2009

Welcome to winter in Corfu.

The torrential rain.

The fifty knot winds.

The astronomical marina fees.

The erratic electricity supply.

The foetid water supply (drinkable costs extra).

The on/off (usually off) internet connection.

The cumbersome, cynical. labyrinthine bureaucracy.

The black hole of a postal non-service.

Oh - and the teargas.

Apparently, the rainy season doesn't kick in until January. Hah! I was just glad we had scuba gear on board.

---

[36] Other effective web-weaving disruptors were benzedrine, chloral hydrate, mescaline and, most of all caffeine. Interestingly, LSD improved the regularity of web design. It is thought that plants evolved the production of caffeine as a defence against insect attack. It seems to be an effective disruptor of many arthropods' metabolisms.

We could use it to get to the shops.

Don't get me wrong, Corfu is a beautiful island, especially in the summer when it's not obscured by sheets of rain. However, as a place to spend the winter on a boat it has certain disadvantages. Most holiday places go to sleep to a degree in the winter, but many parts of Corfu (including Gouvia) go into an unresponsive coma and have to be put on life-support until the spring. Admittedly, Corfu town itself is still an active centre, but you risk a good soaking and the consequent hypothermia trying to get there by bus. Nevertheless it's a sheltered spot with good facilities, so we overwintered there.

Spending a winter somewhere contrasts dramatically with the short, transitory visits made while summer cruising. In the latter, we tend to stay a few days at most, maybe a week to ten days if we are weather-bound or suffer a technical. In the winter we stay in one place for around six months. This makes for a qualitatively different experience - practically, socially and psychologically.

At a practical level, life becomes far more efficient and much easier. Take shopping for example. This is inordinately time consuming in the summer. The first challenge on arrival in a new port is to actually find the shops. Note the use of the plural. Even if we are only looking for basic provisions we will still need to find several shops. The chances of our buying everything at one stop are infinitesimal. The sort of fully equipped hypermarket which sells everything from baked beans through wasabi paste to dehumidifiers and replacement windscreen wipers will, if it exists at all outside of our fevered imaginations, be situated off a multilane gyratory system halfway to the Crab Nebula.

Once in the shop we then face the problem of finding out where they have secreted away the goods we are looking for. At first glance one would think that this would not present too much of an intellectual challenge. One would be wrong.

The major supermarket chains employ a veritable army of psychologists, neurobiologists, time and motion experts, ethologists and data scientists. Their prime objective is to get the punters to spend the absolute maximum amount of money. In this they are similar to Las Vegas casinos and, indeed, employ many of the same tactics – confuse, bamboozle, distract and disorientate. Clocks and natural light sources are minimized in both environments for example.

Supermarket entrances and aisles are usually arranged to encourage anticlockwise circulation, which has been shown to increase sales; apparently by favouring the right hand to pick things from the shelf. The most profitable items are placed on shelves that eye-tracking technology has shown to be the prime positions for being noticed. Describing the full range of tricks and tactics would take volumes and probably induce a fully justified sense of paranoia.

I would have thought that all of this research would have found the near to optimum design and that every supermarket on the planet would buy into it. All layouts would therefore become clones of the big chains' designs. As a result you should be able to walk into any supermarket and know instinctively where everything is.

Outside of Britain and the US, though, this does not seem to be the case. Continental supermarkets, especially around the fringes of the Mediterranean, continue to display the quirky idiosyncrasies of their host cultures. Charming and atmospheric this may be, but it's a bugger if it sentences you to spending a futile hour and a half wandering gormlessly around looking for the bloody toothpaste before finding it cunningly hidden between the drain cleaner and the cat food.

It takes weeks to really get the feel of a place and know where everything is. In summer cruising mode this rarely happens. If you do manage it, say in a small village with only one shop and an itinerant live chicken vendor, you have little time to savour and use your laboriously acquired local knowledge because you're bound to be off the next day.

How very different from the home life of our own dear

wintering cruiser. He has had several months to become a local. He knows where all the supermarkets are and which one he has to go to for what.[37] Hardware stores, stationers, launderettes, post offices and mobile phone shops are all engraved deeply on his mental map; pubs and restaurants even more so. He can even work out the shortest route between any two points in the area by foot or by bicycle.

By the end of the winter the proportion of his life spent on shopping and general commerce has dropped from five hours a day to five hours a week, thus freeing time for such essentially pointless and self-indulgent pastimes as learning line-dancing or writing irritatingly patronising blog updates.

Welcome though these practical advantages may be, they pale into insignificance when compared to the social and psychological effects of the change in seasonal lifestyle.

Humans have a need for company. This derives from the fact that physically we are pretty unimpressive specimens. We can't outrun predators or prey. We are singularly lacking in weapons – fingernails are no match for claws and our stubby little teeth can't hold a candle to a good set of canines.

In terms of musculature we're the original 98 pound weaklings. Depending on how you measure it, the jaw muscle can be considered the strongest in the human body. At full whack it can exert a force of nearly 100 kilograms on the molars. This is actually quite impressive for our size, but it lags behind other apes such as the chimpanzee who can take off a human finger with one quick bite – a fact painfully, if unintentionally, demonstrated by more than one primatologist.

We get round these little local difficulties by working in concert with each other. We form groups that co-operate to achieve the requirements of survival and reproduction. We have evolved to be social animals. This has proved to be a highly successful strategy, but it comes with a cost. In

---

[37] It must be conceded that this last-mentioned characteristic is most likely to be displayed by Mrs Yottie.

parallel with developing it, we have also evolved the psychological need for socialisation. Our brains can neither develop fully nor function effectively if they don't have the stimulation of constant interaction with other human brains. We are genetically programmed to seek out and bond with others.

The cruising life isn't always that conducive to fulfilling this requirement for social stimulation. It takes time to establish social relationships with other people and to cement those relationships with grooming behaviour. Since a lot of social grooming involves language, it's always a lot easier to do this if all parties are fluent in the same tongue.

In summer cruising mode, however, encounters tend to be brief, sporadic, erratic and multilingual. There is usually enough time to cement already-established relationships, but rarely enough to establish new ones. As a result, social interaction tends to be less than optimal. The effects of this can be most effectively demonstrated by observing the extreme end of the spectrum, namely the hardcore single hander.

The hardcore single hander belongs to the extreme provisional wing of the yottie movement. Do not, though, fall into the trap of looking upon him as a separate species. He is merely your average yottie writ large. He takes all of the common yottie foibles and manifests them in extreme form.

The hardcore single handers can usually be recognized by certain common character traits. Whether these traits are a result of his being a single hander, or whether possession of these traits results in single-handerdom is open to debate. Either way there is a remarkable consistency in appearance and behaviour, so much so that he can frequently be identified at a great distance.

The first clue is visual. He will have elevated scruffiness to an art form. I appreciate that this is true of most yotties, but the single hander has no partner or crew to point out that grubby Y-fronts, flip flops and an old string vest liberally bespattered with egg yolk, used engine oil and cheap red wine do not constitute suitable attire for the

Commonwealth Day levée hosted by the local British Consulate.

As he gets closer, the initial diagnosis can be further evaluated by checking for facial hair. Agreed, this will almost certainly be present on any yottie but again the single hander takes this to the extreme. I know I said 'facial hair' but it's just 'hair' really. There is little, if any, actual face to be seen. The wild, straggly beard blends seamlessly into chest hair at the bottom and the eyebrows at the top. The eyes might just be discernable peering through in the manner of an Old English Sheepdog and the ears hazarded at as being the sources of the slightly finer hair sprouting out horizontally from the sides of the head.

The mouth will be invisible, but movements suggestive of small animals scurrying about in the undergrowth can be taken as evidence that he is either eating or attempting to speak. Or, more likely, both. The presence of traces of last night's supper or a fine spray of crumbs can be taken as supporting evidence.

Once the initial assessment has been made, it is worth hazarding a guess as to the sex of our subject. You have a 99.9% chance of his being a him. In the unlikely event of his being a her the aforementioned observations still apply.

It is possible that he will now attempt to engage you in conversation. Even if he appears to be a monoglot Basque with a severe speech impediment, be patient. He is probably British, but his language skills will have atrophied from lack of use. As time goes on he will slowly become more comprehensible.

Do not be alarmed by unusual gestures, vocal tones or facial expressions (if the last-mentioned can be discerned at all through the hair). He will have been deprived of meaningful social interaction for so long that he is no longer able to appreciate or react appropriately to social cues.

A word of warning. Think very carefully before inviting a single hander aboard, even for a cup of tea and a short chat. Once he has overcome his initial difficulties associated with unexpected and unaccustomed social interaction, the dam will burst. Just as he experienced difficulty in initiating social interaction, he will now be incapable of ending it. Social cues and hints such as yawning, standing up and saying goodnight, falling asleep slumped on the saloon table or putting him in a headlock and wrestling him onto the pontoon while screaming 'For the love of God, go!' in his left ear will all have about as much effect as a quiet appeal to Vladimir Putin's better nature.[38]

A good winter, though, can work wonders for the single hander and the standard yottie alike. The difference between them is, after all, just a matter of degree. Winter is when yotties re-charge their social batteries. New social ties are forged and old ones reinforced. Relationships develop over quiz nights, social evenings and extended organised walks. This socialisation even extends to relationships with locals such as marina staff, craftsmen and shopkeepers. Gradually, imperceptibly, the psychological renormalization process progresses. By the end of the winter even single handers begin to exhibit signs of normal personality traits.

Well, normal for yotties

Through the gulfs to the Aegean

The 4th season

May 7th 2009 to June 8th 2009

You know that feeling that something's not quite right, but you can't quite put your finger on it? Something sounds or feels different, but you're damned if you can actually pin it down?

We'd got back from our flying visit to the wilder shores of Western Europe, put the boat back in the water and spent a frantic four days getting everything ready to leave, which

---

[38] All of the above is a vile and unwarranted calumny; a wild exaggeration unsubstantiated by fact or reason. Most single-handers are no more barking, socially challenged or unhygienic than the average yottie. Not that that's saying a lot for them.

we did on the 4th May, for a short hop across to Mourtos. Readers with long memories and little to occupy their time may remember Mourtos as the scene of The Thunderstorm and German Catamaran Fiasco from the previous year. This year the four hour motor across and the two day sojourn there were enjoyable and uneventful. Sadly, this could not be said of the seven hour next stage from Mourtos to Lefkas.

About five hours into this trip I became slightly uneasy. The engine didn't exactly sound wrong, but there again it didn't exactly sound right either. Then I noticed that the oil pressure was steadily dropping. This was not a good sign. Nor was the ever increasing white smoke pouring out from the exhaust. Nor still the fact that we were stuck out at sea fifteen miles from Lefkas without enough wind to maintain steerage.

A quick inspection of the engine bay showed no sign of oil loss, so that was theory number one out of the window. "Hmm", I thought, "Perhaps we've broken a piston ring and are burning oil - hence the smoke" (Wrong colour though). It was far too hot to lay on top of the engine and check the oil level, so we nursed her carefully into Lefkas and tied up to the town quay, nervously waiting for an expensive bang and the sudden loss of control as we were manoeuvring in the restricted waters of the canal and the harbour. Our luck held and we moored up bows to with the stern anchor out.

The next day the oil level was checked and, much to my surprise, not only had it not dropped, but it had actually risen by about four centimetres. It was also worryingly thin. The level of fuel in the tank had also dropped rather dramatically. It was starting to sound like diesel fuel had somehow managed to find its way into the lube oil.

It was time to call in the experts. Contract Yacht Services concurred with the tentative diagnosis and suggested several possible causes, some of which sounded worryingly expensive. If anyone reading this needs any work done in Lefkas we can thoroughly recommend Joe Charleton and his team at CYS. They were friendly, competent and went out of their way to help us, even to the extent of Joe leaving his truck with its used oil bowser at our disposal while he had to scrounge the use of other vehicles.

We started with the easiest and most obvious, the injectors, which turned out to be the case. This came as a surprise as we had had all four injector nozzles renewed that winter as part of the standard maintenance schedule. This had not been cheap. At the same time I had changed the oil and replaced all the fuel and oil filters.

After listening patiently for some time to my impugning the parentage of the engineer who had replaced the nozzles the CYS engineer gently pointed out that the nozzles were all indeed new and had been fitted and adjusted correctly. What had happened was that the needle valves had all seized solid and the injectors were squirting neat, liquid diesel into the cylinders which was then getting past the piston rings and into the sump. The cause, they argued, was fuel badly contaminated with water.

Pulling off fuel from the bottom of the tanks confirmed this. We pulled off five litres of dirty grey water before we got to anything that even vaguely resembled diesel, and even then that was cloudy and heavily contaminated with diesel bug. This was irritating to say the least, as we'd filled the tanks with 1000 litres of fuel just before wintering up in Gouvia marina. Obviously, we had got the dregs out of the bottom of their tank, which I strongly suspect they knew about and had disguised matters by the addition of an emulsifier. I do object to paying nearly one and a half euros a litre for dirty water that buggers up my immaculately maintained engine.

We do, however, learn from our own mistakes if not from other peoples. Every time we refuel now, I take and inspect a sample from the hose at the beginning, middle and end of the procedure. If they get snotty about this then they've got something to hide.

The solution to the problem was four more new injector nozzles, two more oil changes, the renewal of all fuel and oil filters (all of this just fifteen engine hours after it was last done). Then we had to empty the tanks and throw away a thousand quid's worth of diesel, wash out tanks and refill. Altogether the whole shebang set us back ten days and about two thousand euros. Mind you, it could have been a lot worse; we seemed to have got away without significant damage to the piston rings, injection pump and big end bearings.

We hope.

The next twenty hours on engine were spent on tenterhooks as we listened intently for any change in engine sound and kept a nervous eye on the oil pressure gauge and the exhaust. Luckily it seemed to have done the trick.

I spent the first eight trips obsessively monitoring the oil pressure and exhaust smoke, periodically checking oil pressure at tickover, 1000 rpm and 1200 rpm. All remained tickety-boo and we gradually relaxed. We spent a week or so in potter mode, meandering our way down the Ionian, revisiting old haunts. Novelty returned when we turned left into the Gulf of Patras and started off toward the Corinth Canal and the Aegean.

The first stop was Missolonghi, whose brief claim to fame was based on being the place that Byron died. Well, OK, it was also one of the original sites of the resistance to Ottoman rule that led to the Greek war of independence and as a result suffered a prolonged siege in which 4000 Greeks died of starvation and another 3500 broke out. Unfortunately 1500 of those were killed and the remaining 2000 were sold into slavery and had their ears and noses cut off for good measure. Must have reduced their resale value you'd have thought. But what's all that compared with the death of some poetic English toff from what was officially reported as 'a fever' but was probably the clap. You know what these poetic types are like, they're all at it. Any time, any body - any species probably.

Missalonghi is a bijou little university town, which is reached from the sea up a two kilometre canal dredged from the surrounding salt marsh. There was a large basin at the end surrounded by muddy shallows, and a partially constructed marina which offered free mooring and precious little else. Mind you, we did get a visit from a charming gentleman who handed us a leaflet upon which was an 'artist's impression' of the upmarket completed marina. This boasted hotels, shower blocks, shops, landscaped gardens, swimming pool, restaurants, the lot. And, it insisted, all this would be operational by June 2009.

As this was the end of May 2009, we looked around the dusty, barren landscape and wondered at the amazing efficiency by which the three Greek workers equipped with one cement mixer, one pickup truck, two shovels and a broom were to transform it into the described yottie's paradise in a bare five weeks. Look and learn, Bovis, look and learn.

Missolonghi also boasted a rather unusual attraction, a munitions graveyard. Inside an unlocked compound near the quay was a collection of old rusty military hardware - tanks, jet fighters, mobile surface to air missile stations. Of course, we couldn't resist it could we. We clambered all over them, round them and in them, striking silly poses for the camera and making brrrm, whoosh, boom and takatakataka noises.

We got the bikes out for further exploring and discovered another unusual feature of Missolonghi; Greeks on bikes.

Most Greeks wouldn't be seen dead on a bike. Actually, that's not strictly accurate. Given the standard of Greek driving, and the attitude of most Greek drivers to bicycles (namely an irritation of no redeeming significance which should be disposed of at the earliest possibility) dead is exactly the condition in which they'd be seen were they ever to be so *démodé* as to get on one.

Except in Missalonghi, that is. Here there are bicycle lanes and loads of fashionable young things pedalling decorously everywhere. We suspect that it's because it so flat. Salt marsh you see.

You'll remember that Liz was by now doing all the intricate wheel and lever waggling stuff whilst I had taken over the heave-grunt ropes, anchors and fenders business.

It's all very well this changing job descriptions business, but it can have unexpected consequences.

When we left Missalonghi for Patras, Liz took the helm and pootled off towards the canal whilst I untied ropes, brought in the fenders and put everything away. The trouble was that, with all that moving and turning around, I got a little bit disorientated. Looking up from the locker I saw a buoy ahead and said to Liz "That's an Easterly cardinal buoy - we're going the wrong side of it".

Now, Liz did exactly the right thing, which was to express her reservations, but to do as the captain said nevertheless. That's how it is on boats. Unfortunately, what I told her to do was the wrong thing, because it wasn't an easterly cardinal buoy, it was a starboard hand passage buoy, which you have to leave to port if you're going out (don't ask – you just do, alright?).

Things weren't helped by the fact that the sun was now shining straight in our faces so we couldn't read the depth sounder. By the time horrible realisation had dawned, and I had blurted out "it's shoaling, go hard to Starboa..." we ground to a graceful, if undignified halt on the mudbank.

We managed to get off by standing on tiptoe and applying hard astern thrust. We slid out back into the channel, only to notice that the engine didn't sound quite right. Looking over the side, the spurts of cooling water in the exhaust were noticeable by their absence. The hard reverse thrust had stirred up so much mud and silt that it had been drawn into the cooling water intake and blocked the filters solid.

We had to switch off the engine to stop it overheating and seizing, so we dropped the anchor right in the middle of the narrow channel, much to the bemusement of the Greek fishing boats passing by, who squeezed their way through the by now much narrower gap, with much shaking of heads and mutterings about clueless British yotties.

I shut off the seacock and did a record breaking dismantle, clean, seal and remantle of the engine filters, removing half a bucket of vile, sticky mud. I started the engine. All was clear on the water front, so we upped anchor and off we went.

Two kilometres further on, just at the outer end of the canal, we noticed that the cooling water was now just a trickle, so off went the engine again and we drifted whilst I set a new record for , dismantle, clean, seal and remantle of the engine filters. This got out another half bucket of vile, sticky mud. Luckily, Arcadia was standing by while we did this and Keith showed great restraint - no sarcastic comments and not even so much as a smirk. And I thought he was ex Navy.

This seemed to do the trick and we got into Patras with no further incident. I decided that I had better replace the cooling water impellor when we got in, just in case it had been damaged by grit or by running dry. Actually, it was probably a bit of a penance for my original cock up - it's a bloody horrible job.

Still, on the positive side, I did show that although I'm more than capable of getting us into the shit, I'm also capable of getting us out of it.

So far.

Patras is the third largest city in Greece, but it's still pretty self-contained; not a sprawling conurbation surrounded by acres of suburbs like Manchester or Birmingham. You can walk across it in half a day.

Which we did, as it happens.

Patras has charming café/pedestrianised areas, a raffish bohemian quarter, a large roman amphitheatre and a castle overlooking them all. It also has a labyrinthine road system and charming, characterful, humorous locals. Trying to find our way around was made more difficult by the disorientating Greek habit of either covering up road names with signs, trees or posters, or just not bothering to put names on them at all. I stopped at some weather-beaten characterful locals sitting outside a kiosk and tried to get them to indicate where we were on the map.

"Poo eemaste Kyrie?" (Where are we, Sir?) I asked in my best Greek, proffering them the map.

"Patras" they replied, clasping their substantial bellies and falling about with laughter at their own wit and drollery.

I couldn't quite summon the Greek for "Oh you witty, charming, characterful, well-nourished Greek person you. Would you believe we'd actually managed to work that one out ourselves? Any fear of narrowing it down a bit?" Instead I waved the map at them again and rattled off a list of street names until they gave in and pointed vaguely westwards and mumbled something about 500 metres. We got there in the end.

The main reason for staying in Patras was the 'Orthodontos'. This wasn't due to our needing work done on our teeth, but rather 'orthodontos' is the Greek term for a rack and pinion railway. 'Straight teeth' - I suppose it makes sense.

This travels 22 km up into the mountains from an obscure station about an hour's train ride from Patras. It was reputed to be spectacular. It turned to be also very popular and vastly oversubscribed, so Greek Railways, in their wisdom, decided to restrict it to three trains a day, and then only on Saturdays and Sundays. Thinking we'd outsmarted the system by arriving on a Thursday and being flexible over timing, we approached the reservations clerk at Patras railway Station.

No luck. Fully booked.

Saturday and Sunday.

Up, down and across.

"Never mind" we thought. We'll be going through Corinth later and that's on the other end of the line. We'll do it from there". So we watered up and cleared off to the island of Trizonia.

This involved going through the straits of Andirrion, which are spanned by a huge bridge. These straits mark the boundary between the Gulf of Patras and the Gulf of Corinth. Trizonia lies about twenty nautical miles beyond the bridge. Many people had waxed poetic about the charms of Trizonia, so we arrived with high hopes. Perhaps it was because our expectations had been raised so high, but we didn't rate it too much. OK, it was pretty in places in a sort of twee, rustic, picture postcard sort of way, but it didn't do too much for us, so we stayed one night, had a seriously average meal at one of the local tavernas and left the next day for Itea, whence we intended to visit Delphi.

Itea is an example of a common Greek phenomenon, the half-finished marina. These crop up all over the place. After an initial burst of enthusiasm there follows a flurry of activity - pontoons are manufactured and installed to heavy mooring blocks and great plans made for ancillary facilities such as toilets, restaurants, chandlers etc (q.v. Missolonghi). Unfortunately, soon after this the enthusiasm (and, it is scurrilously rumoured, the EU funding) runs out and everything grinds to a halt. Itea had been like this for the last seven years. The pontoons were installed and there was the occasional bollard to tie up to, but very little else - no water, electricity, lazy lines, toilets/showers - anything.

At this point, ownership was unclear, and charges were rarely, if ever, levied. As a result the pack of marine opportunists, that are constantly to be found circling such developments, strike. It may not have any facilities, but there's excellent shelter and by God it's free. It fills up with boats in nanoseconds. Locals mainly, leisure and fishing, followed by skint liveaboards and other ne'er do wells, and finally by the particularly tight-fisted contingent of the cruising yottie tribe (which is most of them).

There was, however, a very sociable local who came along the quays thrice daily in his little diesel delivery truck. The local mayor had charged him with supplying diesel, information and access to a water supply to visiting boats. He gave us the low-down on getting to Delphi by bus. We decided to catch the seven fifteen bus the next morning (My birthday as it happened) and get there before the hordes of tourists descended on the place. (That's crass, sheep-like tourists, of course. Not inquisitive, independently minded travellers such as our good selves.)

The bus wound its way up into the mountains, looking down on an alluvial flood plain (see - I stayed awake in geography lessons) covered in acres of olive trees, and dropped us off in New Delphi (the town, not Old Delphi, the archaeological site) at around 7:45.

Now, we had not bothered to bring maps or guide books on Delphi. Our reasoning went something along the lines of:

* "Delphi is the single biggest tourist attraction and archaeological site in Greece, possibly in Western Europe.

* The town of New Delphi derives almost all of its income from visitors to the archaeological site and museum.

* Therefore they will have guidance, maps, background information and tourist information offices readily and easily available."

As we alighted from the bus we saw that this hypothesis had been tested and found severely wanting. The only two maps we found displayed were one purportedly showing the locations of the several hundred hotels in New Delphi and one showing (again purportedly) the route of the Little Tourist Train around the area. This latter seemed to have been inspired by the famous map showing the London underground, in that it probably accurately represented the sequence of stops made en route, but its concordance with local topography was negligible.

After trudging around for about thirty minutes we were saved by a local authority gardener who switched off his strimmer long enough to explain, in perfect English, that we needed to go right back to where we started and follow the road that our bus took after dropping us off for about 500 metres to the next stop.

Gardener: 2, Greek National Tourist Board: nil

We arrived at 8:15, a quarter of an hour after it had opened and five minutes after the first four coachloads had arrived.

Still, it wasn't that crowded, and the site was stunning.

You can see why the ancients sited it there. The awe-inducing impact of a huge temple complex in that setting must have been huge. It's not just those Johnny-come-lately Abrahamic religions that know how to press all the psychological buttons to best effect.

There is little in the way of explanation or comment around the whole complex, including the museum. We overcame this by fine-tuning the technique we developed in Sicily, namely lurking surreptitiously on the fringes of a couple of large tour groups (from cruises we suspect) and whistling insouciantly in a foreign accent whilst eavesdropping on the tour guides. It seems that most of the lower buildings were treasuries from different city states. The main focus points were the altar, where gifts and tributes were left and slaughtered, and the temple of Apollo where prophecies were divined and prayers offered asking for the Gods' intervention in Earthly matters. My interpretation was that the entire complex was effectively a Mycenaean cross between a Ponzi scheme and a Nigerian boiler-room scam, charging the supplicant to petition the God(s) to temporarily suspend the laws of the Universe on the behalf of an admittedly unworthy sinner. (© Bertrand Russell).

From Delphi we returned to *Birvidik* for a restrained birthday celebration before setting off the next day for Andikirron.

Leaving Itea was slightly delayed by the appearance of the port police, who indicated that we should attend their office *toute suite* and bring our documentation with us. We've honed these procedures down to a fine art and it's usually fairly painless. I have all the required documents arranged in a case, along with quite a few others which are not really required but are sometimes requested. We also have pre-printed crew lists with more personal details about us than you'd find in a Home Office wet dream. All of this is finished with a flourish of our big, sod-off ship's stamp.

We should have known from the uniform. Port police normally dress in a restrained dark blue combat top and trousers, big boots and a baseball cap. They're usually either conscripts trying to work out what to do, or old hands winding down to pension day. The former have an air of nervous confusion and are grateful for any help you can give them in telling them what they and you need to do. The latter affect an air of not unfriendly, world weary resignation and just stamp anything that's put in front of them. Not this one.

He was about 24, and had on a full set of number one whites, immaculately washed and pressed. Instead of the baseball cap there was a crisp, white cap with a peak that, if he walked in direct sunlight, blinded passers by and sent truck drivers ploughing into pavement cafes. There was enough gold trim to rival Fort Knox and a sodding great gun which would have given Dirty Harry Callaghan an inferiority complex.

My, but he was keen. Not particularly *au fait* with the regulations or paperwork, and not much of a linguist, but my God was he keen. Unusually for the Port Police, he spoke very little English and no other languages apart from Greek.

This was a bit of a disadvantage as, ahead in the queue, were a French couple who spoke virtually no English, and a Spanish couple (ditto). I could see I was in for the long haul, and settled into a chair in the corner.

After the same set of forms had been screwed up, thrown in the bin and re-started three times my patience snapped and I joined in the melee. Translating (loosely) into and out of French and Spantuguese via broken English and kindergarten level Greek the forms were eventually completed to official satisfaction.

Then it was my turn. Confidently I laid all the paperwork on the desk: ship's registration certificate, insurance, boat-driving licence, passports and crew list, ceremoniously imprinted with the ship's stamp.

This was met with pursed lips and an intake of breath. Oooh dear, not good enough. Not good enough at all. Despite all the requisite data being on the documents and already printed out and copied for him to cherish and keep, he wanted all the data transcribed to forms more of his liking.

And he wanted me to transcribe it. He lent me his pen, which was white mother of pearl with gold filigree (I suspected sergeant's stripes) and what looked suspiciously like a polished black peak on the cap.

The trouble was that his forms were designed for vessels such oil tankers, VLCCs, and cruise liners. And he wanted every space filled in. No blanks or crossings out.

I answered (almost) truthfully that *Birvidik* carried no large cargoes of crude or distilled petroleum products; neither was it carrying goods classified as hazardous, dangerous, toxic or explosive. Furthermore the number of passengers, including those in private cabins, was zero. The restaurant did not carry bonded stores with a value in excess of 3000 euros (much as we'd have liked that). Shiny boy was obviously unaware of the concept of multitasking as he had difficulty grasping that the roles of Captain, first officer, bosun, radio officer, chief and second engineers, purser and deckhands were all carried out under a crew manifest of two people.

When this had been done to his satisfaction he set about calculating the port and transit levies due. This required several sheets of paper, two calculators and three attempts, after which he came up with the grand sum of eleven euros and eighty eight cents.

I gave him a twenty euro note. He looked at it a little bemused, then unlocked and opened the cashbox on his desk, which was empty. This was strange as the previous two crews had paid him (eleven euros and eighty eight cents each, since you ask). Then he opened his wallet and peered inside. It seemed to contain nothing but old post-its and a twenty euro note.

Then he gave me back my note and told me to go and change it at the establishment across the road, which I did. At first, I took this to be a rather seedy bar but it soon became apparent, even to someone with as sheltered an upbringing as me, that this was the local knocking shop. The pastel colours, opulent red and purple lighting and the voluptuous furniture and statuary sort of gave the game away[39] They were obviously used to doubling up as the local branch of the TSB, and the 'receptionist' didn't bat an eyelid at my request for financial rather than 'special' services. With a cheery smile she gave me a ten, a five and five ones and waved me on my way.

On my return I passed over twelve euros , which prompted a flurry of further searching for small change. Deciding to risk the chance of being arrested for attempted bribery, I told him to keep the twelve cents and left.

The *Birvidik* Theory of Officialdom:

The competence and co-operation of the official is inversely proportional to the flashiness of the uniform.

As it turned out, we didn't stay in Andikirron. We went round and had a look, but the only mooring spaces available seemed to have had lazy lines fitted and then hacked off. This posed the problem of our having to use a stern anchor where it might have got snagged on old mooring blocks and chains, so we turned round and headed off to Corinth, for a second attempt at the orthodontos.

We arrived there and anchored off in the spot indicated in the pilot, just outside the yacht harbour.

The next morning the wind had dropped, the sun was reflecting off the calm water onto the roof of the aft cabin,

---

[39] Prostitution is legal in Greece and it seems that any town worthy of the name has at least one brothel. These are tolerated, if not encouraged and are among the few boom businesses in Greece. They also seem to be among the few that pay their taxes. In 2006 the Greek authorities revised their estimates of GDP upwards to take account of the tax receipts from the industry.

Brothel owner Soula Alevridou even sponsors football teams who have to wear bright pink kit advertising her two establishments, Soula's House of History and Villa Erotica. The line was drawn, though when she donated €3000 to the local primary school to enable it to buy textbooks after the school board said it had no money to fund the school. After news got out, embarrassed local officials ordered the school to return the money.

and we were snugged down for a lazy lie-in after the long day before.

You know that pleasant, hazy semi-dream state as you drift in and out of sleep on a morning like that? Well, believe me doesn't last long if someone blasts a fog horn at point-blank range, making the whole boat vibrate, shaking the screws out of the woodwork and blasting 120 dB down your ears, leaving them ringing.

Three times.

When we peeled ourselves of the cabin roof we scrambled outside to see what the hell was going on, noticing in passing that it was 6:30 in the morning.

"Where's the sun gone?" we thought, before we realised it had been blotted out by the 50 metre high wall of steel that towered above us. It seemed that an 8000 ton Ro-Ro cargo ship wanted to manoeuvre backwards into the commercial dock, and had decided that we were in its way. It was about 30 metres from us. How were we to know? There was no little legend in the pilot book saying "Excellent anchoring spot unless some great steel leviathan wants to execute a pirouette".

You've never seen anyone weigh anchor and skedaddle into shallower water faster. After that we decided that, as we were up, we might as well go into the harbour and see if there was a space. There wasn't. So we went back out and tied up on the commercial quay, at which point a load of boats all promptly left the harbour, so in we went and tied up.

The first job was to explore Corinth, get a map, find the train station and book the orthodontos.

The rough guide said that there was a very helpful tourist police office at number five Ermou Street. "We could get a map there" we thought. The trouble was, how were we to find said Ermou 5 without said map?

This presented the sort of circular problem that confronted the early developers of computers. How do you get a computer to read the instructions on how to start itself up when it needs to have started itself up in order to read the instructions? This was compared to trying to lift yourself up by your own bootstraps so the solution was known as 'booting'. Aptly, it was a computer that came to our rescue and solved our little conundrum.

We had a dongle.

We had internet.

The rate of technological progress in computing and electronic communications is truly staggering. I know dongles seem old hat now, but when we left in 2006, no-one outside of research labs had heard of them.

Cutting edge technology then was wi-fi, which the yachting press assured us would soon be lightning fast, too cheap to meter and installed in every marina and harbour on the planet. Our computer was wi-fi enabled and our plan was to use this facility, so considerately provided by marina authorities world-wide, as our primary communications and weather data portal. It was not to be.

Things started off well enough. Our first stop from Jersey, Saint Quay, had wi-fi access and it worked fine. We looked forward to making use of this miraculous technology throughout our travels. Unfortunately, Saint Quay was not only the first harbour we came across with useable wi-fi but also the last one. After that, we didn't come across it at all until we got into Lagos five months later. Even then it was mind-numbingly slow.

For the next couple of years our dream of fast, cheap, convenient internet access remained just that. Getting access to the net required searching out internet cafes. These are now an endangered species, consigned to the dustbin of history by mobile technology, just like phone boxes. In 2006 and 2007 they were everywhere.

Well, not quite everywhere. First, you had to find them. As they were almost all knocked up on the cheap by skint social outcasts trying to scrape together a halfway decent life, they were almost certainly secreted away down some dingy side street in the cheaper part of town.

In addition, they weren't exactly the most salubrious of environments. The air was thick with cigarette smoke and the furniture grubby and threadbare. If you stood up suddenly the stool frequently came up with you, firmly stuck to your trousers by the blobs of used chewing gum thoughtfully deposited on it by the previous occupant.

The light from the couple of bare, dull orange bulbs barely penetrated the oppressive gloom. Keyboards were sticky with semi-dried coffee and other glutinous residues, most of which were probably best left unidentified. Watching someone type was reminiscent of watching a rat try to extricate itself from a glue-pad trap. The monitor screens were covered in greasy fingerprints and mottled with the spattered debris of years of hawks, spits, coughs and sneezes. After visiting an internet café you had to steep your hands in dettol and fumigate your clothes.

Then you were faced with the problem of transferring data between the boat's computer and the machine in the cafe. This, remember, was in the very early days of laptops, which were expensive and low spec. Bookmarks had to be laboriously written down in a note book. Downloaded data had to be saved on a memory stick with about the same data capacity as a post-it note.

The whole procedure was riddled with compatibility issues. You were lucky indeed if your computer and the one in the internet café had more than one program in common. Weather forecasts had to be saved as a mass of individual files and then pasted into something like word. Sending a few emails and getting a medium range weather forecast could take most of the day.

We were first introduced to the delights of the dongle in Cagliari, eighteen months later. By the time we got to Corinth, just over a year after that, dongles were two a penny and 3G coverage and speed had improved out of all recognition. We now had a yearly contract with a Greek mobile provider and could get onto the internet almost everywhere, including out at sea as long as we didn't stray more than about five miles offshore.

We logged on, downloaded a street map of Corinth and printed it off. Armed with this map, we set off confidently into town and found Ermou 5 in short order.

Unfortunately it was boarded up and derelict, with no helpful sign saying where the helpful tourist police could now be found. Which was helpful.

We went back to the boat to try to find the train station on map. There were two, in fact, in the middle of the city, not far from the port. Bingo! Off we went.

Greece has a fairly rudimentary railway network. There are only 2 lines really, and one of them is narrow gauge. Corinth, however, is at the crossroads of the two lines, and has rail links with all the other major cities - Athens, Thessaloniki, Patras, Kalamata. It's also a large, important city in its own right.

So, what do Greek Railways do with these two highly convenient stations right in the middle of the city and near the port area? Yup - they close them down and leave them to go to rack and ruin. A tattered, fly-blown notice on the paint-peeling, broken window of the station said that access to trains, tickets and advance reservations could now be arranged at the new, 'suburban' train station. No indication of where they might have hidden this, of course. So, it was back to the boat for the internet.

I always thought that 'suburban' meant 'in the built-up, residential areas immediately adjacent to the outskirts of a city or other large conurbation'. Not in Greek it doesn't. In Greek, it means 'four kilometres outside the city limits in a blasted and barren landscape, with the only buildings in sight being two large hypermarkets and a wholesale car dealership'. *"Look upon my works, ye Mighty, and despair"*. They had re-sited the train station as far as possible from any potential customers, so that the only people who could get a train would have needed access to a car in order to get to the station (no bus service, of course). But if you've got a car, what would you want to get a bloody train for? No wonder the place looked deserted.

However, having cycled our way there we approached the reservations office and asked about the funicular. The chap was extremely helpful and friendly.

"It was extremely popular you know" (yes, we knew).

"There were only three trains a day in each direction and it only ran on Saturdays and Sundays you know." (Yup - knew that too).

"Do have any tickets on Saturday or Sunday?", I asked plaintively.

There was much waggling of mouse and tapping of keys, frowning at the monitor and more waggling and tapping. Then some scribbling on scraps of paper.

Finally, with a broad smile and a flourish, he said "Yes! I can get you two tickets going up at 14:10 on Sunday afternoon!".

"Knockout!" We said "And trains from here to the orthodontos and back?"

"Yes" he said "I can do that too." We were on a roll here.

"And what time is the return orthodontos down the mountain?".

"Ah", he said. You know that 'Ah' sound, don't you.

"Ah. All the return seats are full"

How can you get more people coming down a mountain than went up? Are they parachuting in from passing helicopters or just breeding prolifically?

"So when can we get seats for the 22 km down the side of the mountain?"

"The next Saturday."

Not wishing to spend six days stuck at the top of a mountain we declined and cycled back.

The inability to take the orthodontos made us reconsider our immediate plans. Neither of us really took to Corinth too much. Unlike most other places in Greece that we had visited, it had a slightly seedy, delinquent atmosphere, an air of shady characters and feral youth about it. Not quite as feral youthy as the environs of Jersey marina, but getting that way. As an indication, before cycling off we had padlocked all the lockers and the outboard, something we've not even considered doing anywhere else in Greece.

We decided to cut our losses and leave through the Corinth Canal the next morning. This decision was justified later that evening. We'd just had dinner when a couple of lads of about fourteen or fifteen came along the pier on a bicycle. They got off and went just past us to the end of the pier. There was some muttering, and then a red distress flare fired off, lighting up the area and enveloping all the nearby boats, us included, in smoke. They got back on the bike and hi-tailed it off.

A bit later they returned, more muttering, and then an orange smoke flare went off. We were beginning to wonder what sort of arsenal they got access to, or whether they'd broken into a boat and stolen the distress flares. A bit later they returned with a gun. It turned out to be a BB gun and not a proper firearm, but we spent the night wondering when they were going to turn up with the Rocket-Propelled Grenade Launcher.

Never mind – we were looking forward to the Corinth Canal tomorrow and the Aegean the next day.

We transited the canal behind a large coaster at eight o'clock the next morning. It was a spectacular experience, passing between walls eighty metres high cut into the limestone. At times the canal seemed barely wide enough for us, let alone the large coasters and liners that pass through. No wonder parts of the wall are covered in streaks of different coloured paint, just like the sharp turns by the ramps in multi-storey car parks. It would have looked even more spectacular had we passed through later in the day when the sun was higher.

We paid 173 euros for the transit, which works out at about six euros a minute, or three euros for every hundred metres.

Having paid at the other end, and having narrowly avoided being rammed into the quay by an unexpected current, we motored the fifteen miles to Korfos. We were in the Aegean. We tied up to a taverna quay, where we had another seriously average and not cheap meal.

The Aegean

Poros to Kos

June 8th 2009 to July 28th 2009

The Aegean is the stretch of water between mainland Greece and The Peloponnese on one side and Turkey on the other. It makes up over half the total area of Greece. Unfortunately for the Greeks, most of it is water.

This quirk of geography has led to the development of an interesting cultural, social, economic and political phenomenon in Greece, namely the cult of the ferry.

Ferries occupy a special place in Greek society. The reason for this becomes apparent if you ever look at a map of Greece. Most countries, unless they are landlocked, consist of a mainland area with an extent of coastline and a varying number of islands. It is usually the mainland that defines the country. The islands, if present, are embellishments. Look at a map of Greece and you get a completely different impression. The country covers a land area of 132 000 square kilometres. Over 20% of this is made up of islands, and the whole caboodle is spread over an area five times as large as the land area. The overall effect is to make up a country by chopping Portugal into bite-sized pieces and scattering the result over a sea area the size of France.

This gives the whole country a bit of an identity crisis. Peoples' loyalties tend to be assigned primarily to their island. A Cretan usually defines himself as Cretan first and Greek second. This effect is exacerbated by history. The country only really came into any real form of existence in 1832 after the Greek war of independence freed them from Ottoman rule. Even then it was far from what we now know as modern Greece. Most of the islands were still under the Ottoman Turks, some were occupied by the Italians and the Ionians by Britain.

There is also the tendency of the younger islanders to migrate to Athens in search of work, leaving the island communities shrinking and dying (both literally and metaphorically).

The Greek government has developed various strategies to counteract this, among them granting a lower rate of VAT to the further islands such as the Dodecanese. At the core of their efforts are the ferries and, more recently, the internal air links. The ferries are the social, cultural, economic and logistical glue holding this disparate conglomeration into some form of national whole. Ferries are subsidised and are the lifeline to these isolated island communities. Island life frequently revolves around the ferry schedules.

As a result, ferry skippers consider themselves God, or if not God then at least on a par with the Archangel Gabriel. When their several thousand tonne leviathan enters harbour it does so at high speed and with the plain expectation that everyone else will just get the fuck out of the way. With, it must be grudgingly admitted, considerable élan the ferry then executes a handbrake turn, throws on full power ahead and screeches to a halt within spitting distance of the quay. Impressive though this is, it does displace an awful lot of water, which has to go somewhere. Where it goes is all round the harbour and along the quay in the form of a series of metre high waves travelling at about seven miles an hour. This plays havoc with small boats tied up to the quay.

The Aegean is also the windiest part of Greece, a theme that will be developed shortly. Appropriately, then, the met indicated a bit of a blow coming up in a couple of days' time, so we motored on the next day to Poros and dropped the hook.

The forecast the next day was still doom-mongering about force seven to eight from the South, so we decided to make our way over to the pontoon and tie up securely there. We pottered over in ideal conditions and tied up alongside the pontoon, the same as all the other boats. This was ideal for the forecast blow, leaving us secure alongside the leeward side of the pontoon. Having access to water again, we set about basic boatkeeping; sorting out laundry, hoovering the saloon, cleaning the cooker, shower and toilets etc. You didn't realise that cruising was quite such a glamorous lifestyle, did you.

At this point along came the harbour official. "Good morrow, harbour official chappie" I gestured with a smile and a wave, expecting the usual cheery welcome and demand for money. The actual reply was a scowl, a grunt and a "You can't lay alongside. Lay out an anchor and go bows-to!" Then, as an afterthought, "Now!"

We thought this a little unreasonable. We could see the point if it was high season and there were boats backing up as far as Athens trying to get in, but this was Monday the first of June and there were empty spaces everywhere. However, being British, and therefore meek, law-abiding and deferent to authority, we complied with bad grace.

We made *Birvidik* fast and then went for a wander around Poros, which was a very pleasant and picturesque town. On our return, we found that the wind had increased and swung round, and *Birvidik* was attempting to climb nose first up onto the pontoon. The stern anchor had dragged. The pilot did mention that the holding was a bit iffy here. We pulled her back off and the anchor seemed to bite, but we fixed a couple of large fenders between the bow and the pontoon, just in case. This was just as well because the stern anchor slowly dragged again.

During this time, it became apparent that few, if any, of the other boats had taken any notice whatsoever of Mr. Jobsworth's instruction not to go alongside. In fact, six other boats had come in and gone alongside.

This pattern continued over the next few days. The wind rose, the stern anchor dragged and more and more boats came in and laid alongside. By now they were rafted up two or even three deep and no-one took a blind bit of notice of Mr. Jobsworth. I took a photograph of this. On it, you can see all the boats snugly laying alongside, not having to rely on a stern anchor in crap holding. Note there is only one boat bows-to, standing out like a sore thumb. Yes, bloody *Birvidik*.

The wind continued to climb to a seven gusting gale force eight but at least it was now, as forecast, blowing us off the pontoon. We were, however, stuck. If the stern anchor had bitten then we'd have been in real trouble trying to get out in the restricted space, so staying put was the best option as long as the wind stayed from the South. If it shifted to the North and the anchor hadn't bitten it would have been carnage. We worked out ever more elaborate plans to reduce the worst effects should the wind switch. Luckily they weren't needed. Just as well as the wind continued to climb until it was gusting 45 knots at times (force nine).

Boats came limping in to try and hide from the weather and those of us already tied up formed chain gangs to help them in. The forces on the ropes were incredible. At one point it took eight men pulling on two ropes, plus the boat's engine on full power to hold a ten metre boat against the wind. Great care had to be taken to ensure that we all came away with the same number of fingers as we started with. The noise of the wind was so overpowering that all communication had to be by sign language, which is difficult if you're using both hands to hold on to a rope like grim death.

In the middle of all this a large Ro-Ro car ferry arrived and tried to manoeuvre into position. It presented such a huge windage that it was virtually uncontrollable. On a couple of occasions it was carried across the bay by the wind and started drifting sideways down onto the boats in the anchorage. At full power, judging by the smoke from the funnels, it just managed to claw itself off before it ended up mowing down the anchored yachts. It must have been terrifying for them. At its closest it got to what looked like twenty metres or so from the nearest yacht before a lull enabled it to power off to windward. After the second instance of this several yachts decided it was safer to raise anchor and face the gale at sea rather than wait to be crushed into the water by the ferry.

The wind rose even higher and the ferry got into further difficulties and looked as if it was going to plough into us, taking out three pontoons, about thirty boats, including *Birvidik*, and God knows how many people, including us. It just managed to claw off once more. After that it gave up and sailed back to Athens. I suppose there's a limit to how long its fuel will last under those conditions. In the middle of all this, I was helping boats tie up while Liz was on board keeping an eye on *Birvidik*. Not that there was a lot she could do should disaster strike, as became apparent when the snatch forces on the mooring ropes became so powerful that one of our backup lines ripped a fairlead off the boat, taking a large chunk of capping rail with it.

The wind eased a little that night and continued to do so over the next couple of days. Liz doubled her dose of blood pressure tablets.

We decided to water up and move off to the anchorage for the night before heading out for the Island of Kithnos.

As the wind had shifted again and was blowing us onto the pontoon, we let out the stern anchor line and tied up alongside. Then we winched in the stern anchor which slid smoothly across the bottom and came up as clean as a whistle. It hadn't bitten at all. This was true of all the other boats that tried laying out an anchor. I don't know what the seabed was, but I suspect greased sheet metal.

Never mind - the forecast was for light winds and smooth seas.

We'll see, we thought.

Light winds and smooth seas it was, and Kithnos provided an idyllic anchorage. We'd have liked to have stayed on a bit, but what with the various delays and disasters we thought we'd better keep moving in order to get through the Cyclades before the summer weather got too established.

This may seem a strange desire, but it is underpinned by sound reasoning. In the popular imagination, the Greek Islands are a paradise of blue skies, sunshine and still, clear waters. This is generally true in the summer in the Ionian. The Aegean, however, is another story. The Mamma Mia islands have something else to contend with – the *Meltemi*.

Meltemi means 'bad tempered' in Turkish and it is

appropriately named. It is caused by a macro weather pattern which stretches for nearly two thousand miles across the Mediterranean and the nearer reaches of Asia. In the summer months a low pressure system builds over Turkey and the Middle East, whilst high pressure systems frequently form over Italy and the Balkans. Between them they produce strong northerly winds over the whole of the Aegean, ranging from North East in the Northern Aegean, through Northerly in the middle and backing to North Westerly in the southern reaches. The closer together these two systems get, the stronger the winds they produce.

These start to kick in around the beginning of June, reach their peak in July and August and start to ease in September, just in time for the equinoctial thunderstorms. At their peaks they blow at between five Beaufort and seven to eight Beaufort, frequently funnelling to nine Beaufort between the islands and on their lee side.

Big hairy sailors love these winds. We loathe them. Between the Dodecanese and Cyclades the Meltemi blows undisturbed over a hundred plus miles. Within six hours of a 30-knot wind, the waves can reach heights over three meters. Adverse currents make these waves steeper, which can be seriously dangerous for yachts smaller than 10 metres and bloody uncomfortable for bigger ones, like ours.

Anchorages pose problems in the Meltemi. You want to be on the lee side of islands in order to escape the waves but, as mentioned above, this frequently means that you will suffer strong gusty winds even if the sea is relatively calm. Hence our wish to get across the Aegean before June was out.

With this in mind, we weighed anchor the next morning and sailed on to Paros, to another well sheltered anchorage. The met had indicated yet another blow coming up, so we looked at the marina in Paros, with a view to sitting it out there. Unfortunately it wasn't so much a marina, as a tiny, half built harbour with the only *Birvidik*-sized area cordoned off, so we set off for Naxos, which promised better shelter.

Naxos was better, which was just as well as, with one thing and another, we were there for a day shy of a fortnight. This was due to the expected blow (another force seven to eight), which lasted nearly the fortnight, and another little snag that turned up.

Having been very strictly potty trained, I carry out full engine checks after every day's use. On checking the level of transmission fluid in the gearbox I was disturbed to find out that it was a tad low. Further investigation showed that it was leaking from around the selector mechanism and pooling in the bottom of the engine bay.

I made series of expensive mobile phone calls to The Blessed Bill Keating, the engineer in Jersey who had installed *Birvidik*'s engine. Bill pointed us to a worn O-ring which needed to be replaced, so we employed the services of a local diesel mechanic, who took out the selector shaft, toddled off to get and fit the appropriate O-ring and then brought it back and re-fitted it. I watched all of this closely, treating it as a free course in transmission maintenance - which was just as well as things turned out.

The mechanic was a short, stocky troglodyte with a mass of curly, greying hair and a beard that looked as if it might be home to an entire ecosystem of birds and small mammals. He was a reduced version of Robbie Coltrane as Hagrid. Now, I was aware that the pressures in hydraulic gearboxes tended to be a bit on the high side, but I was surprised when mini-Hagrid did up the bolts using all of his considerable strength aided by a socket wrench which could have doubled as a tyre lever for a tractor.

After testing for leaks with the engine running, he wriggled out and pronounced the job done, adding that the gear lever might be a bit stiff for a while, until the O-ring bedded in. He took his ninety euros and toddled off.

When I tried the gear selector, I found that 'a bit stiff' was very much an understatement. It required both arms and the leverage of one foot against the bulkhead to get the thing to shift gear.

Then followed a crash course in hydraulic

transmission engineering, with the aid of several more mobile phone calls to The Blessed Bill Keating. The problem was eventually solved by redoing everything the mechanic had done, taking one bit out and putting some extra bits in and finally bolting the whole thing back together again. (Full boring technical details available under plain cover upon application). So, as I had to do the entire job myself in the end, it turned out that I'd effectively paid ninety euros for a twenty pence O-ring. Never mind, I look upon it as a learning experience.

Despite the disasters, we can thoroughly recommend Naxos. It's the largest of the Cyclades, with lots to see and do. There are concerts on most nights up in the Castle, including a local music and dance evening which was carried out with genuine pride and enthusiasm, in contrast to the tourist pastiches that so often masquerade as local culture. The harbour is well sheltered, apart from some unusual motions induced by ferry wash, and the guy in charge, Kostas, was brilliant - really helpful. When we came to pay he said that he'd give us a special price, and he did; five euros a night, including water and electricity. Bargain.

We set off from Naxos to Patmos, with me nervously checking the gearbox every hour for signs of leakage or catastrophic collapse, but all was well. By the end of the day we were tied up in Patmos, having crossed the Cyclades and, hopefully, escaped the worst area for the Meltemi.

Patmos harbour is a picturesque little place overlooked by a bluff, high rock formation capped by a monastery. It was on Patmos that the Book of Revelation, was written, purportedly by St. John the Apostle, whose earlier best sellers included The Gospel According to St. John, and the three Epistles of John. The Epistles were warm little homilies and the Gospel a call to arms for the early Christian church. The book of Revelation, though, was a humdinger, a dystopian blockbuster of a work. Going from The Epistles to Revelation seems to me like Alan Bennet suddenly coming out with Zombie Apocalypse.

It's not all sweetness and light, though. The Book of

Revelation has to shoulder some of the blame for the Rapture movement in the United States. Members of these fundamentalist Evangelical groups positively support strife in the Middle East, believing it to be a prophesied precursor to Second Coming.

Well, that helps things along nicely, doesn't it.

It was on Patmos that Liz managed a revelation of her own. As usual, she had identified the highest point in a five mile radius and homed in on it. This was the monastery. "I'd like to go up there." She said sweetly. This translates as "We are going up there and don't even think about arguing."

We, and about three hundred other people, steadily trudged our way up the steep, cobbled donkey track until we reached the monastery gates. We passed through the main entrance and it was like being transported into an M. C. Escher lithograph. Arches, steps, windows and doors all intertwined, linking the jigsaw of rooms, floors and gardens, all of which were at different heights.

We went to make our way in. It was at this point that the morality police caught sight of Liz. Ok, she was wearing shorts, but so was I and every other bloke in the place. It was 40 degrees in the shade for God's sake. And it was for God's Sake, apparently that she had to cover up her legs. It's not even as if her shorts were hotpants or displaying tantalizing glimpses of buttock. They were a mid thigh length loose fit.

They were very nice about it, but they insisted she wear the rather colourful, wrap-around skirt they lent her. It seemed that they feared that the sight of her uncovered and shapely pins might inflame the suppressed passions of the monks, thus distracting them from their devotional duties. I could see their point. What I found hard to take, however, was the implicit assumption that my muscular thighs and calves would fail to produce an equally fevered reaction from the hordes of sarong-clad female tourists should I be exposed to their lascivious gazes.

I can dream.

The forecast winds were from the South, so we decided to head North-east to Samos. Naturally we had light north-easterlies on the nose and had to motorsail all the way. We anchored in Pythagorion on the South coast, named after its famous son. Nice little town, but not a right angle in sight.

Pythagorion used to be called Samos and was the capital of the 6th Century B.C. tyrant Polykrates (roughly translates as 'Big Boss'). He decided to make his mark by instigating great public works (a harbour and a 1040 metre aqueduct bored through the mountain) and by persecuting Pythagoras, who responded by disappearing off into a cave on the West of the island.

Samos is one of the bigger islands in the Eastern Med, so we hired a car to take a look around. At Potami on the North coast was a walk along a gorge with a river running through it - cool, shaded and wooded - absolutely exquisite. At the head of this a steep and ramshackle set of wooden steps climbed to a treetop restaurant with views over the woods and out to sea. No disabled access here.

The next target was a deserted village and a church in a cave up in the mountains. Liz likes mountains. Here we came up against the Greek tradition of misleading signposts. This, we suspect, is designed to confuse invading Turkish troops and usually follows a pattern.

Firstly, the existence of some not to be missed site is marked on a map or guide book. As you approach in the car a sign is usually found at a multiple junction, cunningly placed so that it could, depending on the exact angle you view it, feasibly point in any of the five possible directions leading from said junction. Positioning a sign in precisely this way is very difficult and requires three dimensional geometric skills of the highest order. There's probably an entire department in the University of Athens dedicated to it.

Having overcome this first hurdle by employing all available Y chromosome spatial cognition abilities and finding the correct road you come across tactic two. This involves placing the second sign a little after, rather than before, the relevant junction and then adding just a frisson of a challenge by planting a large bush in front of it.

Level three of the game follows with a long stretch of

road with no signs to your desired destination at all. This stretch of road is specifically chosen for having most of its junctions possessing such a level of complexity that it is impossible to determine which road is the main road and which are the subsidiaries. If you manage to overcome all of this they reward you with a sign saying "Churchy villagey thing this way - 5 Km". Soon after that they play their trump card and the road just peters out into a narrow, rutted, boulder-strewn track bordered by precipitous drops.

Not to be outdone we, or more precisely Liz, determined that we should continue on foot. I concurred with my usual good grace.

It got hotter and stickier. We became sweatier and more dust covered. The swarms of flies became thicker and more irritating. After three kilometres (as measured by the pedometers) we came across another sign: "Churchy villagey thing this way – still 5 Km". Were we disheartened? Well, Liz wasn't. Onward and upward we went.

I was getting fed up with this, so I played *my* trump card. Whilst panting my way up a particularly steep, dusty, fly infested section I managed to inhale a rather large flying insect, which promptly lodged itself in the back of my throat. Understandably, it did not wish to disappear further into the hot, damp maw gaping before it, and so it sank its mandibles into where my tonsils would have been had I had any, and hung on as if its life depended on it. Which it did. Unhappily for my unwanted hitch-hiker, however, this tactic was found wanting when I hawked, coughed, chewed and then spat it out.

It came out mangled but, unfortunately, sans mandibles, which remained firmly embedded. Further hawking and coughing managed to loosen them a little but not completely dislodge them. It also managed to produce quite copious quantities of blood.

We'd been unable to determine what sort of insect it had once been, as it was distinctly deformed by the time it came out; so we didn't know whether it had a sting or not. Both of us at this stage thought of the possibility that it might trigger a swelling of the tissues in the throat and compromise breathing. Neither of us, of course, mentioned this to the other.

So we abandoned the exercise and started to make our way back to the car. The things I'll do to get out of one of Liz's expeditions.

As we tramped the track back, Liz surreptitiously checked me out every time I slowed or coughed out more blood. She had all sorts of horror scenarios running through her mind. Trying to get help from up a mountain in a pine forest in the middle of nowhere, especially in Greek would not have been easy. I didn't tell her that this particular problem was unlikely to arise as I had surreptitiously checked my mobile and there wasn't a signal anyway.

Luckily there was no swelling and the bleeding had all but stopped by the time we got back to the car. We called it a day and went back to the boat.

The trip to Kalymnos was uneventful, apart from what we suspect to have been a sonic boom which made Liz jump out of her skin. I dozed on contentedly. We entered a protected anchorage in Emborius and picked up a buoy that had been laid by one of the local tavernas. This, of course, obliged us to go and eat there in the evening, but such are the trials of the cruising life. We were last here on a package holiday in 1998, when it was hitting 45 degrees during the day and 35 degrees at night. It hadn't cooled down much in the interim.

One thing we noticed in the Aegean was the relative dearth of Brits. There are plenty of Red Ensigns, but the boats are all owned and crewed by other nationalities, mainly Greek. It turns out it's the same tax dodge that was operating in Sardinia. With Gordon Brown banging on about tax havens at the time, the words 'mote', 'beam' and 'eye' sprang to mind.

Other than that there were plenty of Dutch, Germans, French, Austrians and Norwegians with a scattering of Swedes and other nationalities, but very few Brits. This isn't much of a problem as all of these nationalities converse with the others in English, but it's not quite as relaxed as conversing all together in the same native tongue.

There was, however, a Brit boat with a Brit crew in the anchorage and they went ashore and took a table in the taverna. We arrived later and sat a couple of tables down. We had thought of acknowledging them and striking up a conversation on the way in, but decided to get a drink first. It was just as well we did.

One of the three had managed to work his way through two litres of wine before the meal had even started. He was one of the most unpleasant, arrogant, pompous, inconsiderate, boastful, loud, obnoxious, overbearing, boorish, argumentative, xenophobic saloon bar bores we've ever been unfortunate enough to come across. His conversation, such as it was, consisted of a repetitive rap of just how much he excelled at everything and just how fucking useless everyone else was. We just sat in the corner avoiding eye contact and trying to look foreign. It is at times such as this that the ability to blather on convincingly in what sounds plausibly like an obscure foreign language comes into its own. Luckily he was so self-obsessed he didn't even give us a second glance, let alone try to engage us in conversation.

We left the next morning for Kos. This is very close to Turkey and there are patriotic symbols all along the coast. On the Greek side this usually takes the form of huge Greek flags (100 + metres across) made up of blue and white stones strategically placed on hillsides facing directly towards Turkey. The Turks counter this by erecting bloody great flagpoles all over the place and flying Turkish flags the size of football pitches from them. The symbolic equivalent of the playground 'Nyah nyah na na na!' . As Bertrand Russell so aptly put it "Nationalism is just tribalism with flags."

Kos is a brilliant marina in a lovely town on a fascinating island. This was just as well as we were stuck here for five days due to yet another slight technical hitch.

I was performing my twice daily obeisance to the ammeter when I remarked "Blimey that solar panel's pushing in a lot of amps." Then I had a think and decided it was too much current even for a 135 watt panel. So I disconnected it. There were still loads of amps going in. "Strange", I thought. So I disconnected everything that could possibly put current in or draw it out. Still loads of amps going in. So I isolated both battery banks - still loads of amps going in.

I was getting quite excited by this time, reckoning I'd inadvertently found a way to circumvent the laws of thermodynamics. A glittering future of limitless clean energy on tap beckoned for mankind, not to mention fame and fortune for me.

I left everything disconnected and went to sleep to have a think about it. I couldn't sleep. But I could think about it.

Which I did, for most of the night.

In the end I gave up, got out of bed and started dismantling half the saloon to expose and investigate the charging circuits.

I found that one of the five series pairs of batteries was a trifle warm. Well, hot actually. Bloody hot. These were rapidly disconnected and extracted. On reconnecting the rest of the batteries and bridging the gap where I'd removed the hot batteries I found the problem had gone away, as had my chances of revolutionising energy technology. It turned out that one of the pair had sulphated, causing a short circuit. This resulted in the other one discharging into the shorted battery, producing heat, a second knackered battery and spurious readings on the ammeter.

All that was needed now were two new deep cycle, ninety ampere-hour wet batteries which fitted into the available space. I went, armed with the specifications and dimensions, but fired more by hope than confidence, to the local chandlery. The man behind the counter said they could have them by the next morning. I had my doubts. Much to my amazement, they did, and quite reasonable at 135 euros each. I stacked them on the heavy duty trolley and lugged them back to the boat.

It must be a frustrating job being a boat designer. The best shape for making a seaworthy and efficient course through the water bears little resemblance to any shape that's even halfway suitable for living in. Power boats have a little more concordance between the two shapes, but for sailing boat designers it's the seaworthy requirement that takes precedence. The hull comes first and determines the shape into which the living quarters are shoe-horned. The consequence of this is that boat accommodation is an intersecting confusion of curves and obscure angles with not a right angle to be seen anywhere. This poses a bit of a problem as many of the items stowed on boat are cuboid and composed entirely of right angles. These include things such as cookers, books, power tool cases, and most boxes.

And batteries.

A further irritation is the stubborn refusal of manufacturers of such items to standardize sizes. This means that you can only get that a replacement to fit if it's the same make, model and spec as the item it's replacing. Even then it's not guaranteed as manufacturers have the annoying habit of changing dimensions over time.

The batteries, of course, did not fit the battery box. They almost did, but not quite. Their documented dimensions, although indicating that they would just slide into the available space if liberally coated with cooking fat, had failed to take into account the fact that they had retaining flanges protruding from the sides. I dug out a saw, a hammer and assorted chisels and hacked off a few flanges round the edges of both batteries. On the third attempt I managed to fit them in and all was now well. *Birvidik* was shipshape and ready for the off.

All that was left to do now was to work our way through the labyrinthine Greek bureaucracy so that we could clear out of Greece in order to be able to clear into Turkey.

Attentive readers will already be aware of the complexities of Greek bureaucracy as it applies to cruising yachts. There was until very recently a theoretical requirement (un-meetable in practice) to visit the port police and clear in and out of every port visited within two hours of arrival or departure. This was honoured more in the breach than the observance, but it becomes more complex when you intend to sail out of Greek waters.

It's bad enough going to another EU country, but to leave for a non EU country sets alarm bells ringing in the bureaucratic brain. If this non EU country happens to be The Old Enemy, namely Turkey, it immediately arouses deep suspicion in what passes for the official neocortex that there is some reprehensible motive behind such a visit. The fact that the Turkish coast is often within spitting distance of the Port Police office seems irrelevant. Or possibly even contributory.

Most marinas have come to some form of accommodation between the ludicrous demands of officialdom and the economic realities of trying to make a living out of the waterborne community. All the paperwork, if done at all, can be done in one go, usually by the marina staff. Kos marina has the (mostly deserved) reputation of being one of the best in Greece. As a result, I tripped with light heart and heavy document case to the marina office to deal with the paperwork and clear out.

At first, all went according to plan. Transit logs were stamped, passports perused, crew lists photocopied to within an inch of their lives and florid signatures inscribed on any blank areas of paper that had so far escaped unblemished. Just as I thought it was all done and I was about to leave, the charming Port Policewoman added as an aside "Oh and you have to pay a tax." This was a new one on me.

"Oh - what's that for?" I asked. She looked a bit confused by this, and said that she didn't really know but thought it might be something to do with light dues.

"OK", I said with some trepidation - "How much?"

"88 cents" (= about 65 pence).

I proffered a one euro coin expecting, based on previous experience, to be sent to the nearest knocking shop to try to get some change.

"Oh no - you can't pay it here" I was told "You have to

pay it at the local tax office." Upon enquiry it turns out that the tax office was local in the same sense that Alpha Centauri is referred to by astronomers as local. It may be the nearest star but it's still three and a half bleedin' light years away.

The exact whereabouts of this tax office appeared to be covered by the Official Secrets Act. The Port Policewoman said something about go out the main gate, turn right and go on until faint from hunger and then ask someone else. I tried the marina office next door. The guy behind the counter was trying to impress a rather attractive new recruit. He smiled knowingly at her and bemusedly at the map - it didn't help that he held it upside down. Then he very confidently said "Ah yes - it's here" and, with a dramatic flourish, drew a circle on the map. The trouble was that this circle covered an area only fractionally smaller than Greater Manchester. I pressed him for more accuracy and got an embarrassed muttering of "somewhere behind Goody's bar" before he hustled the new recruit into the stationery cupboard to explain the intricacies of the photocopier.

Bowing to the inevitable, we set off in search of the elusive tax office. We found Goody's bar about three miles away in the centre of Kos town. Alongside it, rather than behind it, was a large, imposing building with high gates, intimidating steps, a huge, sod off, Greek flag and a sign saying 'Tax Office' in Greek.

I bounded up the steps, approached the young man behind the desk and intimated that I'd like to pay some tax. Offering to pay a tax without the application of thumbscrews and the threat of defenestration was obviously a novelty to the young man who was temporarily flummoxed, but recovered admirably. "What tax?" he asked. I produced the 'instruction to pay a tax' piece of paper that the port police had given me. Unfortunately it had been scrawled on the back of what appeared to be a summons for some major infraction of international maritime law. The Greeks have managed to engineer a system that combines the most complicated red tape imaginable with a chronic shortage of paper.

Once this had been clarified, luckily before the expected telephone call and subsequent arrest, he said that what we wanted was not his establishment, but the LOCAL tax office.

"Where, exactly, was the LOCAL tax office" we asked?

"Behind Goody's bar" he said, as if to a particularly thick and inattentive teenager. We risked official wrath and disdain by asking for more explicit instructions and were told to go out, right, then left, then left again and it's down an alley.

It was, indeed, down an alley. It wasn't marked or signposted. In fact it was one of the few buildings there that didn't have a bloody great Greek flag outside it. What gave it away was a combination of its rather drab appearance and the constant flow of people in and out carrying sheaves of paper and wearing that expression, equal parts anger, irritation and resignation, common to those dealing with tax offices the world over.

I climbed the dingy, claustrophobic staircase and found myself in a large room, cluttered throughout with shoulder high piles of cardboard boxes, all of which were stuffed to overflowing with files, folders and loose papers. They blocked access to the numerous booths, each of which had a long queue at it and none of which had any indication of what they dealt with. There were boxes stuffed under desks and piled up in front of the fire exits. Loose papers that had escaped the overstuffed boxes were trampled underfoot like autumn leaves. "That's where all the paper's gone" I thought to myself. "There are probably hundreds of rooms like this in every Greek village, town and city. The entire country's one big fire hazard."

The question now was which queue to join, only to wait for half an hour and then to be told that you were in the wrong queue and will now have to join the end of that really long one over there. However, I had seen the technique in action at Greek post offices. I looked for the queue which had someone at the front holding up the rest of the queue whilst laboriously filling in some form or other. I then nipped in front of everyone waving my piece of paper and asked the guy if I should join this queue. As expected, the guy pointed me to the longest queue in the room, which I meekly joined.

Upon reaching the front I waved my piece of paper at the woman behind the glass and made 'I want to pay' noises. She looked at me and snarled 'Passport!' It was, of course, on the boat. My Greek wasn't up to bureaucratic wrangling and my nemesis wasn't going to admit to speaking any language other than Greek but I refused to be dismissed and let the rest of the queue through. I was rewarded by a very helpful and probably self interested Greek gentleman from further back who came forward and translated, only to be rewarded by the dragon behind the glass with look like she'd just finished chewing a wasp.

After he'd argued with her for five minutes it turned out that a passport wasn't required at all, she only wanted it to see how my name was spelled. The fact that it was PRINTED IN CAPITAL LETTERS on the piece of paper I'd given her had somehow passed her by. With consummate bad grace she completed a form, stamped it in several places, signed it in two places got me to sign it in three places and gave me the top copy.

I got out my 88 cents and offered it.

"Not here - Pay over there" she said in English, pointing at the longest queue in the room.

It only took another twenty minutes after that.

So - 88 cent tax paid. Now all we had to do in order to clear out of Greece was to deal with the following authorities in the right order: passport control, immigration, health, customs and finally port police to get our transit log stamped for exit to Turkey. As we wanted to leave at sparrow fart the next day, we decided to start early and at 7:30 in the morning we walked into Kos town with our documentation.

We found passport control and immigration straight away. It was easily identified by the 500 metre queue of gently baking, wilting tourists that wound its way tortuously across the sun blasted car park, snaking round rubbish bins, parked cars, coaches and fume-belching lorries. Every fifteen minutes or so the queue would shuffle forwards and two or three people would step gratefully into the air conditioned office. In this time, of course another coachload would have joined the tail.

Working on the principle that the glut of potential day trippers would have cleared in a couple of hours we took ourselves off and spent a happy hour or so strolling around the castle, from where we could keep an eye on the queue. Once we'd seen that it had dwindled to the merely ludicrous we joined the end. As we approached the doors we became uncertain as to whether we were in the right place, as all those in front of us were going straight through after processing and then boarding large cruise boats.

We asked a tour rep who said "Oh no - you don't want to be here - you want to be in the other office by the cafeteria." So off we went. Further enquiries at said office elicited the response that "Oh no - you don't want to be here, you want to be in the other office you've just come from". On our return, of course, another coachload of Germans had joined the end of the queue.

By now it was eleven o'clock and we were getting hungry and thirsty. The sign on the office door said that the office hours were 08:00 - 21:00, so we decided to have a coffee and a bite to eat and come back in about an hour. Fortified with a toastie and a fresh orange juice we returned to find that the queue had completely disappeared. We also found that the door was shut and locked.

An accommodating guy from customs told us that, having just cleared all the daytrippers out, they were now all busy round the other side clearing the Turkey to Greece daytrippers in. He suggested we go and have a coffee and come back in about an hour.

An hour's stroll later found us back at immigration and the door still locked. This time we were directed down the side of the building where we found an open window. Behind this window was an office in which was a uniformed guy sitting drinking coffee and reading a newspaper. Not a day-tripper in sight.

We were just wondering about the advisability of distracting him from his labours, when a local tour rep turned up. She yelled through the window at him and he put down the racing results. On his approach, I explained that we wanted to clear out.

"When are you leaving?" he asked.

"Early tomorrow morning."

"Come back at 7 p.m."

He let the tour rep in then shut and locked the door in our faces.

It's fairly pointless trying to argue with a shut door so we resignedly trudged all the way back to the marina to see the port police and sort out that end of the paperwork. What naïve little optimists we were. It has to be done in the right order. No exceptions. So, we had to go back to Kos at 7 p.m. to get our passports cleared before we could clear out with health, then customs and then finally with the port police.

"Unfortunately," the charming Port Policewoman informed us apologetically, "we shut at 4 p.m."

This was getting quite Kafkaesque.

It turned out, though, that there was a Port Police office in Kos town which was open 24 hours a day, so we resigned ourselves to a lost evening and another long walk into town and back, carrying every piece of documentation we could find, which was quite a lot.

To our great surprise, our evening attempt couldn't have gone more smoothly. I played the Olymbiakos rucksack card and it paid off in spades. Smiling immigration officials cheerily stamped forms and joshed in a manly fashion about my rucksack.

Customs and health must have also been Olymbiakos fans as we sped through there with smiles and jokes and were personally escorted to the Port Police where the same happened and we were spat out the other end after only forty minutes with all the paperwork sorted.

No-one ever did ask us for the hard-earned receipt for the 88 cent tax either.

We left Kos early the next morning in a strengthening wind and started on a cracking sail, reaching 7 knots in a lumpy sea. Just as we were getting the hang of it and starting to really enjoy it, the wind dropped and swung round on to the nose. After that it was motorsail all the way to Marmaris.

And Finally...Turkey

Entry into Turkey requires flying the Q flag and then visiting the following, in the right order: Harbour master (where you obtain a transit log and pay harbour and light dues); health (where you sign an affidavit that you're not importing any unauthorised unpleasant infections); immigration and passport control (where you need to obtain visas valid for 90 days); Customs (where you list every item on the boat worth more than £2:50, along with the relevant make, model, colour, age, serial number and vendor's inside leg measurement) and finally customs patrol who, if they're particularly bored, may want to come on board and have a rummage through your knicker drawer. The peculiar phenomenon of déjà vu strikes again.

The fees for all of this amounted to about 130 euros. For an extra twenty euros you can pay an agent to do it all for you. This involves handing over all your papers, including passports, insurance certificate and boat registration documents, to a total stranger and not seeing them again for 24 hours. We chose an agent linked to the marina. Then at least we know where to point the finger if *Birvidik* suddenly turns out to be owned by an Albanian people-trafficking ring or we get pulled up at any borders because some computer links our passports with actions by assorted terrorists, international prostitution barons, political dissidents, mafia hitmen, money launderers, Mossad agents, illegal immigrants or drug smugglers.

Apart from the boating bureaucracy, moving on to a new country involves a number of other little jobs - new sim cards for the phones, internet access, that sort of thing. Within the EU the phone isn't too much of a problem - you just buy a local sim card and stick it in your existing phone. You can do this in Turkey, but after about a fortnight you suddenly get cut off without warning and neither threats nor bribery will get you reconnected. Local political influence might help, but we're a bit short on that. No-one at the shop tells you about this, of course, and they'll gladly sell you the sim card. Luckily, we had found out about it earlier over the yottie grapevine. Apparently the government is concerned that it might be losing out on some revenue from imported phones. That's guaranteed to concentrate their minds.

There is much less English spoken in Turkey than we were used to in Greece, and it's not too easy trying to have accurate technical and fiscal discussions in pidgin. In the end we managed to buy two new cheapie Nokia phones and local sim cards. Translation services were provided by a waiter drafted in from the café next door.

The internet presented more of a problem. We had been spoiled with our Vodafone mobile phone network connection to the laptop in Greece and wanted to get the same here. We had by now become accustomed to the usefulness and convenience of getting forecasts and e-mails on demand from the comfort of the boat.

The chap in the Turkcell shop was very helpful. We'd found a leaflet about a local USB internet connection service. When we showed it to him he was most enthusiastic, going on in raptures about how fast it was, how many gigabytes we could get, how much they would cost and how we could get more.

"Great" we said, "We'll take it".

He stopped mid flow.

"Oh no" he replied "is finished. All finished. In all Marmaris all finished."

We weren't sure if 'all finished' meant permanently, given the Turkish authorities rather ambivalent attitude to the internet, or whether it meant that they were temporarily unavailable and more would be coming in. We decided to try again in a few days when we got to Fethiye.

Contrary to the expectations of our friends and acquaintances, we had got as far as our limited imaginations had originally stretched. We now had no immediate targets or longer term goals. All we intended to do was spend the rest of the summer pottering up and down the South Turkish coast in a leisurely fashion and maybe check out the marinas for the coming winter. After that, who knew? More to the point, who cared?

We left the bustling tourist mayhem of Marmaris and sailed to Ecinçek, where we anchored for the first time Turkish style – bow anchor deployed and the stern tied to a tree by a long line. Just *Birvidik* and one other boat were there to enjoy the calm of the anchorage. We ate our evening meal and sat quietly, savouring the sounds of the cicadas and the wafted scents of eucalyptus and cistus. Alright, it was only 1800 miles as the crow flies, but it felt like we had come a long, long way.

The next morning I awoke to the gentle sound of wavelets lapping softly on the hull. The goat bells' random song, clear and soft like distant wind chimes, drifted across the water. Sunlight danced off the sea and dappled the ceiling of the cabin with flickering reflections. I turned over and watched Liz sleeping next to me. The reflected light flickered across her face and her soft breathing blended effortlessly with the soundtrack of birdsong and cicadas playing in the background. We were now, truly vagabonds. Of no fixed abode. *Birvidik* was our only home. I had never felt so utterly content and so full of time. My tribe had shrunk to just two people and no other tribe had offered and supported me so much. My tribal range was as small as a suburban living room and as large as the ocean.

Printed in Great Britain
by Amazon